LISTENING TO
ROSITA

❊ ❊ ❊

RACE AND CULTURE IN THE AMERICAN WEST

QUINTARD TAYLOR, SERIES EDITOR

LISTENING TO
ROSITA

❁ ❁ ❁

The Business of Tejana Music and Culture

1930–1955

MARY ANN VILLARREAL

UNIVERSITY OF OKLAHOMA PRESS : NORMAN

(*frontispiece*) **San Antonio *cantante* Rosita Fernández.** Photograph courtesy of the Daughters of the Republic of Texas Library at the Alamo, Elicson Photograph Collection, SCElicson.09.002.

LIBRARY OF CONGRESS CATALOGING-IN-PUBLICATION DATA

Villarreal, Mary Ann, 1971–
  Listening to Rosita : the business of Tejana music and culture, 1930–1955 / Mary Ann Villarreal.
    pages cm. — (Race and culture in the American west ; v. 9.)
  Includes bibliographical references and index.
  ISBN 978-0-8061-4852-6 (cloth)
  ISBN 978-0-8061-5779-5 (paper)
1. Fernández, Rosita, 1918–2006. 2. Tejano musicians—Texas. 3. Women musicians—Texas. 4. Businesswomen—Texas. 5. Mexican Americans—Texas—Corpus Christi—Social conditions—20th century. 6. Mexican Americans—Texas—Houston—Social conditions—20th century. 7. Mexican Americans—Texas—San Antonio—Social conditions—20th century. 8. Tejano music—History and criticism. I. Title.
  ML200.7.T35V55 2015
  781.62'68720764—dc23

                                        2015016354

Listening to Rosita: The Business of Tejana Music and Culture, 1930–1955 is Volume 9 in the Race and Culture in the American West series.

The paper in this book meets the guidelines for permanence and durability of the Committee on Production Guidelines for Book Longevity of the Council on Library Resources, Inc. ∞

❁   ❁   ❁

To the women and their families
who opened their doors to me and
shared stories long ago tucked away.

To my sister Nancy, who made
my world big and full of love.

❁   ❁   ❁

CONTENTS

ILLUSTRATIONS

ACKNOWLEDGMENTS

This book has been in the making for far longer than anyone imagined, especially my grandmother, Mary F. Villarreal. She was determined that I would go to college even as she had no context for what that meant, other than a different and better life. She worked three jobs so that I could participate in extracurricular activities in high school; in college she sent me the recycled beer-can money to pay for books, and occasionally five dollars with a note, "So you can go out to eat." Momo was a domestic worker turned businesswoman. She took over the Pecan Lounge in Tivoli, Texas, when I was five, and it was there that I spent my early childhood years after school doing homework and playing pool. When my grandfather, Raymond H. Villarreal, fell ill in 1996, my grandmother asked me to run the bar so she could care for him. During those four months I truly understood that it was her business savvy that kept the bar afloat.

My sister Nancy also made it possible for me to be the first in my family to graduate from college and to pursue a doctorate. She was my compass, even during my teenage years when I rebelled against every idea she offered. She is a friend who for all of my life has shown up without question. I received the copyedited files of this manuscript one month after she had been diagnosed with a serious illness. My sister is evidence that one person can indeed change the course of a generation. Today we have embarked on a whole new lesson of living, a gift that my daughters will forever remember.

Numerous people have made this book possible. From the beginning of my research efforts, I dragged along my cousin Andrea Leal, who was willing to search out abandoned theaters and dance halls. My friend and *colega* Deborah R. Vargas, then at the University of California, Santa Cruz, and now at UC Riverside, also traveled with me through south Texas as we collected oral history interviews from Carmen Marroquin and Ventura Alonzo. Rosita Fernández and Ventura Alonzo shared lasting memories with me prior to their deaths. Their families continued providing me with stories, interviews, and their time. I always left Sofia Rodriguez's home with a song and a new perspective on her business decisions. Carmen Marroquin's pragmatic approach, "This is the way we did business," was always followed by a good story.

While gathering these stories, I had the incredible fortune of meeting archivists with treasures to share: Thomas Kreneck and Grace Charles of Texas A&M, Corpus Christi; Margo Gutierrez of the University of Texas at Austin; Tim Ronk of the Houston Metropolitan Research Center; and Cecilia Aros Hunter of Texas A&M, Kingsville. Linda Schott, president of the University of Maine at Presque Isle, introduced me to the Rosita Fernández papers at the University of Texas at San Antonio Libraries Special Collections.

My academic journey flourished at Mount Holyoke College, where my faculty advisors, Jean Grossholtz and Martha Ackmann, introduced me to research and made me excited about learning. Jean and Eileen Elliot offered me a home at 10 Jewett Lane, and they both continue to be an important part of my family's lives. My advisors handed me off to Vicki L. Ruiz at Claremont Graduate School (now Claremont Graduate University). I followed her to Arizona State University. Vicki, now at the University of California, Irvine, welcomed me and has been influential in shaping this incredible journey. She has provided guidance and direction since the day I met her while still a senior at Mount Holyoke. She taught me not only the meaning of being a Latina historian, but also *how* to be a historian. Noel J. Stowe, founder of the ASU Public History Program, was a strong-minded committee member and dedicated administrator; his memory lives on in the work of those of us committed to public and oral history. I owe an overdue expression of gratitude to my public-history cohort, who encouraged this project from its early conception: Michele Curran, Rose Diaz, Virginia Espino, Jeff Pappas, and Eve Carr. I cherish the friendships of two incredible historians whose time I know I abused with numerous readings of drafts of this book: Marisela Chavez at Cal State Dominguez Hills and Monica Perales at the University of Houston.

Through invitations to give talks and participate on plenaries at meetings of the Mujeres Activas en Letras y Cambio Social (MALCS, Women Active in Letters and Social Change) and the National Association for Chicana and Chicano Studies (NACCS), I received meaningful suggestions and thoughtful interpretations to consider about the role of family and business. I appreciated the opportunities to share my work with the Latino/a Studies and History Departments at the University of California, Irvine, and the Institute of Latino Studies, University of Notre Dame.

I had the great fortune of being a faculty member at the University of Utah as a joint appointment in the Department of History and Ethnic Studies, and at the University of Colorado, Boulder, Department of History. As a junior faculty member at the University of Utah I received an incredible amount of support, from course releases to research grants, in order to finish my interviews. Former U of U associate vice president for diversity, Karen L. Dace, was instrumental in making the transition into my first tenure track position both smooth and open to great possibilities. My department colleagues, Elizabeth Clement, David Igler (now at UC Irvine), and Matt Basso, read chapters and offered valuable comments. As chair, Eric Hinderaker worked to protect my time as a junior faculty member while supporting my community initiatives. I owe a very special thank you to Ron Coleman for his friendship, mentorship, and especially for introducing me to Quintard Taylor, editor of the Race and Culture in the American West series.

The history department at UC Boulder provided me with a generous library fund, supported my conference presentations, and provided me with a semester leave to complete my revisions. Former chair Peter Boag created an inviting process during my interview. Lucy Chester, Anne E. Lester, Tom Zeiler, and Marcia Yonemoto welcomed me into the department and included me in numerous hallway conversations that gave me opportunities to refine the shaping of my argument. I greatly appreciate the mentorship and time that

Susan Kent, Fred Anderson, and Virginia Anderson spent with me as I thought through my research and teaching.

I entered the final stretch of the manuscript-writing process as I started my new position at California State University, Fullerton. I have had a phenomenal experience at CSUF and so much of it is thanks to the support of the Office of the President staff: Danielle García, Sara Muow, Matt Olson, Monique Shay, Leticia Stotler, Edna Turnbow, Sandy Quintero, Cheri von Mirbach, Presidential Scholar Isabel Serrano, and Guardian Scholar Myla Garcia. I am grateful to President Mildred García and Chief of Staff Ann Camp for a new professional home where I have thrived and grown under President García's leadership. I am especially grateful for their insistence and encouragement that I finish this book. President García's "Dream Team" cabinet members have shared tremendous energy and courage with me as they lead CSUF to become the national model public comprehensive university.

While my grandmother, Momo, and sister, Nancy, have played a huge part in my life, this book would not be complete without the support of our other family members: Jennifer and Joe Jimenez, Henry and Yolanda Flores, Leticia and Gary Cederquist, and Jo Ann Perez. Henry and Yolanda invited me to give a talk on Rosita at Los Sembradores of San Antonio, an organization that promotes higher-education opportunities for students. What an exciting afternoon that was, with new stories shared and a number of new sources to consider. Our extended family that has grown out of our lives in Massachusetts, Arizona, Utah, and Colorado is filled with deep love. I am fortunate that our paths have crossed and our friendships remain so rich: Maria, Dave, Joaquin and Solana Garciaz/Galvan, Mistalene and James Calleroz-White, Orly Hersch, Angie Dill, Lisa Vasquez, Gina Alavarez, David Quijada, Ruby Chacon, Lisa Woods, and Tereso Hurst. The final push in this project came from Jenn Aglio, who read my work carefully and provided me with detailed comments during the revision process.

My partner, Lisa A. Flores, and daughters, Amaris Noemi and Aliana Sofí, have sacrificed my everyday presence so that I could pursue an incredible opportunity in the Office of the President at California

State University, Fullerton. My love and gratitude are inadequate in thanking them for their adaptability and courage to embrace change. Lisa has also read every version of this manuscript and has heard me talk through each change made over the years. I am fortunate to have her love and support in seeing me through this project.

When Quintard Taylor put me in touch with Jay Dew at the University of Oklahoma Press, I had no idea the lengths that the OU Press would go through to see this manuscript to this end. I want to thank acquisitions editor Kathleen A. Kelly for pursuing my reader responses following Jay's departure, and for guiding me through the initial process and supporting my manuscript. I have had an incredible experience working with manuscript editor Emily Jerman Schuster. Thank you, Emily, for making this process so easy and providing me with outstanding support from copyeditor Katrin Flechsig and marketing assistant Amy Hernandez.

Portions of this book appeared previously, in modified form, in the following articles: "Finding Our Place: Reconstructing Community through Oral History," *Oral Historian* 33, no. 2; "Becoming San Antonio's Own: Reinventing 'Rosita,'" *Journal of Women's History* 20, no. 2; and "Life on the 'Hill': Entrepreneurial Strategies in 1940s Corpus Christi," in *An American Story: Mexican American Entrepreneurship and Wealth Creation*, edited by John Sibley Butler, Alfonso Morales, and David L. Torres (Lafayette, Ind.: Purdue University Press, 2009).

INTRODUCTION
NO ORDINARY PLACE

This project began with questions about how the few records by women performers made their way into the jukebox at the Pecan Lounge in Tivoli, Texas. The jukebox was a high profit-earner for the Pecan Lounge and served as a collective source of community entertainment during the week. Everyone in the bar was required to put a quarter on the table—or be shamed by my grandmother—a kitty that would then feed the jukebox for the next couple of hours. One quarter bought two songs, and two quarters bought five songs. My grandparents sold the idea that the more coins folks pitched in, the more songs they all got. The message was, "this is not about money, but about more songs," but the jukebox paid for my college textbooks every semester. Before those days, it paid for my school clothes. I recall my grandfather checking the number of hits on each song and pulling records he did not deem popular. Money mattered. I loved watching him decide which records made the cut from inventory to inventory. A variety of women singers populated the jukebox, but four women lived in that jukebox from the day their records were loaded into their slot until the day the bar closed: Lola Beltrán, Lydia Mendoza, Amalia Mendoza, and Dolly Parton.

I sought out women *cantantes* (singers) by using an unusual research style for a historian, a type of fieldwork that José Limón utilized and that can be described as ethno-autobiography, anthropology, and cultural theory.[1] It included talking to the women who frequented spaces considered off-limits to them, driving their possible travel routes throughout south Texas, and visiting bars, dance halls, and the performance stages—some still standing and others now in ruins—frequented by the cantantes themselves. In asking them to step back on stage or behind the bar, I heard their stories weave together the physical, geographic space with cultural, generational space, joined through memories and oral histories, but separated by time and history. These spaces, which created an informal economic infrastructure dependent on the consumer, turned out to be the center of this study. Similar to the way cantantes relied on their audiences, Texas Mexican entrepreneurs initially turned inward to the Spanish-speaking community to build a foundation, with an eye toward their own upward mobility.

Spanish-language music, though not at the forefront of my study, nonetheless acts as a cultural connector for all the parts of this book. Both bilingual and monolingual Spanish-speakers also sought cultural spaces, from entertainment venues to commercial stores that sold ethnic goods. Cultural studies theorist James Clifford writes, "We cannot ignore the full range of expressive culture, particularly music—a rich history of traveling culture-makers and transnational influences."[2] Thus, I borrow Clifford's metaphor of travel as looking through a kaleidoscope. As the pieces of the kaleidoscope move independently of one another, the connections get lost. Similarly, the lens for examining performances at times gives the impression that the individual movement of groups means that they do not work within a network of communities. My research contests that conclusion and uncovers those networks, intangible though they may be.

In this book, I use the term "Texas Mexican" to signify an identification with the cultural heritage of Mexico, and yet, with a tie to Texas as a homeland, a geographically tangible space with the privileges of U.S. citizenship. This cultural production of a Texas Mexican identity was rooted in both nineteenth-century Tejano history and in a contemporary fight for full rights of citizenship.[3] Politically and economically, Texas Mexicans could not always escape being "Mexican," which for the larger Texas Anglo population carried stereotypical associations of dirtiness, poverty, or delinquency. However, families launched small businesses that created a legitimate industry of Mexican goods and music. They discovered that segregation did not negate the purchase by Anglos of Mexican goods such as tortillas and bakery items. Essentially, some ethnic goods were somehow disconnected from Mexican people. The production of Mexican identities, goods, and services opened a door for capitalist ventures that sold an exotic social and consumer product. As double outsiders—not Mexican, not Anglo, but "other," a Spanish-speaking local community within a larger community dominated by Anglos—their business move remade their identity into a cultural product, one that could be sold as an authentic good or even a social necessity. For example, San Antonio built its tourism industry on selling the idea of an "authentic Mexico" with Spanish-language entertainment at the heart of its identity. In other situations, language often served as a barrier between Texas Anglos and Texas Mexicans, and audiences sought out their own Spanish-language music social spaces.

Both men and women in the music industry saw discrimination limit their opportunities. Oral histories and other primary sources make it clear that some hostile areas existed, but each of the women I discuss duly handled the encounters with a segregated society, knowing that "that's the way things were."[4] Texas Mexican women recognized the racial barriers present in the Texas landscape and made smart decisions by creating opportunities and capitalizing on any breaks that came their way. Their gendered experiences as cantantes and *mujeres* differed depending on the individual circumstances of their lives, including such factors as marital status and familial obligations. These factors affected their responses to any ill treatment.

During the oral-history collecting phase of this project, I remained conscious of the need to separate myself from the community of those whose stories I was trying to unearth, yet I discovered that I could not entirely detach myself from these women and the communities they call home. Women like Señora Ventura Alonzo and Señora Carmen Marroquin gave me their stories, their memories—and these are intricately intertwined with my own and those of my grandparents. I also had the fortune of accessing interviews with Fernández, Marroquin, and Alonzo in various archives. Hearing their life stories firsthand provided me with an understanding of their early experiences in the music business. Indeed, oral history "connects generations" and allows for a "self-reflexivity" that questions any assumptions I had about the music business and the personal decisions of the women interviewed, and also makes it possible to position the women and their businesses in larger "historical and theoretical contexts."[5]

Writing about home, the everyday lives of people as they sought success, to make ends meet, or simply to live, has required developing the art of listening. I have tried to integrate and interweave the oral histories of individuals from quite distinct communities, and who had no formal connections, into a theoretical framework aimed at creating a critical discourse of space, gender, and cultural production, while at the same time giving weight and significance to their voices. The foundation for developing an analysis comes in the listening, in connecting the dots of their stories with places and people. It comes in the need for the telling, not the knowledge that scholars bring to the table. As Mabel McKay, a Pomo basket weaver and medicine woman, rightly states, "You have to know me to know what I'm talking about." It is my job, then, to introduce the men and women who opened their doors to me and other historians, to allow others to know them.[6] I do not move chronologically or in a linear fashion as I put together the history of the "Texas Triangle." This is the name I use to describe the area of south Texas defined by imaginary lines drawn between Corpus Christi, San Antonio, and Houston.[7] Building on the voices of mostly women singers, musicians, and small-business owners who were not part of the traditional social or economic landscape meant that I had to listen closely; I had to know the people to know what they were talking about.

At times my interviewees struggled to recall details, thinking that they had to find something significant to tell me. What I could not explain to them was that the search for the ordinary tasks of travel, performing, and running a business produced a picture yet to be painted.[8] It is the ordinary, the act of just doing whatever came their way, as housewives, mothers, commercial actresses, singers, and dance hall owners, that I wanted access to. Not knowing what their individual histories would reveal, I followed up on leads from the conversations, seeking other women I could interview and drawing connections between them. The details of their narratives generated a web, bringing in other women artists, hinting at some of their relationships, revealing stories about audiences and specific communities—little of which appears in archival sources or secondary literature. Through the kaleidoscope lens, my research differs from and informs already-existing scholarship on Texas Mexican identity. The seemingly trivial and mundane details of cantante life speak to the ways in which the larger cultural presence and identity are knitted together.

My narrators gave valuable details about dance halls, theaters, and bars throughout the Texas Triangle. However, if asked a direct question about a particular site, many would respond that their memories could not go that far back. When I inquired about where they performed, I would get responses like, "It's not there anymore, but it was on the corner of ——." The youngest cantante I interviewed was already in her early seventies, so at times their memory about a specific street or the names of dance halls failed them. However, as most of these spaces had literally vanished, finding surviving social spaces in rural areas proved difficult. Instead, I had to rely not on memories grounded in physical space, but memories that gave spaces meaning temporally and visually. The unheard—until now—oral histories of the women in this work produced a "re-membering" of a socially engaged economic past that illuminates present conditions of abandoned sites and some understandings of those conditions. The memories of these women helped to paint a picture of community life not available in text or photographs.

The oral histories on which this book draws also reveal how cantantes have enacted their own collective memory in contrast to how writers have recreated it. As erstwhile performers, the majority of these women displayed a continuing interest in the audience of their oral histories, thinking about entertaining their listeners more than becoming a part of the historical narrative. They did not see themselves as significant players in the music industry; instead, they saw themselves as women trying to make a living by perfecting their performance and music business and raising a family.

This complex renegotiation of identity is exemplified in the life of Rosita Fernández, "San Antonio's Rose." Born in 1918 to Petra and César Fernández in Monterrey, Mexico, Rosita came from a family of sixteen children accustomed to creating their own entertainment, from puppet shows to singing at family gatherings such as birthday and holiday parties. Rosita received her primary education in Laredo, Texas, before her family moved to San Antonio. Shortly thereafter, at the age of nine, she started traveling as a singer with her uncles in the group Los Tres San Miguel. As a child, Fernández found the travel lonely, but that loneliness turned to excitement in her teenage years when she began performing live on WOAI radio, which featured soap operas and news hours. She began to receive invitations to appear on behalf of the stations and the city of San Antonio, and she fostered those relationships for the lifetime of her career. Fernández cultivated her career by taking advantage of the uniqueness of the times and region, when the growth of the Spanish-language radio and record market sent her voice over the airwaves to households in Texas and across the border. She considered her voice a "God-given" gift, but a gift that she often cited in newspaper interviews and that she refined and shaped according to the political-cultural climate.

A self-created singer, Rosita found that her love for music presented her with many paths, from recording artist to radio star. Each path took her on a different journey, both literally across Texas and figuratively in the media. Recalling her 1950s touring schedule, she remarked, "Later on I started to work with the Eduardo Martinez Orchestra and we did travel . . . mostly Dallas, Houston, everywhere around here close to home." When she died in 2006, Rosita Fernández left a legacy of music and culture that has marked her place in Mexican American history. Her career spanned six decades with venues including everything from 1930s *carpas* (tent shows) to San Antonio's Riverwalk.[9] Significant to this book, Fernández's career offers a glimpse into the role of women- and family-controlled businesses in forging the social and economic network that brought together Mexican American communities in the Texas Triangle.

Fernández started her journey in the small towns of south Texas, following the carpa shows from San Antonio to Kingsville. She often endured discrimination and segregation throughout the Texas Triangle. If she ever faced immediate physical danger, she never publicly revealed the details of the risks that she and her uncles encountered every time they traveled through areas known for their anti-Mexican segregation practices. She recalls, "We had our [hard] times, of course. Somehow we didn't feel hurt in a way, because I guess we knew it was their [Anglo] way of thinking and our way of being."[10] Though appearing to accept the status quo of the time, the choices Fernández made as a performer suggest that she used the status quo to reinvent herself at various stages over her career.

Fernández's story, like that of many Texas-Mexican business owners, both male and female, reveals the intricacies and complexities of race, gender, geography, and business. Fernández appears throughout the narrative of this book because her career development exemplifies the various aspects it examines: cultural identity, business orientation, entrepreneurial vision, and racial and ethnic negotiation of public performance, business, and domestic spaces. Her travels and experiences with segregation, her efforts at making a place and name for herself in public venues, and her negotiation of family life are all well documented in this book and the UTSA Libraries Special Collections. Her interaction with the larger Anglo community, both as entertainer and businesswoman, offers insight into how Texas Mexicans positioned themselves to capitalize on entrepreneurial opportunities. Emerging on the San Antonio cultural tourism scene in the late 1930s, Fernández enjoyed a long career that also represents and reflects changes over time within the parameters of this study.

By recounting the histories of figures like Rosita Fernández, my research examines three unexplored areas of Mexican American history: the development of business communities in the Texas Triangle, the emergence of women as entrepreneurs, and the growth of family-owned businesses. The women's stories not only establish their regional presence in the music industry, but also intersect with the narratives and experiences of people fleeing the Mexican Revolution during the early twentieth century, of migrant laborers during the 1930s, and of the later rural-to-urban transplant population. Although local newspapers and photos tell us much about the movement of people, the formation of communities, and the impact of informal economies at the local level, the oral histories—specifically of women whose voices have not yet been heard—are crucial to a fuller understanding of local communities and commerce. In this way, narratives and movement, time and place provide a new understanding of temporal space, especially as it played out in the Triangle area.

In an examination of Fernández's professional life as well as that of Texas Mexican women and business owners that emerged in the

1930s through the 1950s, I shift the public lens from the more com-
monly studied politics and labor to the economic and social arenas.[11]
In doing so, I have ended up in a radically different place from where
I began. My early research started with oral histories of legendary
women cantantes, some found in archival collections and others that I
collected in the field. In the first phase of my research, I chose to focus
on women cantantes because men were still considered the "real" pioneers of *la música tejana* in Texas and local history.

As I focused on the early Spanish-language music industry, what I
saw as the background story was the existence of numerous Mexicano-
owned businesses that had withstood decades of change in the cultural
landscape.[12] Thus, my project left the music industry on the periphery
and instead turned to family- and women-owned businesses. The
stories I trace unfold over a racially confused, hostile Texas economic
landscape where middle- and working-class Mexican Americans
labored to build a local economic infrastructure dependent on the
Spanish-language market. Women such as Carmen Marroquin,[13] member of a singing duo and later owner of the dance hall La Villita, made
a place for themselves wherever they traveled, and they established
businesses in whatever setting they found themselves in. Like Fernández, customers who sought services or goods often faced segregation
due to their economic status and ethnic and language backgrounds.
At the same time, an emerging professional and entrepreneurial class
with roots in Mexico made continuous attempts to separate itself from
the *patria* and integrate into the larger Euro-American narrative as
Texans. The success of these Texas Mexicans ebbed and flowed with
the economic and political climate; those businesses that targeted or
made room for Spanish speakers saw continuous fluctuations in their
customer base.

Looking at Mexican American history through the lens of business owners places the reader at the intersection of multiple themes
of migration, identity, opportunity, and consumer culture. Whether
operating as business managers or business partners, Texas Mexican
women negotiated a domestic sphere that grew to include their public
life. Viewing Texas Mexican family businesses in this way provides a
lens to examine how Mexican American women laid claim to business

spaces, how they responded to the demands of family, and how their entrepreneurship appropriated and articulated cultural identities.

The role of memory—of a past that has shaped an identity layered in class, political, and social conflict—has yet to be applied to the area within the Texas Triangle. The mostly untold history of Texas Mexican segregation and discrimination in the twentieth century leaves many gaps in the written histories of the everyday—the ordinary making of Texas Mexican and Spanish-speaking communities. Those left out include the businessmen and women identified in this research. The oral histories and other primary sources used to tell this story at times supplant, or at least expand on, the available (male) narratives and memory that have become "official" collective memories.

Early studies of recovered, oft-neglected Mexican American history focused on urban settings such as Houston, San Antonio, and El Paso. Historians of nineteenth-century Tejano history have illustrated how Texas Anglos engineered racial and ethnic categories to alienate Texas Mexicans from the political process and ostracize them socially based on language differences. Tejanos responded by creating their own mutual aid societies to economically assist the disadvantaged working classes, social groups that offered separate entertainment spaces, and political organizations that sought to end discriminatory practices in public spaces and public schools.

Business people who worked to integrate into the larger business community that catered to both Anglo and Mexican customers ran the risk, however, of failing to meet demand, as was the case with La Malinche Tortilla Factory. Unable to expand the factory to compete with larger tortilla-makers, La Malinche could not meet the commercial demand due to its costs. Ultimately, the survival of businesses that expanded their customer base rested on their negotiation from an ethnic or neighborhood business into one accepted into the mainstream, a delicate politicking of promoting the sale of culturally assigned products or services.

During the period I investigate, 1930 to 1955, new opportunities developed for ethnically defined businesses, Texas Mexican political involvement increased, mobility between socioeconomic classes was augmented, the adaptation and safeguarding of cultural practices grew, and local community populations rose and changed as both rural and urban migrants traveled across Texas. In the decades following the Great Depression, as Mexican Americans continued to grapple with questions of citizenship, American identity, and integration, their struggles highlighted the contradictions that divided and yet brought together Mexican Americans and Mexican immigrants. Through the formation of businesses and the perpetuation of cultural practices, informal routes of travel and exchange emerged. While the Great Depression halted much travel as musicians faced a number of obstacles in finding modes of transportation, some evidence suggests that specific carpas enjoyed a popular following by the end of the decade of the 1930s. For example, Anglos such as "Stout" Jackson, who did not participate in the segregation of Mexican Americans, created new spaces but also made a small profit from the demand for recreational events. My work locates this economic, social, and cultural production in the area I designate as the Texas Triangle.

Mexican migrants' decisions about where to live and work had a profound impact on the formation of south Texas communities in what geographer Daniel Arreola calls "perimeter" counties—those adjacent to what he calls "Tejano South Texas,"[14] but nevertheless excluded from it because of their small Mexican-American populations. Building on his groundbreaking cultural-geographical analysis, I posit the idea of the Texas Triangle as a cultural space defined by multiple layers of negotiation in the public and private sectors. The geographic area Arreola identifies, but does not fully explore, comprises the perimeter counties north of Nueces County, including Bexar County and extending east to Harris County. Arreola argues that "Mexican South Texas is a distinctive borderland, unlike any other Mexican American subregion."[15] Precisely because this region did not have a large Mexican American population, yet still maintained strong "Texas Mexican" identities, its dynamics were unique.[16] Its competing environmental, cultural, and political identities resulted in shifting perspectives inside the region.

Building on the geographical parameters of "space," geographer Richard Schein suggests a reading of the landscape through an examination of who has lived in the area and how it has been occupied. He writes that the outcome, "as unwitting autobiography," reveals both the "practice and ideals" of race in the area.[17] I expand his argument and hold that such an examination of the landscape produces a picture of the not-so-visible sense of community, expressed through the meaning of community as it was produced and shaped among the various locations where Texas Mexicans lived, worked, and traveled. The expression of sentiment, a sense of home and place, changes over time, as seen explicitly in segregation. Thus, physical spaces are not merely geographic, but temporal and historical. In this study, I want to add the layer of the temporal sentiment of space, its meaning, which despite the destruction of physical places or the desertion of small communities persists in memories.

For example, as the demarcating lines of segregation are erased, the importance of "Mexican only" areas is relegated to the past; however, the relationship of people's experience to the "Mexican only" phenomenon remains. Historian Matt Garcia reiterates that "landscapes are not 'neutral' or blank sheets on which human history is written; rather, their form and process of creation often possess keys to understanding the type of social relations that exist within a given society."[18] Retracing the routes driven by workers, performers, and other travelers requires imagination, suspending the notion that interstate travel meant quick gas fill-ups and food stops. Signs reading "No Mexicans or Dogs Allowed" stood in storefronts and restaurants, reminding Mexicans that their business was not wanted.

Discrimination, segregation, and the ongoing building of an alternate community shaped the Texas Mexican experience. These experiences drew connections of sentiment between audiences and cantantes. Through the expression of sentiment it is possible to explore the interactions that occurred in public places, from those spaces off-limits to women to spaces shared by both genders.[19] Frances Aparicio makes an argument for the value of understanding how cultural expression has created spaces for a collective identity and the self-reflective practice of Latino cultural traditions. She writes, "The arts are not only entertainment, but also expressions through which U.S. Latinos, both as performers and as audience, can reconnect—either symbolically or through their bodies and senses—to their traditional cultures of origin, to their heritages and language."[20] In order for my analysis to reposition women in the larger context of the informal business structure of Texas Mexican communities, then, I had to go beyond naming them. The businesswomen and men in this study moved beyond connecting to their cultural experiences as they created new spaces that took advantage of marginalized sectors to expand their own personal wealth as well as community resources.

This work builds on the available historical scholarship in the last half of the twentieth century, which has uncovered the past through the organizational success of the League of United Latin American Citizens (LULAC) and its high-profile members; though the story of Felix Longoria, a World War II hero who was denied a funeral service because of a "whites only" policy in a Three Rivers, Texas, funeral home; and through labor activists such as women of the San Antonio Pecan Shellers Strike. My own work complicates the neat categories of civic participation by inserting and reexamining the entrepreneurial class whose efforts at integration included social mobility and access to resources beyond those guaranteed by citizenship, and more closely aligned with capitalism.

An important marker of historical space in the Texas Triangle is the founding of small businesses that served an important function in light of de facto segregation and the maneuvers Mexican Americans had to perform in the face of both gendered and racial resistance. The path toward self-employment or sole proprietorship widened for all who could amass the initial start-up capital. Women who claimed a role in business affairs were engaged in redefining gendered spaces as they expanded their domestic role to include a public presence tied to their place of business. In bars, markets, restaurants, dance halls, curio shops, and a variety of other small businesses, Texas Mexicans practiced a cultural production of Mexican American identity both varied and, at times, self-contradictory.

I examine the development of Mexican American family- and women-owned businesses in a region of Texas heavily populated by both rural and urban communities over a twenty-five year period. While I do not offer an analysis of Spanish-language music, I bring cantantes into the discussion, for they managed their careers over varying lengths of time and located and secured performance stages vital to their work. Part of their success came from their use of different strategies for marketing their businesses and establishing their niches. They created a family image shaped by proper notions of sexuality and built their businesses based on ethnicity or nationality.

Matt Garcia's *A World of Its Own* explains how Mexican Americans utilized windows of opportunity to move into spaces that allowed interethnic relationships. These relationships did not lead to resistance, nor did they symbolize a working-class struggle. Instead they give a glimpse into the ways that Mexican Americans integrated and shaped their communities based on these interethnic exchanges. Similarly, Texas Mexicans used various business strategies to build relationships outside of their segregated communities.

The growth of family- and women-owned businesses had no set pattern, as many of the case studies I discuss demonstrate. Fernández, for example, never imagined she would have a long career performing and serving as her own manager. As a child in the late 1920s, she traveled from San Antonio to small towns such as Robstown, singing with her mother's brothers, Sotero, Santiago, and Fernando San Miguel—the "Trio San Miguel." She emerged from those early touring performances as a young star, building her success on selling her name to a local market and to a national tourism industry in its prime. Fernández exemplifies the business skills that women utilized as they navigated among circumstances such as gender expectations and discrimination based on language and ethnicity.[21] At stake for many of these women, regardless of their occupation, was their reputation, due to concerns about their ability to integrate family and work. Fernández preempted possible criticism of her balance between family and work by creating a professional media image integrally linked to family and strongly tied to her heritage. Other women who proved successful in their businesses and careers faced sanctioning by family and outsiders who misinterpreted their defiance as disregard for their domestic responsibility. They had to work in tandem with their husbands so as not to appear to challenge his masculinity or the public's perception of who was in charge. At the same time, they had to keep their customers happy with their service, maintain the audience's satisfaction with their performance, and respond to criticism of their public behavior.

Women understood the risks of appearing in places that might generate a lack of respect toward them, especially on the part of men who did not believe they should share the same spaces. The women whose stories I tell ran the bars and dance halls and remembered their women customers' names. Collecting these stories reinforces the act of naming names.[22] Mary F. Villarreal, my grandmother, recalls a time when most of her regular customers were women, young and old, who felt safe at her bar. "[There was] Chata, Elena, Dominga, Chepa, Mary, Simona, Anita, Connie. . . . Most of them played pool, drank beer, and put money in the jukebox just like a man."[23] Women in this narrative disrupt strict notions of private and public places and images of the traditional homemaker who adheres to regulated dictates of femininity. The response of their husbands, fathers, and other male relatives varied, but in many of these cases their family business was dependent upon embracing the participation of the women and girls.

When Ventura Alonzo's husband became jealous of the attention she paid to her male customers at their dance hall, La Terraza, she would remind him that it was her job and that if she didn't pay attention to them, the men would not return.[24] Her conversation with them did not promote promiscuity, but she knew that her husband interpreted her interaction with male customers as potential for gossip. All of the women I discuss responded to negative perceptions of their status by employing traditional business strategies, whether in sole proprietorships or partnerships with their husbands or other family members. Some sidestepped problems by using their husbands as the face of the business, a protection against questions about their public presence. Such measures, however, did not keep outsiders from commenting on these women and their appropriate place.

Pulling women in from the margins of the historical narrative required making their history the center. Susan Drucker and Gary Gumpert in *Voices in the Street: Explorations in Gender, Media, and Public Space* offer an examination of ideas of space as they address the gender gap and analyze how public spaces—associated with a sense of ownership—split along racial and gendered lines. They also raise questions about women's safety in certain public spaces and point to the institutionalization of gendered spaces as agents in reinforcing male privilege.[25] For example, women who worked in bars not only had to justify their presence but also their authority. Here, I place them in the context of their struggles and the challenges that they faced as women, mothers, and Mexicans.[26] Their narratives provide a unique opportunity to examine the establishment of Texas Mexican business communities. When placed on a map of south Texas, their life stories, over time, illustrate the links between the changes occurring in rural communities and the changes occurring in urban areas. History in this case adds the dimension of temporal space, where the experiences of the people I interviewed inform an event or place and endow it with significance. Together, seen through the lens of a geographical mapping, their oral histories chronicle the emergence and growth of businesses specific to cultural and economic development among Mexican Americans.

The issue of gender was, for many, not a matter of fighting for the right to fit in, but fighting for survival. Bar owner Mary F. Villarreal would scoff at the notion that she promoted women's rights. However, as a business manager, she insisted that women in the bar be treated with respect; she believed that if she allowed men to be abusive toward other women, then she gave them permission to treat her the same way. By controlling men's behavior toward their wives and girlfriends, she set the tone for the whole bar. Similarly, former cantante and nightclub owner Sofia Rodriguez recalled running into women at the grocery store who begged her to reopen her nightclub because they did not have a place to go where the men did not bother them.[27] Feminist or not, women bar owners literally created places where women were treated with respect.

The history of Mexicans in the Southwest continues to unfold through the gendered, racialized, and economic experiences of Texas Mexicans. The story of the Texas Triangle region has only begun to be uncovered and told. I hope to show that the physical location of the Triangle area gave Mexican-identified populations the opportunity to craft a personal and cultural distinctiveness that attracted both English- and Spanish-speaking customers.

Over the past three decades, an increasing number of Mexican American women activists, labor leaders, and educators have appeared in historical works covering American, Texan, and Mexican American populations. These women have come to the fore in part due to their successful management of their public and private lives. Historians of women's history, specifically Latina and Chicana history, have noted these women's successful integration of kitchen and family responsibilities as essential parts of the social and political movements they undertook—whether organizing from the home or bringing their children to the picket lines. Reading the lives of the women in these new histories underscores the importance of their work and counters previous ideas about the passive, docile nature of Mexican women. The histories of Texas Mexicans, Mexican Americans, Mexicanas, and Chicanas continue to reveal a constant in their survival—they sought in whatever way possible to utilize and act upon their rights of citizenship as a means of displaying their right to be a part of conversations and seek equity.

Historian Maria Eva Flores's work on the west Texas community of Fort Stockton reminds us, as well, of the significance of the national climate. "While the Depression touched the lives of all Americans, Mexican Americans in Texas and the American Southwest faced the movement from a rural, agricultural world to an urban, industrial lifestyle and the subsequent separation of families, and the additional hardship of repatriation and deportation."[28] Between the economic hardship of the Depression, when musicians curtailed their travel, and the growth of urban communities impacted the demand for rural social spaces, entertainers had to find other means of income. Hence, the rise of small businesses that catered specifically to segregated and marginalized populations. Texas Mexicans took advantage of the demand for ethnic and cultural goods and services on the part of Spanish-speaking populations marginalized by segregation.

The former owners of these business spaces produced accounts of travel, interaction with customers, and in the case of cantantes, experiences both onstage and running the stage. Sarah Deutsch offers an example of women's uses of public space in nineteenth- and twentieth-century Boston: "Women did more than respond to shifts in urban geography, however. They took a hand in altering the map of the city and in defining its meaning."[29] Like the Boston women Deutsch examines, the Texas Mexican business owners I discuss, men and women alike, altered the map of segregated spaces. One of them, Rosita Fernández, performed in auditoriums and on stages frequented mainly by white audiences: for example, the Arneson River Theatre and Municipal Auditorium in San Antonio, Texas. She adapted her style to the audience's tastes, turning these stages into her own, even taking responsibility when issues of funding for preservation arose. As Deutsch argues, women did not simply fall into a prearranged place; they participated in appropriating new places for women. She explains: "Space does not have independent agency. Its meaning or power is determined by the way groups of people organize their social, political, economic, and other interactions."[30] Throughout Rosita's career, we see such processes at work. She transformed a space through her constant negotiation of identity.

While not all of the stories and lives of people in this book navigated their careers with great success, they did employ various strategies of moving through a segregated terrain. Looking through the kaleidoscope of the south Texas landscape, the reflection of the shiny silver glass that is Rosita is the first reflection that reveals the dynamics of time, geography, place, and space; so too do the ways in which Rosita moves and repositions herself change in the context of the ever-shifting Texas Mexican identity.

Chapter 1, "Business First: Becoming San Antonio's Rose," examines the success of Rosita Fernández as a businesswoman who marketed her name to help build San Antonio's cultural tourism. Though criticized for participating in San Antonio's re-creation of a palatable Mexican influence for its cultural tourism dollars, Fernández found a place on San Antonio stages for over six decades. During her career, she reinvented her "Rosita" character to attract audiences both local and national. Assuming a non-threatening public persona to speak publicly about what she viewed as the loss of valuable cultural space, Rosita and her personal politics remained unquestioned when she performed at political rallies. Though she never claimed feminist politics and has often been overlooked in Tejano music scholarship,

Fernández reclaimed through her media relations a public space generally reserved for Texas Anglos.

Chapter 2, "A 'Proper, Fitting or Moral Occupation' for Women: Gendering the Space of Business," examines the unconventional strategies of women in the bar and dance-hall business. Some of these women began their careers as singers, eventually leaving the stage for the chance to stay put and run their own businesses. The women in this chapter found a place in their bars and dance halls, though they encountered social stigmas and legal obstacles. The five bars discussed reveal a history lost in the erasure of Mexican American women from the twentieth-century Texas narrative.

Chapter 3, "The Business of Culture: Selling Politics and Cultural Goods," expands the examination of the market to include traditional Mexican-American businesses that catered to both Mexican Americans and Texas Anglos, while also discussing issues of identity production. The majority of these businesses can be found in the Corpus Christi region, an area known as the home of the early political activism of LULAC and the American GI Forum. These organizations served the community by seeking fair and equitable treatment through the legal system. The region also had a solid base of Mexican-American-owned and Spanish-language businesses. Corpus Christi's location at the southern tip of the Triangle, or the beginning of the transfer zone—the area through which people traveled for work or to locate a new place to settle—marks it as a significant point in teasing out how identity and action define "place." The success of these businesses in this region cannot be determined exclusively by financial gains, but also, and more importantly, by their longevity and the meaning of their presence to the community.

Chapter 4, "Figuring Space: The Texas Triangle," explores the significance of the culture area between San Antonio, Corpus Christi, and Houston. I argue that the location of the three cities and their shared rural spaces created a cultural production of identity significant to the making of Texas Mexicans, both urban and rural. The 1930s and 1940s afforded Texas Mexicans new business prospects as they responded to the demand for services not easily accessible outside of the Spanish-language community. Texas Mexican men and women took advantage of these new opportunities to serve the needs of their larger local Mexicano community and build business alliances with the Euro-American community. These alliances raise questions about the economic influence on the transformation of Texas Mexican and Mexicano cultural identities. Surveying the Texas Triangle through community histories serves as a foundation for examining the cultural, social, and economic landscape that created a demand for business and social venues catering specifically to Mexican American consumers. Networks that developed between communities and performers opened the door for women business owners and the development of informal business associations.

Chapter 5, "Mapping Communities: Race, Gender, and Place," examines migration, discrimination, political activism, and the network of urban-rural relationships that developed out of the response to segregation and economic demands in the Texas Triangle region. This study starts in Corpus Christi with the longest-running Spanish-language newspaper, *El Progreso*, and travels along the coast on Texas Highway 35 toward the Houston region. By following both a narrative description and the experiences of those who rode the highways, it illustrates how people identified with their local communities and with a larger cultural connection as Texas Mexicans.

Carrying the story of Rosita Fernández throughout this book serves as the sliver of the kaleidoscope, the reminder of the spaces that Texas Mexican-American women made their own to refashion themselves and foster a sense of community. They constantly faced the question of where they fit as women and Texas Mexicans. In the bigger picture, Texas Mexican families responded to segregation by recognizing a need and demand for ethnic and culturally based goods, and they developed their businesses accordingly. As their enterprises grew and the racial and ethnic makeup of neighborhoods changed, business owners found themselves competing with corporations that took over the ethnic goods market at much lower costs. Neighborhood business owners were left without neighborhood customers when the businesses chose to integrate into the larger economic structure. In other words, building bridges, as Fernández often spoke of doing, sometimes led businesses to lose their market niche.

In using the term "Texas Mexican," I hope to show that those who entered the arena of business ownership placed value in an ethnic notion or idea, not in the actual people who made up the community. Historian Cynthia Orozco argues that the term "Mexicano Texano," not Texas Mexican, was the self-referenced label used in the 1920s, and while I do not disagree with her analysis, her term applies specifically to the decade prior to the core of my study. Also, she examines community formation through a different lens, as I argue that business people, whether families or individuals, men or women, made choices that gave them social mobility. However, Orozco's description of "Mexicano Texanos" as people who "were typically born in the United States, and/or their life experience was largely within Texas," is useful in describing the same population I label Texas Mexicans in this study.

Significant to their business relationships was their life experience in Texas as Mexicans.[31] Like the beers in my grandparents' bar, choices were limited in rural, agricultural areas. Texas Mexicans acquired social mobility through building economic infrastructure that provided a social network and visibility, thus expanding their customer base and permitting economic survival. Rosita the singer built Rosita the business and in turn grew a career that covered time and space over periods of ethnic tension in Texas. Starting with her story, this book illuminates the role of a select group of women whose families were shaped by their entrepreneurial vision in the Texas Triangle.

LISTENING TO
ROSITA

❋ ❋ ❋

1

BUSINESS FIRST
BECOMING SAN ANTONIO'S ROSE

A la encantadora estrella
Rosita Fernández
En este homenaje de reconocimiento por su gran labor
artística a través de los años. Radio, cine, televisión, discos,
variedades. Por llevar el talento artístico de nuestra raza y
nombre de San Antonio más allá de nuestra frontera. En
nombre de sus numerosos admiradores.

KCOR Radio

To the charming star
Rosita Fernández
This homage is in recognition for her great artistic work
through the years [in] radio, movies, television, records,
and variety shows. For taking the artistic talent of our *raza*
and the name of San Antonio beyond our borderlands. In
the name of her numerous admirers.

KCOR Radio

When Rosita Fernández began traveling with her uncles, the band
Los Tres San Miguel, she had little idea of the music world that lay
before her. As a nine-year-old, she suddenly had new opportunities
to sing in front of audiences other than her family. She never spoke
publicly of herself as someone who pioneered access to performance
spaces, nor did she associate herself with the Spanish-language music
industry that catered to working-class spaces such as bars or *cantinas*.
Instead, as she often insisted in newspaper and oral history interviews,
she simply loved to sing. Her singing ability in both English and Spanish produced more than just a sixty-year singing career; she also built a

business of "Rosita" on a divisive cultural landscape that often revered its "Spanish past" and dismissed its Mexican American present.[1]

Building and managing her varied and well-received career across music, tourism, advertising, and even film industries, Fernández earned her place in Mexican American history. Consider, for instance, KCOR's 1967 public recognition of her, which not only reflects her reputation among San Antonio's Spanish-speaking listeners as an artist and performer, but also hints at the influence she had outside of the city.[2] The award came to her mid-career—at the height of her public visibility as a constant source of entertainment on the Riverwalk, at conventions, and at local and regional charity events. Another high-profile award was the naming in Fernández's honor of "Rosita's Bridge" in 1982 for her annual participation in the Fiesta Noche del Rio. The bridge spans the San Antonio River and links to the Arneson River Theatre.[3] The plaque on the bridge reads: "Dedicated to ROSITA FERNÁNDEZ, singer of songs which have helped to build the bridge." Fittingly, this was the same bridge her father worked on in 1939 when it was built by the Works Progress Administration (WPA). Located on San Antonio's Riverwalk (Paseo del Rio), which attracts approximately 5.2 million visitors each year, Rosita's Bridge represents the twenty-six years of Fernández's performances at Fiesta Noche del Rio and the strong connection between the city of San Antonio and its popular entertainer.[4]

The narrative of this relationship however, does not emerge as a central storyline in the development of San Antonio's tourism industry. Although Fernández received numerous awards from the city and local organizations, and was honored at her death by political officials, her name and contributions are not publicly remembered in the same vibrant spirit with which San Antonio is known to celebrate its numerous iconic legends. The bridge named after her is one reminder of her cultural impact, but it stands alone, offering little hint of Fernández's civic contributions to the preservation of San Antonio's historical sites and cultural traditions. When laid out over six decades and viewed through a wide lens of music, culture, philanthropy, and civic engagement, Fernández's career provides a rich, little-explored layer of San Antonio's social and economic growth in the twentieth century. Her participation in numerous parades, her travel as a delegate of San Antonio's cultural tourism efforts, her performances at dinner clubs and military shows, and her support—financial and otherwise—of public performance space in San Antonio informs scholars of the politics of representation in San Antonio in the formative years of its entertainment industry.

Appearing continuously over a period of six decades on stage and in recordings, Rosita Fernández became a popular icon among Euro-American San Antonians as a representative of "Old Mexico." She was versatile in repertoire, providing accompaniment to orchestras, singing a range of boleros and rancheras. In her compilation of greatest hits recorded by Ideal Records, songs like "Mi Fracaso," "No Faltaba Más," and "Adiós Felicidad" were well known to her audiences. Early in her career, Fernández used her "Latin" look and Mexican heritage as a way of showcasing her talents. Drawing on her cultural background, her status in San Antonio radio, and the city's relationship to Mexico, she promoted herself as a representative of San Antonio's Mexican culture. While she did not resist the stereotypical images promoted by public relations representatives in San Antonio, she also shaped images of herself starting as early as the 1930s. Commercial spots and appearances on hour-long shows gave Fernández a boost toward establishing her local celebrity status, building upon her popularity among American audiences.

Early in her career, Fernández starred on live local radio stations, posed for city tourism marketing pieces, and acted as a spokesperson in advertising campaigns. As manager of her own singing career, Fernández led the life of a professional businesswoman who adapted to her changing audiences and clients. Fernández began appearing in public advertisements sponsored by the city of San Antonio in the 1930s, using her reputation to shape her niche in the market and direct her career according to her own desires. During her early years in the spotlight, for instance, she appears as an anonymous figure in a 1936 postcard. The back of the postcard reads: "A Senorita of Old Mexico in gala dress standing in front of picturesque Old Missions that are so numerous in this historic old land."[5] Although unnamed on the postcard, Fernández was on the verge of becoming a popular

Rosita Fernández is the unnamed model on this 1936 postcard (front). Rosita Fernández Papers, 1925–2000, MS 18, Special Collections, University of Texas at San Antonio.

public figure. Catering to San Antonio tourists, she reinvented herself culturally, mixing her "Spanish" heritage of music and dance into her roles as entertainer and hostess. Her innocent 1930s image, though transformed from señorita to señora over six decades, became the symbol of "Rosita." Her conscious decision to make San Antonio her home speaks to the significance of the making of place. In particular, the Riverwalk became Rosita's place. She became a fixture at the Arneson River Theatre, the historic outdoor theater spanning the river, where guests could sit on terraced steps or listen while floating in boats.

Fernández's career highlights the layers of negotiation within a male-dominated industry when viewed against a backdrop of

1936 postcard (back). The handwritten inscription (in Spanish) reads, "Rosita: Pleasant surprise to find you around here even if only on your card. Regards, Ramiro." **Pub. by Sandoval News Service, El Paso, Texas.** Rosita Fernández Papers, 1925–2000, MS 18, Special Collections, University of Texas at San Antonio.

discrimination and stereotypes. Fernández did not use those descriptors in stories of her career nor did she frame her experience in a narrative of racialized segregation; however, two pictures become clear from the news articles generated throughout her career. One, gendered language referring to body size and how she balanced work and family pervaded all news articles about her. Two, if she ever responded negatively to participating in places that played on stereotypical assumptions about Mexicans, she did so only privately. The second is evident, in that Fernández's place in the history of Mexican Americans and Chicanos does not fit the traditional mold of struggle and response to discrimination. In fact, she did not claim to have lived the life of negotiating between working-class roots and a Tejana identity. In addition, she traveled long enough with her uncles to acquire recording contracts, though she certainly faced discrimination during her travels, as did her predecessor, Lydia Mendoza. Instead, Fernández employed a professional image, playing to Euro-American stereotypes while not giving up her Mexican identity. What Fernández shares with Mendoza and other women performers of her time is that they negotiated a livelihood on the stage in the face of gendered and racialized assumptions, and while dealing with family obligations.

In interviews, photographs, and newspaper stories, Fernández promoted the stereotypical image of a submissive, quiet Mexican woman who did not question authority. Although in the 1930s and '40s divisions along lines of race, class, and nationality characterized the cultural landscape of the Texas Triangle[6]—the area of south Texas between Corpus Christi, San Antonio, and Houston—such was not always the case in the business world, where Rosita Fernández sang the jingle for the nationwide company Fritos. She also acted as the face of Gephardt Chili, whose commercial character "Rosita" reached everyone, regardless of citizenship.[7] The story of becoming "Rosita" speaks to the productive use of stereotypes for marketing purposes. Fernández's husband told the story of how Rosita went to "an audition for a Gephardt Chile Powder program. . . . They told her she would have to change her name from whatever it was to Rosita."[8] She replied that her name was indeed Rosita, ostensibly not challenging the company for its stereotypical request. Though these images might suggest a voiceless person, such a conclusion is premature, for Fernández, particularly early in her career, used her influence to raise money for charities and bring attention to the city of San Antonio's need to address the loss of important entertainment sites.

In 1967 Fernández renegotiated her place in San Antonio's tourism market, dabbling in acting, and creating her own "crossover" image that included accessing space on the convention and cocktail dinner scene. As an entertainer and singer, Rosita Fernández claimed spaces operated for and by white audiences. Her strategies parallel the actions of Paduanos, the name given to performers who appeared in shows at the Padua Hills Theater for more than four decades in Claremont, California. Historian Matt Garcia's work on the Paduanos offers

Rosita Fernández poses for an Amigos Tortillas ad, 1950. Rosita Fernández Papers, 1925–2000, MS 18, Special Collections, University of Texas at San Antonio.

an example by which to frame Fernández's rise. The Mexican Players of Padua Hills found their opportunities during the same period as Fernández, beginning in the 1930s.[9] Garcia contends, "Given the context of discrimination, segregation, and repatriation, many Paduanos valued the opportunity to perform in a public space rarely accessed by Mexican Americans."[10] Fernández laid claim to public space in a similar fashion. Given the discriminatory climate of the time and place in which Mexican artists lived and performed, the act of claiming space for performances played an important role in community building. Though both Rosita and the Paduanos performed for mainly white, middle-class audiences, they had clear strategies for successfully making a name for themselves in entertainment circles.

From the beginning of her career, Fernández asserted that she had the future of San Antonio's Mexican heritage in mind. She saw her contribution as important, especially in later years, given the explosion of the competing genre known as Tejano music, which integrated U.S. styles and fashions into Mexican-influenced music. She created her own mark with her handmade sequined dresses sewn mostly by her mother, The singer built her success on her choice to stay in the San Antonio area and cultivate an audience specifically to create a "legacy of Mexican singing and dance."[11] She once told a reporter that she "would like to leave a show or wonderful group of (performers who will carry on the) more typical roots of our culture so that the heritage—our dances, music and costumes of Mexico—don't die away in San Antonio, and so that it is not modernized so much that it's not our heritage anymore."[12] This legacy embodied a middle-class ideal, traditional in form, and tied to an often idealized and romanticized Spanish past. Her prominent visibility led to appearances across the United States as well as to the role of cultural icon among San Antonio's Anglo and Mexican American populations. The irony is that Fernández has been discounted as a part of the history of *la música tejana* (Tex-Mex music) because of her relationship to American middle-class audiences. Until recently, scholars have treated her as a popular figure known mostly among Americans and not as one of the prominent Mexican American singers in twentieth-century history. Returning to the kaleidoscope metaphor (see introduction to this book), it is evident that the various lenses through which audiences viewed Rosita's narrative did not change. And the parts that composed the whole of Rosita Fernández's story did not change.

The process of "becoming San Antonio's Rose" brings together the overarching themes and arguments of negotiated spaces, cultural production, and the significance of place and region that I make throughout this book. As an entertainer, Rosita demonstrated how she strategized and cut new paths as a businesswoman who created a marketable icon for audiences across age, race, and language.

This chapter, through oral histories and other archival materials, breaks Fernández's career up into three stages with overlapping chronology. First, as part of San Antonio's "Old Mexico," seen through San Antonio tourism advertisements, and as spokesperson for a variety of products including milk, tortillas, and beer. Second, as the performer "Rosita," who located her "Spanish" heritage of music and dance within U.S. culture and played hostess to San Antonio tourists. Third, as the "family before fortune" representation of motherhood and domesticity. Her constant refashioning of herself as a public persona often required that she open up her private life for outsiders to see, and thus she projected an image of a Mexican woman devoted to family. Specifically, through the local media, photo opportunities, and city affairs, Fernández crafted an image of a superwoman—mother, wife, and performer. Fernández not only managed her career as a songstress, but more significant to this study, she also self-managed and orchestrated her own persona—Rosita—in the public eye. As her own best public-relations agent, she used the media to remind them of her long-standing relationship with the city, as well as her friendship with various political and religious leaders in San Antonio.

Before moving into the three stages of Fernández's transformation, it is important to get a sense of how she described herself and how the media read her. While she attributed her success to God and family, the fact remains that Fernández held a clear vision of how she should promote herself. She often told reporters, "God has given me this, and I like it!" Neither in press nor in oral history documentation did Fernández state directly that her ambition included becoming nationally renowned, but her actions to become part of San Antonio's entertainment industry demonstrate her ambition. Indeed, Fernández often played on her "God-given talent"—her voice—as a way to explain her supposedly unanticipated venture into performance. Like other women performers and business people, particularly Mexican American women, she had no formal training in either arena, leaving journalists wondering how she had found such success. In an undated biographical flyer, the description of the singer begins: "Not dreaming that singing would become a life-time career, Fernández started singing with her uncles.[13] Arguably, this tale of her beginnings might have been true when she was nine years old, but later Fernández was clearly both ambitious and strategic in her ability to sell ideas and images relevant to the Mexican community.

Fernández's strategies at times created a tension between luck and aptitude. Journalists often noted her husband's professional position and identified her as "the wife," overlooking how she deftly handled the broadening of her performance spaces and her status as a married woman. The gendered and racial language used to describe her tended to depict Fernández as a fragile flower with surprising talents given her lack of training. A caption under Fernández's picture in *The Indianapolis Star* illustrates this point. "Her [Rosita Fernández's] sweet, strong voice is untrained but 'lovely things keep happening' to dark-eyed Rosita."[14] In one sentence, the writer alludes to the fact that Fernández has more luck than talent. In case the reader cannot tell from the photo, she does have dark eyes, like a true "Latin." With examples like this from *The Indianapolis Star* prevalent throughout her career, Rosita capitalized on the desire of tourists and middle-class San Antonio to capture a romanticized picture of Mexico through her music and her persona.

Fernández's success reflected her personality: a child who loved an audience, she started performing for her family's entertainment and what followed just happened from there. In an interview, she stated that all of her siblings had some sort of acting or singing talent, as they often put on shows for family members and neighbors. She thought her sister Bertha exhibited a natural singing ability, while she herself enjoyed the performance side of their shows. In 1936 the Entertainment Committee of the Texas Centennial Exposition chose the Rhumba Kings as the official orchestra of the exposition and Fernández and her sister Bertha as the featured solo singers. Bertha left the duo after a brief stint. Fernández believed that Bertha's decision to leave the stage had to do with not wanting to respond to the demands of a singing career.

Fernández's own career advanced rapidly as she moved from live singing to radio and eventually to film in the 1950s. The growing radio and recording industries, in conjunction with her live performances, gave her new venues to enhance her relationship with audiences.[15] At seventeen years of age she sang live on San Antonio's KONO radio station for $2.50 a week, and by 1932, she had the lead role in a WOAI radio show, also in San Antonio. Fernández sang to an anonymous public when she began singing live on the radio. This was some of her hardest singing, she claimed, since it took her voice hours to warm up in the morning.[16] Though little known at the time other than by her voice, she began making appearances for the radio stations and became the face for local advertisers. Her continued live performances gave listeners the feeling that they knew her personally, and through the performances, she imparted her love for Spanish-language music. Similar to the relationship Paduanos had with their audiences in California, Rosita's popular culture image and her music ultimately gave Euro-Americans access to a part of Mexican American culture that they might not have known otherwise.

REPRESENTING OLD MEXICO IN SAN ANTONIO

Perhaps one of the most telling examples of the negotiation of cultural space emerges from Fernández's skill at crossing and perhaps even erasing cultural and literal borders. Her ability to cross borders without ever leaving San Antonio came from her singing on shows such as "Border Magic," which aired on Tuesday evenings from six to six-thirty, a perfect time for dinner or after-dinner entertainment. To many listeners, she offered moments in which the boundaries between Texas and Mexico simply disappeared. A critic wrote, "When Rosita sings there is no border between Texas and Mexico."[17] The border, its precise location a subject of historical disputes, had long represented a line between "us" and "them." Fernández's insistence on framing her musical performances as a cultural bridge lifted a border between many people in two countries, though momentarily. Fernández drew on her Mexican heritage to attract an American crowd that was both curious about her ethnic roots and comfortable in her presence.

As "Rosita," Fernández continued to cultivate her name, look, and talent to become San Antonio's entertainment-industry representative of Mexico. In 1952, she and bandleader Eduardo Martínez attended the Washington, D.C., Board of Trade's annual midwinter dance as music representatives of San Antonio. In a "Confidential Report to Chamber of Commerce Board of Directors and Sponsors," photos show Fernández and Martínez dressed in traditional Mexican performance attire. The pair provided the entertainment for the Texas Frontier Frolic, attended by more than eight hundred guests in cowboy and Mexican dress. Although the state of Texas was the center of attention, San Antonio stole the show in demonstrating its position as the "gateway to Latin American trade."[18] San Antonio officials effectively marketed the city's romanticized historical legacy and prime geographical location by hiring people like Rosita to celebrate San Antonio's culture. An interesting juxtaposition: as Rosita was marketing and defining herself as the "bridge" between cultures and identities, the city in which she lived was positioning itself as a geographical gateway.

Fernández's career highlights in the 1960s included promoting the 1968 HemisFair in San Antonio, advertising the HemisFair on Mexican national television, and participating on the city's float during the Macy's Thanksgiving Parade. Fernández also recorded the English-language song "San Antonio," written specifically for the HemisFair event. The city made a "flexi disc" single of the "San Antonio" record that could be mailed. The decorative collector's item included photos of Rosita on the Riverwalk, the Alamo, and other San Antonio attractions.[19] Though disappointed by San Antonio city officials' failure to ask her to actually sing at HemisFair, Fernández continued to perform the song at city events for years to come.[20]

Fernández recognized the difficulties of capitalizing on the local market but also understood the nuances of the performance industry, which led to new opportunities. She established her reputation with her expansive song repertoire, ability to work with a variety of bands, and regular headlining of performances. As she reiterated in an interview, "I love San Antonio, I would never leave San Antonio," and that strategy proved to make her the star of her show and "San Antonio's Rose."[21] Her legacy and connection to San Antonio fans are illustrated in three murals in the city: "La Rosa de San Antonio–Rosita Fernández," "La Musica de San Anto," and "American Dream."[22]

ROSITA

Fernández's second strategy of success was to create the performer Rosita. This persona illustrates an uncanny ability to move the spotlight to the role of mother and the performance of domesticity. In 1963, an article in *The Indianapolis Star* points to her busy personal and professional life. "Rosita, in private life the wife of a department store executive and mother of two, nevertheless finds herself with 12 radio programs, one TV show, some conventions, a few radio commercials and San Antonio's 'Fiesta Noche del Rio.'"[23]

Several years after World War II, Fernández expanded her travel schedule beyond the boundaries of San Antonio. She and her husband, Raul Almaguer, moved their family to New York in 1953 at the urging of her uncle. "My uncle Sotero said, 'Rosita, come on, we need you here in New York,' so we decided to go."[24] A 1953 tax record in her archives indicates that she was in New York, participating in the show "Live Like a Millionaire." She received a small wage of $39.70 for her work. But San Antonio proved to be more than just a home; it was where the couple felt they belonged. Rosita laughed, while recounting their short stay in New York, "We just couldn't be away, away from San Antonio really. In two months we were back!"[25] Leaving San Antonio had not only meant leaving her extended family behind, but also her role as a San Antonio favorite. Fernández missed the interaction with her audiences and the attention she garnered in public. The city had been Rosita's home since 1928, and one of her marketing tools had been to establish herself as a representative of San Antonio's public image of Mexican culture, a role she assumed with seeming ease and comfort.

Fernández gained additional national exposure by appearing on other television programs, such as those hosted by Arthur Godfrey, Gary Moore, Barbara Britton, and Raúl Velasco.[26] As a result of her 1953 performance on the Arthur Godfrey variety show, a representative from CBS wrote the show requesting information about the song she sang and her record label. Fernández recorded a commercial for Mercury automobiles on the Ed Sullivan Show in 1955. Over the next decade she made additional national appearances, usually promoting her first name as her stage name, "Rosita."

Fernández continued to build her career, making two important decisions that put her back at the center of San Antonio's cultural spotlight. First, she took over her own bookings. Media relations and booking gigs essentially became her full-time job. Acting as her own manager and booking other acts to join her, Fernández also acquired new contracts by word of mouth. People knew her and her work and would call her at home for a booking. She hired a manager for a short period to handle her calls but found that she was losing business. She recalled that, after asking people to call her manager, "they wouldn't call him. I would lose the job."[27]

Second, she developed a working relationship with the Kiwanis Club in 1957 that proved to be strategically successful, as they developed the summer-long program Fiesta Noche del Rio. This partnership guaranteed her the role as the headliner for summer tourists. Fernández's partnership with the Kiwanis Club served as more than a source of regular income. In her continuous charitable resourcefulness, she used the event to impart on her fellow cast members the importance of the fundraiser. She recalls, "I would take them to the shelter and explain, 'this is what you are working for. This is what you're helping, you're helping children here.'"[28]

As a third strategy, she appeared regularly as a singer both in and around San Antonio with several well-known *orquestas* and big-band leaders such as Eduardo Martínez, Xavier Cugat, Sammy Kaye, Herman Waldman, and Tex Beneke. Her ability to do so was remarkable, particularly given the context of the times, when women singers in general remained nameless in photographs and pamphlets. Historian Manuel Peña has illustrated the popularity of orquestas among the middle class, and Fernández reiterated that there were many to choose from during that period. She loved singing surrounded by well-known groups, which she believed were true orchestras, "orquestas de quince, veinte músicos" (orchestras of fifteen to twenty musicians). She chose to sing with the Orquesta de Eduardo Martínez on most occasions, a strategic move given his band's popularity among Texas Mexicans.[29]

Fernández continually fostered her public persona's wholesome image. When the Walt Disney studio first hired her for a small part in a movie, they had not done so with the intent of offering her a singing engagement. Her ability to market herself as "pretty, Latin, and petite" expanded her image from San Antonio's embodiment of Old Mexico to Hollywood's stereotypes of Mexicans. Fernández remembers receiving a call from a Disney representative one night after nine o'clock. After a local radio station had given him her name, the representative phoned her at home, looking to hire a bar girl for *The Alamo* (1960). She recounted the phone conversation: "He asked, 'Are you Rosita the actress?'" She responded, "I'm Rosita. I'm not an actress. I'm a singer."[30] They hired her as one of the bar girls anyway. If she had any concerns about how such a role might tarnish her image, she quickly turned the situation into an example of how her traditional look made it difficult for makeup artists to turn her into a bar girl. In interviews she often told the story of how John Wayne would send her back to the trailer "to put on more makeup, and say, 'No, she doesn't look like a cantina girl.'"[31] She obviously did not fit the stereotypical "painted" look of a *cantinera*. In relaying this story, Fernández suggested that her wholesome appearance was inherent in her character. Just as important, this wholesomeness was a quality she often played up to court her audiences.

Fernández enjoyed acting, and her willingness to embody the image of a *señorita* earned her supporting roles in Hollywood both in television and on the big screen. She earned a larger role in Disney's film for television, *Sancho, The Homing Steer* (1962), in which she was slated to lip-synch the song "Tortilliaso." Apparently, the producers had not paid much attention when she said she was a vocalist. Nevertheless, she was willing to follow their direction. She described the voice of the original artist: "I heard a beautiful little voice of the young lady, but her pronunciation in Spanish was a little [off] . . . this is my job, singing." During the shooting, she attended a party on location in Arizona, where she had the opportunity to sing for Walt Disney. After that, he said to let Rosita sing whatever she wanted to sing.[32] She was paid a flat fee for her singing and appearance, but she joked, "I didn't get rich." The next year, Fernández played the mother to Tony Orlando's character in the CBS drama *Three Hundred Miles for Stephanie*. Despite being an untrained actress, Fernández parlayed her reputation as a well-known singer to be selected for film roles, though her roles stereotyped her as a traditional Mexican mother.

Evidence of Fernández's successful creation of herself as Rosita can be seen in her selection as the headlining entertainer for local conventions. Rosita assumed different performance "looks" without negative publicity and represented San Antonio in all venues where she performed. Fernández told Deborah Vargas that she estimated she performed at more than eighty conventions per year: "y con esos era muy bueno. Porque San Antonio era siempre de turismo" (and with that it was really good, because San Antonio was always a tourist spot).[33] Tourists on the Riverwalk saw the refined "señorita," an image she shed when she appeared on the cover of *Finan-seer*, the official publication of the Texas Finance Institute, and moved beyond typical Mexican fashions. In the issue, dedicated to an upcoming annual convention with Rosita as the headliner, she wore a form-fitting sequin cocktail dress and struck a seductive pose, an image opposite of her *folklorico* style and *trenzas* (braids). Because she was, of course, the virtuous Mexican woman, she could appear in a seductive gown, since it was recognized as a performance. Her role as the virtuous "San Antonio Rose" possibly diverted attention away from her revealing costume and the fact that the photo appeared on the magazine's front cover. By relying on a performance persona that operated within the parameters of stereotypical images of the Mexican woman, she achieved the freedom to push the limits of traditional dress and the larger stereotypes associated with less than wholesome images of women.

Fernández negotiated new spaces for Rosita beyond the stage of the Arneson River Theatre. She sang in private clubs and at dinner clubs in San Antonio: "I started singing with [the] Eduardo Martínez orquesta and we were playing for all the most beautiful clubs, not [dinner] clubs . . . for dances really." Almaguer, Fernández's husband, pointed out that "There were only two, the Kit Kat club and the Seven Oaks," but she performed there regularly.[34] In February 1960 she performed at the Midland Club and was also described as the "darling of supper clubs" by the Colonial Country Club in Fort Worth, Texas.[35] In a 1967 newspaper, Fernández appeared in an advertisement for a holiday sale at Joske's, a major department store that employed her husband for more than twenty years; the ad is a pencil drawing of Fernández with Mariachi Chapultepec.[36] This same drawing had graced the jacket cover of her 45-rpm record "San Antonio," which came out in 1966. While the 1960s were filled with conflict over access and civil rights for Mexican Americans, Fernández had become a prominent name in entertainment circles among affluent Texas Anglos.

Conscious of the racial politics that had emerged over time, Fernández believed she could serve as a cultural bridge, able to provide a link between Euro-Americans and Mexican Americans. She promoted herself as a representative of the city and claimed that she did not align herself with any political party. She also constantly referred to the bridge that bore her name, which linked amphitheater seating with the Arneson stage, as the tie between herself and her audience. She said in interviews, "I would always cross that little bridge. I crossed that little bridge for years and years and years. I would always sing a song at least on the bridge and then talk to the audience and then go back to the audience. That's where I would take a bow and then I'd bow at the stage. I thought it would be nicer to be closer to the people."[37] For Rosita, the bridge, built by her father and eventually named after her, made San Antonio hers. It served both figuratively and literally to connect her to the people in the stands. As she crossed back and forth, she reached out to her audience, calling on them to participate and join her in conversation in song, using her bilingual performances to emphasize a connection of cultures.[38]

Fernández's name allowed for several references to her image as a "Rosa" in both English and Spanish, a reference that she clearly enjoyed. Her name became an icon in itself with the rose's many associations, in particular the "Yellow Rose of Texas." A document dated

July 18, 1959, announcing the release of her new record, refers to her as "La Rosa de San Antonio."[39] Even though she personally enjoyed the title, it had multiple meanings that objectified and exoticized her. During a San Antonio welcome for ambassadors, Lady Bird Johnson introduced Rosita Fernández as the "Yellow Rose of San Antonio." Fernández modestly recalled with a smile, "She [Lady Bird Johnson] referred to me as 'First Lady of Song.' It just happened that all the news . . . from the newspaper . . . it just took like that and I'm glad."[40] Her other nicknames included "Alamo City's Ambassador of Good Will," both titles she had begun cultivating since her days as a representative at Washington's trade convention in 1952.

Fernández's engagement in politics beyond San Antonio's boundaries occurred mainly on the performance stage. She entertained world leaders such as Pope John Paul II and Prince Charles when they visited San Antonio.[41] At her first of multiple retirement parties (her public would not let her stay retired), held at El Centro de Artes at El Mercado, attendees included local and state officials and Mexican dignitaries.[42] Though she entertained politicians who used the Arneson River Theatre for political rallies, she always considered her own participation as entertainment and never as a political endorsement. Never acting as spokesperson for any political party or candidate, she maintained her position of staying out of politics. She stated in an interview that when she performed for President and Mrs. Johnson, she did not engage in conversation about politics. She could talk about her music, but she claimed to leave politics to the politicians.[43] In a biographical sheet distributed for the press, she rebuffed any idea that she had political connections, instead reiterating her cultural responsibilities as a performer: "a song stays longer in the heart, than a speech in one's head." For her, song had the strength to bring people together, unlike mere words.

Fernández and Almaguer built on her strategy of crossing borders when they shifted markets from the Spanish-speaking audience to a larger audience and decided to create a compact disc of Rosita's music. In 1999 they compiled and released a CD of her well-known titles, incorporating songs in both Spanish and English. When asked how she came up with the CD, she responded, "I chose [songs for] one of the albums because it was in English and Spanish and I am so lucky to have such beautiful friends, mexicanitos y americanitos, so I thought it would be just right."[44] Fernández's attention to her audience, in particular their language preferences and nationality, reiterates her strategic approach to making her audience feel that she was performing solely for them in the comfort of their home.

Fernández's negotiation of the political scene and her constant presence during the city's showcase events illustrates that she successfully mapped out her role in the city's identity. In the 1980s, she utilized her connections to city government when she felt that the Arneson Theatre needed repairs.[45] She wrote a letter to Mayor Henry Cisneros and City Councilwoman Maria Antonietta Berriozabal to propose a solution. Councilwoman Berriozabal replied, "I believe what you suggest is a good idea and I have contacted staff for information on the feasibility, practicability and cost of such an endeavor. . . . I recognize fully your many contributions to our community and I appreciate your suggestions."[46] Fernández's relationship to the mayor is evidence of the connection she had to city leaders. She recounted the time the mayor called her to help prepare for the visit of Prince Charles in 1986: "Henry Cisneros . . . called and said, 'Rosita, I want you to get about fifty mariachis.' Le digo yo, 'muy fácil, muy fácil Henry' [I told him, very easy, very easy Henry]."[47] Her ability to pull together a show eventually secured her place as one of the major forces behind the restoration of the Arneson Theatre. Her efforts at times focused on the Mexican American community, but the majority of her energy was devoted to children, the Catholic Church, and the renovation of public performance sites such as the Arneson and the Municipal Auditorium. When raising money for the Arneson, she would attend summer shows there and then pick the best troupes to perform in her Fiesta Noche del Rio fundraiser show.

Although Fernández spent much of her career proclaiming an apolitical position, her recording and performance decisions clearly show that she had identified the cultural gap between her audiences. Indeed, ever the link between two cultures, when she felt the need to point out the loss of a valuable cultural space, she would write a letter to the San Antonio newspaper. If, as she believed, a song stayed in the heart longer than a speech, then public spaces gave her the stage for those messages. She did not write with any sense of privilege or arrogance; rather, she would point out what she saw as an unfortunate mistake. In one case, she wrote a letter to the editor expressing her concern that the Main Plaza was not receiving the same attention as Alamo Plaza, the Riverwalk, or El Mercado. The tone of her letter suggests that it was both a financial and public relations matter, and she wanted to bring it to the city's and the media's attention.[48]As part of her civic responsibility, Rosita also wrote a letter to the newspaper as a call for help to restore the Municipal Auditorium. She told readers that they needed to support the proposed bond issue. Although she insisted that she remained outside of political circles, her letters to the newspaper illustrate her political involvement on behalf of the arts. Her name brought support from people like Jim Delaney, owner of Machinery Company, who wrote her personally and agreed to help, adding "you are wonderful in my book." Her ability to persuade through her letters reflected clout earned through the intercultural legacy of her performances.

Her success at crafting the Rosita brand was made clear at her first retirement party.[49] Newspaperman Rodolfo Resendez reported that "occasionally she will come out of retirement for special functions."[50] Her guest appearances continued into the 1990s, as she was often invited to perform as Rosita, the public persona she had cultivated for more than sixty years. Furthering her iconic status, the San Antonio Convention and Visitors Bureau re-released a recording of Fernández's "San Antonio" in December 1995.[51]

SAN ANTONIO'S ROSE AS WIFE AND MOTHER

Fernández's third strategy of self-fashioning came shortly after her marriage to Raul Almaguer in 1938. At this point, a third facet of the character she had created emerged, compatible with both her "Old Mexico" identity and her Rosita persona: the family woman. This makeover, a dramatic shift from professionally oriented to family-focused, portrayed her as a dutiful daughter, wife, and mother committed both to her family and to San Antonio and gave her credibility as a "good woman." The actual events in her life and her public image reveal a series of contradictions, including the wife who tried to give up her career for the sake of her marriage, the daughter who served her parents unquestioningly, and the mother who shielded her children from the public while simultaneously sharing "Rosita's family" on stage. When Lady Bird Johnson referred to Rosita as "San Antonio's First Lady of Song," she perhaps gave Fernández the highest honor of personal achievement, as the title captured both the place Fernández sought as part of San Antonio's cultural heritage and the elegance and refinement of womanhood she sought to portray publicly. Such an honor came with much negotiation at home.

In an attempt to stay home and become a full-time wife and mother, Fernández disappeared briefly from public view after her wedding to Raul Almaguer. The experience brought two surprising results: first, her health and spirit suffered in the transition, and second, the *San Antonio Light*, the city's major newspaper, took notice of her absence. Almaguer later revealed that Fernández experienced a terrible depression, and it became evident that her return to the stage was the solution. In response to the newspaper's questions regarding her whereabouts, Almaguer responded that Rosita was alive and well, and according to the article, "he should know because he is her husband." Together, Almaguer and Fernández played on the newspaper image of Rosita as the "petite, coy Latin" but added "wife" to the balance. Their response to the public shows a determination to bring her role as wife to the forefront, a move that makes her success seem even more unusual given her primary responsibilities as a daughter, wife, and mother. The purity of her image as a traditional housewife who just happened to have a phenomenal singing talent helped her to avoid scrutiny.

Almaguer and Fernández negotiated their gender roles so that Rosita did not have to give up her career, even though Raul initially attempted to redefine Rosita's place as being in the home and off the stage, demanding she drop out of show biz. The drive to maintain a virtuous image, which arguably helped her status, meant that even questionable acts of machismo by her husband were turned into "success" stories. Throughout Fernández's activities, newspaper reporters took great interest in Almaguer's position on her career. He repeatedly told them that he was the one with the "regular, full-time job." After first working for Joske's Department Store, Almaguer moved into the position of area store manager for Sears, a position from which he would retire in the 1980s and secure his family role as the breadwinner. Raul told sociologist Deborah Vargas, "We had an agreement that I would take care of my job and she would take care of her job."[52] "Breadwinner" in this case suggests the supplier of a steady income rather than the provider of the most money. With his job allegedly being to ensure that money came regularly into the household, the status of Rosita's income was positioned as "supplemental."

A second significant media strategy Fernández and Almaguer employed was the public use of her maiden name. She and Raul believed that "Fernández" was perceived as more authentically Mexican than Almaguer. The *San Antonio Express-News* noted that, "Married for over 48 years, she and husband, Raul, came to an agreement that she should continue using her maiden name of Fernández because they realized that Rosita had a very good opportunity to open doors for other Mexican American[s]. At that time only a handful of Almaguers were listed in the phone book and the name Almaguer did not sound Mexican enough."[53] This move marked the first conscious decision they made as a married couple to promote Fernández's career.[54] They successfully created a performance persona that the public read as representative of her private life. The personal note that Fernández received from San Antonio residents Walter and Joan O'Connor, who pledged their full support of her efforts to raise money for local spaces, illustrates how the public bought the idea of Rosita. The O'Connors felt they knew Fernández from her singing: "We do know your name is, properly, Mrs. Rosita Fernández—but to many of us who have enjoyed your singing these many years, and who love you—you are, always, Rosita." This reference to Fernández as her married name shows Rosita and Rául's success in marketing what the public perceived as the more Mexican-sounding name.

The birth of her two children, Raul Javier and Diana Rosa, created another opportunity for the business of making Rosita. Her new image played on the delicate balance of daughter, wife, and mother, thus making her husband's support integral to her public-relations success. Throughout her career, journalists wrote that Fernández put her family before her profession. One local newspaper headline read, "Fernández chose family over fame, fortune." Although Fernández made it known to reporters and interviewers that she had gone to New York, acted in films, performed internationally, and received numerous invitations to tour, she often followed such admissions by insisting that none of that gave her the satisfaction of having performed on stage with her daughter, or of rearing her children and being near her family. Fernández also reminded reporters that she had tough decisions to make while expanding her professional life: "I think about the big disappointments entertainers go through . . . things that happen with marriages and families when entertainers are performing that much on the road."[55] If a band made her an offer, she weighed her options: "I'm not saying that I wasn't tempted to go. . . . What I liked all the time was to sing, and I was always able to do that here in town—without getting all that money—but still, I was doing what I liked and was able to be here with my family."[56] Her public commitment to her family elevated her image as a pure, well-behaved wife and mother. Even on stage, she made her business a family affair, with both Raul, Jr., and Diana occasionally performing as dancers.[57]

Fernández's marriage and family captured the attention of San Antonio residents. Press clippings from the *San Antonio Light* and *San Antonio Express* show news coverage on everything from Rosita's family Christmas parties to her latest performances. She often publicly credited her husband as her strongman, the center of her support: "I married him 61 years ago. He's been my *como dice esa canción* [how does that song say it?] the wind behind [beneath] my wings. He's been my memory; he's been everything to me."[58] During an interview with Deborah Vargas, Rosita and Raul continued to finish each other's sentences as they told of how she performed live for the Armed Forces on an open-air stage.

Raul's support of Fernández earned him respect in newspaper articles where journalists praised his encouragement and modesty. Almaguer joked, "At work I'm Mr. Almaguer. . . . Outside of work I'm Rosita's husband."[59] He was also Rosita's biggest supporter and helped manage her career, though "In a 1989 interview with the *San Antonio Light*, the self-effacing Almaguer called himself his wife's 'prop man.'"[60] Her reply to the "prop man" reference: "No, you're everything."[61] Almaguer's strength shows up in his skillful use of newspaper space. In the following poem printed in Spanish with English translation in a local paper in the early 1990s, he takes advantage of a toast to his wife's retirement to remind the public of her contribution as a bridge builder and her tireless efforts as a longtime performer:

Rosita Fernández	Rosita Fernández
—cantante—	—singer—
Después de sesenta años	After sixty years
Rosita se retiró,	Rosita retired,
y paso a paso escaló	step by step she climbed
de su gloria los escaños;	to her glory inspired;
qué lástima que su voz	What a shame her voice
cristalina como fuente,	crystalline like a fountain,
ahora nos diga adiós	now says farewell
para construir una puente;	to build a bridge;
yo, a mi manera de ver	the way I look at things
le digo con mucho celo,	I tell her with great envy,
que cuando ya esté en el cielo	not to forget Almaguer
no se olvide de Almaguer.	when she is in Heaven.[62]

Almaguer's public pronouncements of love and respect for Rosita had a long history, so it seemed only fitting that he would send her out with this poem.

When Lady Bird Johnson proclaimed Fernández "San Antonio's First Lady of Song" and when local, regional, and national media all referred to her as "La Rosa," they captured what we might think of as the "essence of Rosita and all that she hoped for and came to mean. In her remarkably long career, Fernández traveled from the rural areas of south Texas to the big screens of Hollywood, naming and claiming space, crossing and challenging borders and boundaries, and negotiating gender, family, career, and business along the way. Her struggles and successes illustrate the many ways that Texas Mexican women singers and business owners created capital, both in their own individual and family ventures and in their larger communities. She catered to many audiences, from her start singing with her uncles in the Trio San Miguel, performing for migrant communities, to her final concerts on the patio of Mi Tierra, a landmark San Antonio restaurant catering to both local San Antonians and to many of the more than two million tourists who passed through San Antonio's popular El Mercado tourist center in 2006.[63] Fernández had to develop strategies for mediating the different needs and wants of her various audiences. And her success emerged in part from those business skills.

Fernández's travels, both geographic and cultural, literal and figurative, meant that she had to be a bridge builder, if not a bridge herself. It is no coincidence that the bridge in downtown San Antonio, near the Arneson River Theatre, was named "Rosita's Bridge," for not only did she regularly walk across it during her performances, but throughout her career, she strove to model what it would mean to cross between what we might think of as a divide between Texas Anglo and Texas Mexican worlds. On the occasion of her fiftieth anniversary as a performer, she was clear about the goals she had held so many decades earlier, in 1930: "Proud of her Mexican heritage, she wanted to be not only a singer but a representative of Mexican-Americans."[64] She believed that her Mexican heritage had much to offer through whether through performances or through letters to the editor. In an interview, she reiterated her desire to help her community: "I've always thought if I can help it any way, I will do it, and it just makes me feel good inside. I think it's our duty to help with anything we can."[65] Her impact, however, would never have extended to national recognition had she not made her public image as an entertainer an integral part of her life. Record contracts and radio programming changed the face of the music industry by the 1960s, and as she saw fewer opportunities to perform live and with various radio stations, Fernández found other avenues to foster relationships with her audiences.

That she was named "Woman of the Year," by San Antonio mayor Henry Cisneros tells us much about her success in managing gender. Early on, Fernández had to make choices about how to be "Rosita," the performer, Rosita the businesswoman, and Mrs. Almaguer, the wife and mother: "'There's two of us,' she said in 1990. 'First, there's the

Mrs. Almaguer, who does the dishes. Then, there's a Rosita Fernández who sings. The separation is such that, when our kids were small, they would say: 'Come on Mom, hurry up with the dishes so we can go see Rosita Fernández.'"[66]

Fernández's public statements about her early vision to identify and build a community of performers of Mexican heritage demonstrate how she laid claim to the invention of herself as Rosita. She often told stories of her early childhood, of her performing at home for family and in variety shows, to reinforce her sincerity and authenticity in the art of Mexican music and dance. Evidence of her success at making Rosita a "pretty, Latin, and petite" legend surfaced one last time in a tribute to the singer in the *San Antonio Express-News:* "She sang for a simple reason. 'God gave me a voice that is pleasant to hear, and I want to share it,' the petite singer said."[67]

Fernández's voice carried beyond audiences and borders. She gave spaces meaning both when occupying them and when speaking to their importance in maintaining cultural identity. She made certain that the public never forgot her ability to navigate home life with support from her husband and mother. She let her audiences know how meaningful they made each moment while she was singing. During the span of her career and in the spaces she touched, other women performers and business owners in the region between San Antonio, Corpus Christi, and Houston emerged and crafted similar storylines and personas. They redefined and performed intertwining public and personal identities that made them successful in negotiating gendered spaces.

As discussed in the next chapter, the conventional small role of women was integral to the growth of family-operated establishments and in challenging narrowly defined gendered work. Businesses that served as social spaces managed to survive for decades under the same owners despite numerous changes in alcohol laws, music styles, and business costs. Though these family businesses have given way to new social spaces or simply folded, lacking an heir to continue to run them, they illustrate a moment in time that provided ripe opportunities for social and economic engagement in local communities.

A "PROPER, FITTING OR MORAL OCCUPATION" FOR WOMEN
GENDERING THE SPACE OF BUSINESS

"Michigan could, beyond question, forbid all women
from working behind a bar."

Six months prior to her death, Señora Ventura Alonzo sat at the keyboard by her bed. Neither age nor arthritis could keep her from this mini-performance. She warmed up for a few minutes and then began playing, no longer paying attention to the small audience that surrounded her. Perhaps she imagined Alonzo y Sus Rancheros on stage forty years earlier, she at the microphone with her accordion, singing dance favorites requested by her fans. At ninety-four years of age, Alonzo displayed an attachment to her keyboard that revealed the depth of her love for music. Her bedroom became her stage, transformed in her imagination into a space open to public admirers. Although four decades had passed since her public performances, Alonzo still thought of herself as an entertainer. Her bedroom performance parallels that of other cantantes I interviewed: they all spoke of their public and responded to my questions with that audience in mind.

The early Spanish-language music industry opened small windows of opportunity for women to begin singing careers. Their travels with family members, as they followed migrant labor camps in the 1930s, laid the groundwork for future permanent work and recording opportunities. Unfortunately, the music industry and research on la músíca tejana[1] has focused less on the singers and more on the musicians or genres, leaving most women vocalists nameless in photos and in historical scholarship. Although their roles as "the only" or "the

29

first" have captured the attention of music buffs, they have not been written into the critical discourse of women's or Mexican American history. Yet this history is one that needs to be told, as the stories of these women reveal the many negotiations they made as singers, businesswomen, wives, and mothers. Their stories also bring to light the intersections of space and place that this book investigates.

Cantantes-turned-businesswomen continued their work in the music industry by taking advantage of a niche market of consumers from both the local and surrounding communities of the Texas Triangle defined by Corpus Christi, San Antonio, and Houston. Expanding their roles in the music industry by shifting their control to music venues such as bars and nightclubs, these women worked to claim legitimacy within the music industry by cultivating business strategies to give bands and their music live airtime. Even as they negotiated their place as women, they fashioned their businesses with a family image, promoting these locales as safe places for single women to socialize.

Legal parameters bound women to male oversight and protection in the early twentieth century, especially in the bar business, but many women in the Texas Triangle made their own decisions about the types of ventures they operated in partnership with their husbands. Among other issues, court cases raised numerous questions about how Mexican American women negotiated their role as sole proprietors, co-owners, and mothers in places considered damaging to their reputations and that of their families. The history of the Triangle area also exemplifies the ways in which Texas Mexican women actively participated as entrepreneurs in the entertainment field. Their histories are told through places like La Villita, La Terraza, the Arneson River Theatre, and Sofie's Lounge. When club owner Sofia Rodriguez opened her first tavern in the late 1940s, for instance, she first had to convince her father that she was not doing anything against the law. She believed that she had the legal right to make a business decision with her own money regardless of any existing legislation that sought to regulate her behavior by limiting the establishments she could enter, much less run. And yet the obstacles were significant, involving as they did not just the businesswoman and her family, but also her clientele. Because these women bar owners overwhelmingly targeted working-class populations as their clientele, they could also be accused of contributing to the delinquency of their working-class patrons.

An examination of women bar and dance hall owners illustrates their business foresight. Regardless of how outsiders viewed them, these women used the alternative social spaces of nightclubs, dance halls, and bars as profitable endeavors. Their experiences in starting their businesses differed based on whether the women served rural or urban populations, and on their customers' tastes in music. In addition to owning and operating these enterprises, they managed money and inventory, and threw out incorrigible drunks. The details of their narratives reveal how rural communities survived discrimination and isolation. Their stories bring to light the importance of their role as businesswomen as well as the importance of consumers in an informal economy—neither of which appears in other secondary literature or most newspaper articles.

A central and significant theme running through these stories is that the women, often working-class and under-educated, developed strategies that led to successful businesses. These women knew how to appeal to their customers, building long-standing businesses, and they had to exercise complete management of what happened inside their establishments. They persevered, often against considerable odds, over the forty-year period analyzed here, from the 1940s through the 1980s, in south Texas. For many of them, the neighborhoods and towns they had seen flourish began to disappear with the advent of urban renewal and the building of new state and federal highways starting in the1940s. An examination of their roles in the music industry shifts Mexican American historiography away from a focus on politics and labor, which currently dominate scholars' attention, and toward the development of Mexican businesses and their relationships to Mexican culture, in particular to an industry based on music and socializing in Mexican American communities throughout south Texas.

This chapter turns the kaleidoscope of Texas Mexican identity, allowing Rosita Fernández's piece of the larger narrative to bump into the pieces of other cantantes' stories. Though Fernández's marriage in

1938 caused a short hiatus in her singing career, the couple's ultimate decision to situate Rosita as part of the performance world provides a snapshot of the intentional focus the couple exhibited in investing in both her singing talent and the opportunity to build a business on that talent. The way in which Fernández marketed herself to *mexicano*, Mexican American, and Anglo audiences exemplified Mexican women's ability to understand their audiences and adapt to requests for particular genres of music, and in some cases, to converse in both English and Spanish. Fernández also successfully maintained a public image of a lady beyond reproach, though she traveled extensively and, at times, catered to audiences comprised mainly of men.[2]

Although women remained largely invisible in the mainstream entertainment industry, the women discussed in this chapter flourished as owners and operators of bars and dance halls. As business people, women faced a double standard, for they had to be both strong businesswomen and "ladies." Culturally, they had to expand the narrow boundaries allowed for Mexican American women's participation.[3] Regardless of laws that excluded their formal participation, de facto segregation in the economic political realm, and their status as Mexican women, whether single or married, they borrowed strategies from their male relatives and neighbors as well as Anglo business people to carve out business spaces of their own. Such tactics included building on the idea of being "family oriented" and creating spaces where their commercial advertisements included either their own children or photos of couples.

In 1948, a Supreme Court ruling upheld a lower court decision "that women did not have the right to serve as bartenders unless they were related to the male tavern owner."[4] The ruling stayed in place until 1970, indicating that prior to that time, laws limited the involvement of women in the bar business, specifically the women in this chapter. Although some husband-wife exceptions existed, as a whole, women were formally shut out of the industry. The lives of the women in this chapter, however, highlight their public relationships: performers-turned-businesswomen who negotiated their presence in spaces that traditionally excluded them and where, because they were "illegal," they possessed fewer rights before the law.

Women interested in owning, running, or working at particular businesses faced considerable legal challenges during much of the early half of the twentieth century. Taking their appeal to the Supreme Court, the appellants in the 1948 case *Goesaert et al. v. Cleary et al.* hoped to reverse Michigan law that discriminated against women bar owners. Although male bar owners could hire their female relatives to work in bars, female bar owners could not. Ruling on December 20, 1948, the court upheld a Michigan statute that stated that women in the state of Michigan could own their own bar or hold a liquor license, but could not work for themselves or hire their daughters to help run their bar. The grounds for affirming the statute, as well as extending its discriminatory practice over all women, suggested that the Court had a vested interest in protecting women's chastity. The Equal Protection Clause of the Fourteenth Amendment did not apply to what the Court considered societal vices. Since *Muller v. Oregon* (1908), many states had developed laws that "protected" women in the workplace, usually from hard physical labor and long hours, but also from "moral" dangers. Ironically, these moral dangers reflected men's advancement and sexual desires.

The plaintiffs did not base their appeal on alleging sex discrimination, but instead argued that male bartenders had lobbied to have such a law put in place in an effort to corner the bartending market. The Court's response dismissed such allegations of lobbying and expanded the scope of the case as a judicial public statement of women's peculiar moral vulnerability and the right of states to protect women based on their sex. Justice Frankfurter's opinion conflated sex and gender: "The fact that women may now have achieved the virtues that men have long claimed as their prerogatives and now indulge in vices that men have long practiced, does not preclude the States from drawing a sharp line between the sexes. . . . Since bartending by women may, in the allowable legislative judgment, give rise to moral and social problems against which it may devise preventive measures, the legislature need not go to the full length of prohibition if it believes that as to a defined group of females other factors are operating which either eliminate or reduce the moral and social problems otherwise calling for prohibition."[5]

The statute, as the high court reaffirmed, protected women from the alleged social ills brought about through the sale and consumption of liquor. Male behavior never came into question as being out of line or out of character; rather, the Court expected and confirmed that alcohol led to physical violence or sexual immorality. The Michigan statute, the Court believed, ultimately served to protect women's reputations and bodies. Women who worked under the direction of male relatives were exempt. After all, male family members had always been the first line of defense for women's virtue. The assumption that a male's presence offered protection raises questions about whether the male relative's reputation would suffer as well. The Court stated, "It is a question of public expediency and public morality, and not of Federal law."[6] Unspoken assumptions about gender and contradictory positions regarding personal definitions of moral behavior and women's respectability informed the 1948 ruling on many fronts. One outcome was that women could serve alcohol if they worked as waitresses, since the protection clause (*Muller v. Oregon*) did provide equality in some work situations.

The 1948 Supreme Court case came out of precedents set in 1890 and 1904, both of which excluded women from the liquor industry. Both of these earlier rulings identified an entire class of people who could not drink liquor: women. In the 1890 case, the Supreme Court also determined that a certain class of people, not just women, could be denied service: "Not only may a license be exacted from the keeper of the saloon before a glass of his liquors can be thus disposed of, but restrictions may be imposed as to the class of persons to whom they may be sold, and the hours of the day and the days of the week on which the saloons may be opened."[7]

For women and men who got around existing liquor laws, the bar business served as a means of making money and promoting community relationships, and not always prostitution. The bars and dance halls of the Texas Triangle represented a cultural production of Mexican American identity through music.[8] They were places open to women and the larger Spanish-language community, both of whom fell outside of the population normally included in public places.[9] Customers as well as bar and dance hall owners repeatedly tell of the

demand for space, of the local and rural consumer base able and willing to pay for dances and drinking, and of how business owners stayed
within the bounds of reputable behavior. Each oral history I conducted
signifies how the women I study marked ethnic and cultural identity,
as well how they kept their space distinct and separate from other
public spaces in the vicinity.

The core of these businesswomen's success lay in retooling their
skills to function in the business world; they had to sell a reconfigura-
tion of womanhood that included a negotiated reputation and increased
public responsibilities. They moved from the stage to behind the bar,
and in some cases, moved between the two. For several women, success
came from their experience early in their careers as cantantes, when
they built their audiences by cultivating a sense of a personal relationship
with them. Rosita Fernández's relationship with her audiences proves
the importance of creating a persona, however stereotypical, and connecting with audiences through that persona. Developing rapport with
customers came easy to these who treated their careers like a business,
catering to audience preferences. Their touring and cutting records
strengthened their ties to their listeners, because cantantes depended
on an ever growing audience to buy their music. This connection translated into the everyday retail business where they built both a clientele
willing to pay for drinks and a space dedicated to drinking and dancing.

Women entrepreneurs engaged in businesses that lay outside of
acceptable gendered boundaries. They defied the general presump-
tion of the 1940s and 1950s that women did not belong or could
not endure in the music industry, as well the notion that they could
not make profitable business decisions that would enable them to
stay in operation for decades. While employing traditional business
strategies, these women targeted a Spanish-language market that also
integrated English-speaking customers, including working-class folks
across ethnic lines.

DIME CON QUIÉN ANDAS Y TE DIRÉ QUIÉN ERES

Laden with moral judgment, the Mexican dicho (saying) "Dime con
quién andas y te diré quién eres" (Tell me whom you walk with and I
will tell you who you are) captures certain beliefs about how to judge

a person's character by the company he or she keeps. Arguably this sentiment sends a strong message to women who step out of their gendered conventions to enjoy a night "out on the town." "Dime con quién andas" dismisses women like Sofia Rodriguez, owner of Sofie's Lounge in Corpus Christi, Texas, whose father immediately thought that his daughter would be seen by neighbors as corrupt when she chose to run a bar. "Y te diré quién eres" meant these women were also judged solely on the basis of their clientele who were also their friends. Their hangouts, in this case, the "joints" they operated, were off-limits to "moral" women. Their women customers, themselves of questionable repute since they chose to go to a bar alone, thus offered further indictment of the bar owner's character.

Taking advantage of the possibilities open to them, however, businesswomen effectively merged their domestic roles with their new public positions. For women who chose to build careers beyond the traditional roles assigned to them, the choice meant a constant negotiation between proving they belonged behind the bar, and maintaining the "dignity of a lady." Mexicanas and Chicanas have been compared to La Malinche for acts considered oppositional to traditional Mexican ideals.[10] The virgin-whore dichotomy that these bar- or club-owning women faced appears repeatedly in their life stories, as many of them met criticism from men. Regardless of how they constructed their public identities, these women resisted categorization within the virgin-whore model even as their strategies challenged traditional notions of "women's work." Both cantantes and businesswomen faced specific challenges such as having to be accompanied by a husband or respected male figure to keep their good-standing intact. They resisted societal gender roles that confined them to particular spaces; yet they also played on their "womanhood" and their cultural identities to promote their careers. They often chose to tour with their families and favored spaces accessible to a Spanish-speaking clientele. Their decisions, while not assertions of independence per se, demonstrate their ability to make astute choices, both personal and professional.

The women I interviewed made varying decisions about their participation during World War II. At the same time as Sofia Rodriguez decided to join the call for women workers, the Mendoza sisters were singing at Club El Bohemio. María Mendoza recalls that "the war was going on at that time, and there were so many soldiers around. The soldiers were the ones who go and hang out in the beer joints, drink beer, and Juanita [her sister, with whom she formed a duo] and I were girls. They would go into the club on account of us."[11] Such strategies indicate that these women were not blind to the gendered nature of the new work opportunities.

Whether earning a living as a cantante or as a businesswoman, Texas Mexican women set their sights on developing a niche in the music and entertainment industries. They entered into music-oriented enterprises: Ventura Alonzo opened a dance hall, for example, and Sofia Rodriguez ran a bar. Without altering their traditional roles, they refashioned themselves as women who could create a night of entertainment, sometimes as cantantes, in other cases as managers and promoters for the artists and venues. Many of these women exhibited financial savvy in spaces where women should not be: bars or similar establishments. Through bars and dance halls, they combined work and family, striking a balance by meeting their traditional roles while finding ways to make a profit.

The establishments they ran emerged from a pattern of Mexican American businesses that catered to Mexican American communities. In 1934, San Antonio's West Side had several active businessmen who not only belonged to the Mexican Businessmen's Association but also "functioned as the intermediaries between the Mexican and Anglo communities."[12] Women were not listed as members, which suggests that men controlled the public relations of their businesses, despite the involvement of their wives or other women family members.

Women entered the music business, a field with a reputation for immoral behavior, and refashioned its definition of womanhood by maintaining the principle of family as defined by them. They thus claimed a place in their community's informal economy. Their decisions were not motivated by "women's rights," but by the idea that women, single or married, made good customers—and good business owners. In addition, these business owners identified a need for public spaces—the same spaces that had given some of them the opportunity to perform in earlier years. These spaces served to build community bonds and led to further opportunities for expansion. Women business owners recognized that men were often disrespectful to women who frequented bars, because of the association of bars with prostitution and other disreputable behavior. Instead of blaming their women patrons, mexicana bar owners made the men responsible for their actions by requiring that they behave appropriately and respectfully toward their women patrons.

Although the women I talked with denied holding positions of power in their communities, their descriptions of their activities and the reactions of others in the community belie their modesty. Local politicians who needed votes recognized that the patrons of these establishments were valuable unclaimed votes. Candidates for sheriff and county commissioner often asked Mary F. Villarreal, proprietor of the Pecan Lounge in Tivoli, to remind her customers to vote, especially since she already had a reputation for helping people obtain their absentee ballots or driving voters to the polls. Sofia Rodriguez also became active in politics and offered her business as a meeting place: "A lot of politicians started to come in and it was really, really nice."[13] Though often ignored by the business elite, and frequently denying that they held any real power, these women had the attention of leaders in both the Anglo and Mexican American communities.

Their cultural power emerged in part through their strategic social and cultural negotiations. For instance, "San Antonio's Rose," Rosita Fernández, negotiated not only her worth but also the payment for groups she hired to work with her. In 1980, John J. Hutton, who was in charge of securing entertainment for the International Meeting of Medical Specialists (IMMS), enlisted Fernández's help to arrange a variety show in San Antonio. Comments at the bottom of the lineup that Fernández drew up illustrate her thoughts as she made a note to herself calculating costs:

6 Mariachis
6 Mx. Dancers
6 Spanish [dancers]
a guitarist
M.C. & Rosita
20 people—for 2 hrs. $1,000 (not included spot lights and sound)[14]

This note provides a glimpse of her business acumen but also raises questions about how she played to the cultural tourism audience.

The intricacies of space, place, and community development are revealed in the different kinds of businesses and the different populations they relied on. The Corpus Christi dance halls drew their customer base from surrounding rural areas, while Houston and San Antonio drew from sizable populations both inside the city limits and in small towns on the outskirts. Cantineras, or women barkeepers, served predominantly Mexican American communities and usually operated on a small scale. They faced considerable opposition, as their businesses were generally considered off-limits to women of virtue. A critical look at the establishments included in this book reveals several distinctions in the labels attached to women who entered these spaces. Bars and taverns generally served beer-drinking customers, usually regulars who stopped by after work. They shared a lowbrow, working-class clientele, although women who owned these establishments never viewed their businesses or customers as beneath them. Nightclubs, on the other hand, catered to a night crowd that wanted live music for dancing. Nightclubs served mainly local people—unlike dance halls, which attracted people from the entire region, sometimes from as far as a hundred miles away. Dance halls had a higher social standing than bars; nightclubs stood somewhere in between. Given the rural population's lack of live music events to enjoy, dance halls such as La Villita gave surrounding farm communities access to bands stopping through on tour. People frequently caravanned in a group of vehicles to nearby dance halls, especially on weekend nights when they could count on hearing a popular band.

Places such as churches, privately owned buildings, and open public spaces played a vital role in meeting the demand for Mexican-oriented entertainment spaces. Churches held a special meaning as places where many of the women had started out singing in public and to which they returned at the end of their careers. Corpus Christi's Lupe Góngora, of Las Hermanas Góngora, was singing in the choir of La Sagrada Familia Catholic Church,[15] thirty-eight years after leaving her career. Fernández also maintained a close connection to her parish church, St. Paul, throughout her career, performing at several church fundraising functions. The legendary cantante and guitarist Lydia Mendoza recalls, "We would arrive at a town, a little town, Marfa, for example, that is on the way to El Paso, and Montes [their manager] would go directly to the church to speak with the priest, 'Do you have a hall, ¿un salon?'"[16] Churches offered direct access not only to space but also to audiences in the form of parish members. In addition to church spaces, abandoned buildings and empty lots sometimes provided necessary entertainment space.

Mendoza's stories about traveling to north Texas illuminate the way she and other performers fit into the schedules of farmworkers. She recalls that during those days, there was enough work for numerous groups: "We all got work. We'd each get only three days. Three days for us, then the next group. . . . And you'd work all week . . . because it was just packed with all those people."[17] They would gather at Lubbock's "Teatro del Lobo [Wolf Theater], which was a huge beautiful theater; nowadays it's a dance hall." In this description, Mendoza draws a picture of the interaction between performers and audiences where social gatherings created community.

Demand for Spanish-language entertainment in rural areas was so great that several Anglo entrepreneurs decided to get into the business as well. Robstown resident Thomas Jefferson Jackson, also known as "Stout" or "Strongman" Jackson, operated a number of well-established *carpas* (tent shows). A local biography of Jackson reported that "The coming of the Depression brought other changes to the entertainment world. . . . He [Jackson] sought another form of enterprise. He became attracted to south Texas, and realized that the many Spanish speaking persons in the area had neither low cost entertainment within their price range nor presentations in the language they could best understand. He acquired several large tents from the Old Tom Mix Circus, and as permanent entertainment features, set them up in Robstown, Kingsville, Alice, Falfurrias, and Carrizo Springs."[18]

The early success of carpas and the high demand for entertainment laid the foundation for the establishment of permanent dance halls. Stout Jackson is only one example of several carpas in the area that brought in Spanish-language movies and famous artists from Mexico. Several were established in the 1930s. By the 1940s, a smattering of Mexican-American–owned dance halls would emerge throughout Texas in rural towns and cities with pockets of Mexican American populations, as entrepreneurs built on the ongoing appetite for entertainment. Following World War II, permanent dance halls began to emerge in response to the continued demand.

Two dance halls owned by married couples and one woman-owned nightclub, all located in the Triangle region, found success in both their immediate and neighboring communities. While the location of the establishments provided relatively easy access for Mexican American customers, these places also shared a strategy of creating family-owned businesses that relied on family labor. The owners' children or grandchildren often worked collecting money, cleaning, or parking cars. These strategies helped generate an attractive public image: if these parents allowed their own sons and daughters to be in the place, others could do the same.

VENTURA ALONZO

The careful negotiation between family and business was crucial to the success of these women. Contrary to the story told in much of popular media, that women can either be successful professionally or as wives and mothers, the women I spoke with often managed to do both. Consider, for instance, the case of Ventura Alonzo. A hundred and fifty miles away from Sofia Rodriguez, Alonzo lived her final years in her hometown of San Antonio, with her daughter, Mary Sanchez.[19] Born in Monterrey, Mexico, on December 30, 1904, Alonzo was the fifth of eight children born to José Mártínez, a musician, and María del Pilar Cuevas Escamilla. Ventura and her family migrated to Brownsville, Texas, during the Mexican Revolution, when she was five years old. Shortly thereafter, they continued on to Kingsville. Her brother had ordered a piano from New York, and he often scolded Ventura for playing it in his absence. She was only twelve years old when a piano teacher came from Mexico to teach several children, including Ventura and her sister. Although she just wanted to play piano and did not want lessons, the piano teacher told her parents that she had an ear for music. Alonzo recounted, "Entonces vino el profesor y me examinó en el piano. . . . Él dijo, 'Esta muchachita no es de nota, es de aquí de la cabeza.'" [Then the professor came and gave me an examination on the piano. . . . He said, "This little girl does not go by note, but here, in her head.] Like many of her male counterparts of that time, she had talent but little formal training. As with Rosita, her family's acknowledgment of her talent was crucial to her development.

The young Alonzo was unable to make use of her talent, however, because her father died at the outset of the Great Depression, and her mother moved the family to Houston to find work. There, Alonzo married and had three sons with a man who could not stay employed and neglected to support the family. As a result, she filed for divorce. She began working at the National Biscuit Company, where she met and later married Francisco "Frank" Alonzo.[20] Thus, before she ever picked up the accordion and became lead singer in Alonzo y Sus Rancheros, she had divorced her first husband and assumed the role of head of the household with three young sons in tow. Señora Alonzo gave birth to five more children with her second husband.

In the mid-1930s, the Alonzos put together their orchestra, Alonzo y Sus Rancheros, and later Alonzo y su Orquesta, including Señora Alonzo on vocals and accordion. One story recounts how Alonzo made her singing debut while performing as a musician at the Immaculate Heart of Mary bazaar: "During one set, Alonzo's arm got tired from holding the accordion and she put it down, stepping up to the microphone to sing publicly for the first time. She was a hit." Alonzo left her mark on Tejano music, crafting a legacy as both singer and songwriter, with her credits including the hit "Magnolia Park," named for their Houston neighborhood and recorded by the family *orquesta*. Alonzo's status as the "first" and "only" woman accordion player for many years earned her the title "Queen of the Accordion." The orchestra recorded several albums with a variety of labels, including Falcón (in McAllen) and Rio (in San Antonio).[21]

Alonzo knew what it meant to be financially independent because she was raising her sons as a single parent after divorcing her first husband. She, Francisco, and sons, as Alonzo y Sus Rancheros, traveled the circuit in the 1950s, going through approximately forty-seven cities in a year including "places like Fort Worth, Austin, Kingsville."[22] For special events like Cinco de Mayo and other Mexican holidays,

Ventura Alonzo plays the accordion. Ventura Alonzo Collection, MSS 02020–04. Houston Metropolitan Research Center, Houston Public Library.

the group traveled to small cities south of Houston, like El Campo and Sugarland. She was a hit wherever they toured, from Ft. Worth to Kingsville. Also during the 1940s, the orchestra's musicians performed live on the radio to try to increase their popularity and to promote music they had recorded. Ventura Alonzo continued to work to keep family and business obligations tied together, now opening a family-operated dance hall. When they opened La Terraza in Houston's Magnolia Park neighborhood in the 1950s, they became the house band.[23] By initially attaching a café to La Terraza, the Alonzos responded to a ready-made customer base composed of people hungry after a night of dancing,.

Alonzo's talent on the accordion gave her respectability and status, but her commitment to family, singing, and the family business, La Terraza, remains overlooked. Yet Alonzo's deftness at business negotiations offers another example of women laying claim to space in the music industry. Playing a central role as a singer, agent for the band, and dance hall manager, often cooking at the café after a night of dancing, and ultimately taking charge of La Terraza's operations, Alonzo did more than play in the family band. Her granddaughter, Rosa Linda Alonzo Saenz, writes, "She was the one in charge of booking security officers, waiters, bartenders and other[s]."[24]

For more than fifteen years, the Alonzos would play Tuesday through Sunday nights, with people coming, in part, to see her play the accordion. Equally important, however, La Terraza served the local community as a popular social gathering space, seating close to a thousand people on the weekends. Alonzo understood how to meet her customers' demands, including their music requests. She recalled the story of the *troquero* (trucker) who would tip her five dollars to play his favorite song. He would come into town on the weekends: "Llegaba al Acapulco night club, allá por la Washington, 'Señora Alonzo, tóqueme mi pieza,' iba y me dejaba cinco dólares, se la tenía que dedicar, y sí le cantaba el son troquero. Es canción ranchera. ¡Tienes que darle gusto a la gente, si no, ya no te quieren!" [He arrived at the Acapulco nightclub, there by Washington [Street], 'Mrs. Alonzo, play my piece,' he would go and leave me five dollars, I had to dedicate it to him, and I sang him the trucker song. It's a ranchera song. You have to please the people, if not they won't want you any-more!][25] Alonzo also guaranteed her audiences that whatever songs she did not know, she would learn by the next time she played, usually the following week. Negotiating between her roles as performer, busi-nesswoman, and wife, she reminded her husband that on stage she had the obligation to satisfy her customers. She knew the importance of keeping her audience happy, playing the songs they requested and keeping the regulars coming back the following week.

For a number of years, Alonzo's son and his family lived in an apartment above La Terraza, where her granddaughter remembers helping to clean up in the late hours. Such family involvement signals Alonzo's success at merging her family and business life. La Terraza gave her a venue to perform, operate a business, and at the same time raise her children and manage the household.

The Alonzos' lives in the family business changed after La Terraza's lease expired and the landlord sold the building. Alonzo claimed that the owner of the building sold it without informing her or her husband of his decision, bringing an end to her career as a musician and nightclub owner, the latter venture having provided an alternative to a schedule of touring. The family retired from the night-club business and disbanded the orchestra in 1969.[26] Music had been Alonzo's business, but it did more than just bring in money. La Terraza had served a community of families, providing space for a night out together to enjoy the spirit of dancing and music live—and filling a void felt strongly by Texas Mexicans denied access to other forms or places of entertainment.

CARMEN MARROQUIN

Carmen Marroquin's experiences as a performer and a business owner in Alice, Texas, offers a snapshot of the social and economic exchange in urban and rural areas. These experiences also reveal how marriage and family redirected the course of some women's careers, like that of Carmen's sister, Laura Cantú, who later "fell out of sight."[27] Carmen and her sister initially sang as the duet Carmen y Laura. Little infor-mation exists about Laura, as many scholars and journalists have over-looked her role as part of the duet. The success many of the female *duetos* of the 1940s enjoyed was short-lived in comparison to those singers and musicians who found a regular audience.[28] Another sister act, Las Hermanas Góngora, for example, had a fourteen-year stint on the circuit, ending their career in 1956 when Luisa married. In his article on Las Hermanas Góngora, Vicente Carranza highlights the weight of societal expectations and rewards that Texas Mexican women encountered. He writes of the sisters, "They married great men and raised educated, moral Christian families. When Luisa married she was given a choice between continuing with her singing career, raising a family or both. She chose to raise a family."[29] Though he does give them credit for venturing into public spaces secured only for men, Carranza also reinforces the traditional hetero-normative ideals of womanhood and marriage.

Carmen y Laura toured with Ideal Records two months at a stretch, going through small towns where they could find pockets of Mexican American communities, but they did so with their husbands, which put them under less scrutiny. In fact, they worried more about the impact of segregation than they did about their reputations as women. Generally, Carmen claims that they did not let discrimination deter them from choosing their destinations. Northwest Texas towns such as Lubbock had reputations for strict segregation in living and social spaces. Although Marroquin recalled a stop in Lubbock, she remembered little except that people stared at her as she walked through downtown. She stated that she did not pay attention to discrimination if she encountered it, and it did not keep the duo from performing. However, they still had to find makeshift locations, as Marroquin recalls playing in school gymnasiums where they "would play in jeans because there were no places to make dances," and clearly, few places to change into performance clothes.[30]

Although Marroquin began her career singing with her sister, she found her greatest success as owner and operator of La Villita dance hall in Alice, Texas, approximately 102 miles southwest of Tivoli.[31] Tired of being on the road, Marroquin and her husband, Armando Marroquin, hired an architect from Monterrey to design their new business. Carmen Marroquin stated that they opened La Villita in 1952 "because we saw the need for the hall. We knew we could make money out of it."[32] Understanding that they could not rely solely on the population of Alice as their customer base, they attempted to attract customers from the surrounding towns. The *terraza* (patio) style evoked a sense of dancing in a garden, with plants and trees everywhere; however, weather eventually forced the Marroquins to add a roof. The club proved popular, drawing people from as far north as Victoria (114 miles away) and as far south as Brownsville (158 miles away). The opening night show included Beto Villa, the "father" of the *orquesta tejana.* During the first years that La Villita was open, bands from south Texas dominated the stage.[33] Her break into the dance hall business as part of a husband-wife operation highlights how women integrated their immediate family into their business ventures. Her ability to raise two sons while managing La Villita, as well as caring for her husband during his battle with Alzheimer's disease, demonstrates an uncompromising success in light of personal challenges.

Public resistance to women in charge nevertheless posed ongoing problems for bar owners. Like other Tejana businesswomen, Marroquin set the rules: "You have to let the public know quién manda [who is in charge]. I put a lot of guys in jails. If they wanted to show off, show off in jail. I run my place with rules. The public is not going to tell me what to do. I do what I want to do and the public had better respect my rules."[34] Marroquin protected not only her own business and reputation, but also the reputations of the women and families who patronized La Villita. The market she catered to wanted not just live entertainment, but family-oriented entertainment. She succeeded at making La Villita a family place where people could have weddings, anniversary parties, and *quinceañeras.* The inclusion of such parties suggests one means by which women could incorporate family functions into businesses that nevertheless depended on the sale of beer and other liquor.

Carmen Marroquin's operation of La Villita over the course of forty years demonstrates her ability to keep her dance hall current and popular, as she regularly brought in new talent to attract a younger generation with a taste for Tejano music. La Villita has withstood competition from two other local dance halls, one belonging to the Knights of Columbus and the other to the Veterans of Foreign Wars (VFW), both of which eventually became shared spaces that drew both Anglo and Mexican American patrons.

With family life as her focus, Marroquin came to see the La Villita building and business almost as a daughter in need of protection. Only half jokingly, she admitted, "I look at it like La Villita is my daughter. I have two sons, so La Villita is my daughter. So you better be nice at La Villita or I'll kill you."[35] She believed that any violent activity brought into La Villita equaled a personal affront—both to herself and to her family—one that she regarded as her responsibility to prevent.

SOFIA RODRIGUEZ

While Carmen Marroquin anchored her career in Alice, Sofia Rodriguez's success as a café- and bar owner started in San Antonio. After she returned from living in San Francisco and Chicago, still in her early twenties, she entered into a contract, leasing a tavern called the Frisco Bar. As expected, the new venture did not please her father, Luis Rodriguez, who argued with her for several hours about becoming a cantinera. Sofia, however, did not believe that her new venture would taint her reputation. She explained to him, "'No, I'm just going to sell beer.' He said, 'Well, that's a cantinera.' I said, 'Well, it's legal. It's legal to sell beer. I'm not doing anything illegal.'"[36] Using the specifics of the law, Rodriguez attempted to convince her father that what she planned was neither wrong nor damaging to the family name. His focus on reputation, countered by her argument about the legality of her decision, created a loophole that she exploited. Following legal parameters and reminding him of the American ideals she strove to achieve, Sofia pacified her father. Although questions about whether she actually did follow legal procedures remain unanswered, she certainly fought and won the first round. Perhaps fortuitously, her father did not realize the truth of the situation: Sofia had already purchased the license and signed the lease.[37]

The new bar, on Ruiz Street in San Antonio, served predominantly working-class Mexican Americans. She remembers that the parking lot filled up after three o'clock in the afternoon, when most of her customers got off work. Most of her business was based on selling beers like Southern Select and Lone Star, which sold for twenty cents a bottle. The more expensive brands, Schlitz and Budweiser, sold for twenty-five cents, and beer on tap sold for ten cents. While she served mainly working men from the neighborhood, she soon added another section to the bar that attracted couples. The space for the men included the bar and pool table areas, while the women sat at tables at a distance from the bar.

Rodriguez continued to operate the bar mostly on her own but hired her brother and another man to help out with the cleaning and stocking. Her father ran the pool table area, more to keep an eye on things, although it had become apparent that Rodriguez could manage well on her own. He watched over her carefully, and while his presence may not have signified approval of her operating the bar, it likely kept her reputation intact. The father-daughter relationship was complicated by the fact that the tavern where he worked belonged to his daughter; she made the final decisions as well as hiring her own employees. His role as the informal overseer continued even after her first marriage in 1949, to San Antonio policeman Ruben Rodriguez.

Married for less than three years, she had a son, Luis Rodriguez. When asked about her first husband's feelings about her running the bar, she replied frankly, "That's where he met me, so there wasn't anything that he could do about it."[38] In the 1950s, Rodriguez's decisions to divorce, move out on her own, and continue in the beer retail business did not align with the experiences and decisions of most other women, whatever their ethnicities. Again, as she had earlier with her father, Rodriguez approached the decision to divorce as a legal one. Had she done something illegal, she might have felt guilty, but in her eyes, the marriage had failed for other reasons. After deciding that her marriage would not work, she decided to move on. If there were consequences for choosing to divorce, Rodriguez never let them deter her. In 1953, Sofia Rodriguez closed her San Antonio tavern and took a chance on a move to Corpus Christi. There she became an important local figure as she discovered that politicians and other city leaders wanted the votes of her customers.

After looking at some properties, Rodriguez made an offer, purchased part of the building at 1107 Kinney Street, and eventually took ownership of the entire building. Her purchase of both the building and equipment illustrates her business acumen, as well as her disregard for how she might be perceived as a woman. As Rodriguez recalls the transaction:

> There was a Greek guy running the place, and I said, "How much are you selling this place for?" He wasn't selling the building, just the equipment. I said, "Well, don't you own the building?" [He replied], "My wife and I own it, so you have to lease it from us." I said, "Then I buy the stuff from you and I lease it from you?" He said, "Yes." I said, "I want the whole thing. How much do you want for the building and the equipment?" He said, "Eight thousand dollars." It was just a little place. I said, "Okay. You're on." I gave him a check for two thousand, five hundred dollars. "I'm going to San Antonio, I'm coming back with my boy and my clothes. I'll give you the balance when I get back. Make preparations." In less than thirty days I was in here.[39]

Rodriguez's ability to make a large down payment and pay off the building within thirty days speaks to her business savvy. Rodriguez also knew the advantage of purchasing as opposed to leasing the building, because doing so gave her the option of making changes and additions without having to request permission from the landlord. After retirement, she rented out a portion of the building as space for a lesbian bar, proving that she could make a valuable long-term investment to supplement her fixed income.[40]

By the mid-1950s, Rodriguez struck a profitable balance between her business responsibilities and her family obligations.[41] Her early investment in her business had meant long hours, because it included a café. As a single parent, she managed well even though she worked eighteen hours a day. Her son ate "his breakfast [at the café] and went to [the nearby] school, came home for lunch, went back and then ate supper."[42] She used the flexibility of her work routine in the bar to create a family space where her son could easily walk home for meals and she could keep tabs on him during the day. Willing to take risks proved important to Rodriguez's ability to build success in later years, as she remained active in the music industry and traveled across Texas with a band that she managed.[43] She would schedule two-to-three-day tours, all within driving distance, so she could be close to home and return for long stretches of time.

MARY F. VILLARREAL

Decades later and seventy miles north, Mary F. Villarreal, my grand-mother, made similar choices that helped her stay in the business for almost three decades. People in Tivoli did not approve of her taking over the bar, the Pecan Lounge, but she later said, "I didn't care."[44] When she took over in 1976 to help save the floundering family business, she also became the bill collector, telephoning and going to the homes of customers delinquent on their tabs. In typical "Mary" fashion, she would park her car in the driveway or on the street and honk until someone would come out to deal with her.[45] Twenty-six years later, when she faced retirement due to her failing health, she continued to amaze her friends with her strong-willed approach to recalcitrant customers.

Like other women proprietors of bars and dance halls, Villarreal faced being labeled not only a cantinera but a *callejera* (streetwalker or prostitute) and had to defend herself against rumors of promiscuity, since she often ran the bar on her own. Gossip about Mary abounded, while her husband's behavior rarely was questioned. But she did not back down from her right to operate a business, which she saw as merely selling beer, not herself. Even after twenty years in the business, Villarreal still faced criticism, particularly from men. She recalled a particular man on a Sunday afternoon: "Era un señor de Port Lavaca y me dijo, 'Qué esperanzas que dejara que mi mujer estuviera aquí sola.'" [It was a gentleman from Port Lavaca and he said to me, 'Not a chance that I would leave my wife here alone.'] She explained that she was not alone—family, friends, and other regular customers were present. She listed them, "Chata, Don Juan, some women from Refugio," and added, "Y usted que está aquí de las diez de la mañana ¿donde está su mujer?" [And you who are here since ten o'clock this morning, where is your wife?] He replied, "En la casa donde debía estar." [At home, where she is supposed to be.] Villarreal felt that she had little choice but to defend herself by putting him in his place and

Mary F. Villarreal. A rare moment of my grandmother relaxing before the start of a busy Sunday at the Pecan Lounge, circa 1977. She was probably having barbecue and drinking a Coke before stepping behind the bar. She is wearing jewelry, which means she had just come from church. Author's collection.

retorted, "¿Como sabe usted? Ya se fue con el Sancho y vino y usted ni cuenta se dio." [How do you know? She already left with her boy-friend, came back, and you did not even notice.] She ended her story, "He never came back."[46] She chuckled to herself as she told the story, both because it amused her that she could frustrate a man with her wit and because she was successful enough not to need his business.

While rumors circulated about affairs she had had with custom-ers who, though they stopped by regularly, were at best close family friends, some customers joked about her virginal characteristics as a form of making her name untouchable. A frequent male customer from Victoria, Texas, would announce "Entró la luz." [The light walked in] upon her entrance into the bar.[47] She liked to tell this story as a reminder to her customers not to take his announcement of her virtuous status lightly. Not only had a man proclaimed her virtue, but an out-of-towner at that! Characteristic of Villarreal, she won these battles on the principle of respectability and her ability to refuse service to anyone she considered disrespectful.

Once Villarreal began managing the bar, the money, and the inventory, she cared little about losing customers whom she deemed not worth *los nicles que gastaron* [the nickels they spent].[48] Her attitude often led to gossip by outsiders about both her private life and her activities inside the bar. Although she ultimately saved the family business, preserving her good reputation among the wives of her male customers may have been the greater accomplishment. This personal success also translated into more business for her, as wives felt comfortable and welcome in Villarreal's place of business. Her good standing meant that single women also somehow fell in line. "Dime con quién andas" worked to her advantage, as she was the one who drew the line of respectability. Specifically, she knew that she had customers, particularly women customers, to protect. Even when Villarreal decided to rent out the Pecan Lounge, she thought long about agreeing to a request by a local couple to lease the bar for a year, because she did not want her clientele to be driven out of a place she felt belonged to her customers as much as to her. Her old customers often commented that they missed her presence at "The Place," as they called it: "I don't know if they tell me to make me feel good or because it's la verdad [the truth], but they tell me que El Lugar [that The Place] is not the same without me." At the end of our interview, when I inquired whether she would do anything differently now, she stated that her intent "era a enseñar los hombres que yo era la que mandaba allí [was to show the men that she was the one in charge there] and I think I did that."[49] So while she may not have regarded herself as woman-conscious, she knew from the beginning that her success depended on her ability to keep her male customers aware that she was the boss.

Villarreal's account of her choices and priorities, particularly her gendered choices, offers insight into the complex daily negotiations of space, identity, and business that women business owners engaged in in 1920s–50s south Texas. Demonstrating commitment to a comprehensive ownership of her space—The Place—Villarreal was willing to risk alienating those few patrons who might disagree or disapprove, in order to protect her larger system of values. That is, in her own space, all women were welcome and all women deserved social respect. Intentionally or not, she used space in ways that challenged the virgin-whore dichotomy and that ultimately generated greater business and loyalty.

CONCLUSIONS

In retirement, Sofia Rodriguez rented her club to a lesbian couple who turned it into a bar. She understood that her place was always "safe," and that as the only lesbian bar in Corpus Christi, it had the potential to be successful. In the meantime, Mary F. Villarreal's renters decided not to renew their lease. Their departure coincided with the opening of a new bar in Tivoli, surprisingly, by a gay male couple. After visiting the bar, Villarreal decided that she would rather have her regular customers go there than turn to her rival, Adolf Villarreal (no relation), who owned the Pan American Ballroom.

I asked all of my interviewees the same final question: "If you could have done something differently, what would that be?" Three of my strongest interviews, all with women business owners with twenty to forty years of experience in the music and entertainment business, reiterated my grandmother's point, that they would have done nothing differently. They had no regrets, and while they may have argued the semantics of what it meant to be a businesswoman, they clearly placed themselves within their local Mexican American business community. With all of them using music as their connection to the larger entertainment industry, Sofia Rodriguez's sentiments highlight how they staked their claim in the Spanish-language music market: "I can't imagine [doing anything else], because I'm in love with music. I love music. I can't get away from it. As a matter of fact, I miss it so much I wish I had a place right now. You know, that I could be listening to music and talking to people, making friends."[50]

As in Michigan and many other states, the Department of Alcoholic Beverage Control in California sought in the 1970s to protect women's virtue, providing a section of written code that revoked the liquor licenses of those who had hired women bartenders not legally married to the licensee. Thus the law set a precedent for judging women's sexuality and confining them to men's guardianship. In *Sail'er Inn, Inc. v. Kirby* (1971), the next critical case on this issue, the petitioners challenged the code on the grounds that they had to choose between following the state mandate or federal law, for the Civil Rights Act of 1964, which specified a nondiscriminatory hiring policy, conflicted with the state code. Bartending as an occupation was not illegal; thus, under the new federal laws, women could become bartenders. The challenge in the *Kirby* case (from which the title quotation of this chapter is taken) finally overturned nearly eighty years of bans on women working in this morally "dangerous" trade in California.

Rodriguez was the only owner I interviewed to note the impact laws had on her ability to have full and legal ownership of what was simply a beer joint. The other women were impacted not by judicial regulations, but by societal constraints that created false boundaries and conjured up pejorative stereotypes of their character because of their business decisions. They simply ignored, or at least sidestepped, such accusations and capitalized on the moment to build a much-needed sense of community in a local, familiar place.

The next chapter, an examination of Corpus Christi newspapers in the 1930s and 1940s, offers striking examples of how these women responded to new economic and social possibilities in spite of the continued racially insensitive and sometimes aggressive segregation policies of local institutions toward Texas Mexicans. This book's focus on women is expanded to include both male and female business owners. The growth of Mexican American businesses in the Corpus Christi region during this period, for example, reflects a dependence on neighborhood customers originally from "the Hill," an area on the bluff behind an affluent neighborhood. Its borders were Leopard Street to Tancahua Street. The intersection of political history with the business development of Corpus Christi illustrates the complicated layers of ethnicity, citizenship, and socioeconomic mobility.[51] The Hill remains an economically deprived part of Corpus Christi, but stirrings of a downtown revival have emerged, and the Mexican-American business families have been integrated into upper-scale neighborhoods.

Those family businesses that have remained in the demographically associated, poor part of town have nevertheless demonstrated a long run.

Businesses such as La Malinche Tortilla Factory lost the basis for their success as they either moved to other parts of town or had to compete with the local business community at large, which had begun catering to Mexican Americans. The loss of this neighborhood also decentralized the economic base of many of the small businesses. Sustaining family-owned and -operated businesses on a local level meant that scant new money was generated; however, the internal flow of cash and goods helped neighborhoods maintain a sense of autonomy. Archival photos and Spanish-language newspapers offer lasting reminders of a once bustling downtown, filled with rural laborers doing their weekend *compras* (shopping); the open doors of businesses; and the emerging conflict over racialized treatment in receiving services.

3

THE BUSINESS OF CULTURE
SELLING POLITICS AND CULTURAL GOODS

We Invite You To Visit
Tex-Mex News Stand
"Little Mexico in Corpus Christi"
316 N. Staples, Dial 7887

The struggle of early twentieth-century Texas Mexican civil rights organizations produced not only activists, but also a class of entrepreneurs committed to achieving ideas of social mobility. Social justice incorporated more than a fight for equality; it also included a push toward integrating the meanings of citizenship and cultural identity. This chapter pays particular attention to the Corpus Christi region, where the rights of citizenship were debated in local newspapers, raised within organizations, and claimed through business ownership. Although the city's formal economic infrastructure and cash flow stemmed from its natural resources of gas and oil and its ocean port, the growing Mexican population established a business presence to serve a local and regional customer base. The relationship between civic activism and entrepreneurship in south Texas crystallizes most clearly in the Corpus Christi area.[1]

The quest for the American Dream through establishing businesses reinforced the claim to the rights of citizenship for Mexican Americans. The growth of family-owned and -operated businesses proved to be one avenue of gaining access to socioeconomic mobility and social status. Small business owners on "the Hill," the predominantly Mexican American side of Corpus Christi, created a new class of professionals without higher education degrees, such as Joe Rodriguez, Jr., who had just a high school diploma. His achievements as an athlete earned him respect when he became active in the business community as well as in the League of United Latin American Citizens (LULAC) and the American GI Forum. Unlike the cantina and dance hall businesses, which targeted a specific clientele of Spanish speakers, these small, conventional retail stores catered to an integrated market. They thus acted as "crossover" businesses whose owners were usually middle-class Mexican Americans with access to the privileges of society at large. They exercised the rights of citizenship and free enterprise, also identifying themselves to a degree with what may be called a discourse of whiteness.

Mexican Americans' claim to whiteness manifested itself through numerous political positions taken by Mexican American community leaders. Their views conflicted with most federal and state government efforts that sought to maintain a satisfactory relationship with Mexico, yet ignored the plight of Mexican Americans. Even more insulting was when government officials referred to Mexican Americans as "good neighbors," rather than recognizing their U.S. citizenship. When Texas farmers failed to uphold fair labor practices, the Mexican government banned the use of Mexican workers in Texas agricultural industries. The chairman of the Good Neighbor Commission in the United States dismissed the accusations as insignificant and at the same time mistakenly referred to Mexican workers as "Latin Americans," a title preferred among "American citizens of Spanish extraction . . . not 'neighbors.'"[2] The Good Neighbor Commission, created by Texas governor Coke R. Stevenson, had been in effect five years by this point. One of the original design points of the commission was to give rights of citizenship to Mexican Americans by classifying them as Caucasian in the census.[3] While declaring Mexican Americans to be white might not have changed their living conditions, advocates believed that the change in classification would change Texas Anglos' perception and treatment of Mexican Americans. Dr. J. A. Garcia fought to drop the term "Latin American" as a classification for county Health Department services, "El Dr. Garcia le recomendó . . . sólo dos clasificaciones—blancos y negros—y que suspendieran el uso de la clasificación latino-americano."[4] Garcia argued that the use of "Latin American" hurt the image of the Mexican American community.[5] The tension over names and the treatment of Spanish-surnamed populations surfaced not only between Texas Anglos and Texas Mexicans, but between Texas Mexicans and Mexicans who maintained ties to Mexico.

This chapter examines the merging of Corpus Christi's Texas Mexican civil rights and business communities through two local newspapers and three small businesses that sold an "authentic" line of products identified with Mexican culture. In the course of this examination, this work highlights two important business goals: one, a commitment to bettering neighborhoods and building a sense of community; and two, an effort to capitalize on immigrant and Spanish-speaking patrons. I use two Corpus Christi newspapers, *El Progreso* and *The Sentinel*, to examine how their perspectives embody the contradictions of citizenship and ethnic ties and later look at the newspapers in terms of ownership. *El Progreso*, the only locally run Spanish-language paper, was owned by a husband-and-wife team. *The Sentinel* was published by two American GI Forum members after World War II who wanted to bring attention to the continued discrimination against Mexican Americans and highlight the work of Mexican American civic and social organizations.[6]

The public discourse of community visibly played out in the two Corpus Christi newspapers in the period between 1938 and 1948. Rodolfo and Dora Cervera Mirabal used *El Progreso* to push a social-activist agenda that spoke to a wide range of Spanish-speaking readers. The newspaper represented only a small branch of the family business, the Mirabal Printing Company, the only Mexican-owned and -operated printing company in the Corpus Christi region.[7] The Mirabals represented the Mexican entrepreneur class, whose affluence gave them access to capital for investment and who enjoyed a positive reputation with the Anglo business world.

In the following decade, however, the other paper, *The Sentinel*, publicly championed the rights of Mexicans Americans but made clear its position on the need for Spanish speakers to make English their primary language. Newspapers such as *The Sentinel* alluded to the discrimination that business people experienced, such as that their office locations and largely Mexican clientele sometimes rendered their businesses "suspect" or disreputable. According to one of its editorials, *The Sentinel* used its pages to supply "'news about ordinary people' and 'authentic information and statistics pertaining to the abusive mannerisms practiced by selfish, ignorant bigwigs who think little if anything about the small fry's privileges and Constitutional rights.'"[8] *The Sentinel* reflected the views of its editorial board, the Phillips brothers, Oscar and Charles, both men active in the social and political life of the Corpus Christi community. Through the course of a two-year period, the newspaper reached out to the community to encourage local activism. The newspaper functioned as witness and evidence to the political and racial tension of the area. As the newspaper businesses grew as well as the influence of Mexican American organizations and Mexican business owners, the question of identity became ever more important.

In the political arena, civil rights organizations such as LULAC argued for the rights of citizenship for Mexican Americans. They fought for social justice in education and health care. Made up of entrepreneurs and professionals, these organizations demanded that Texas Mexican children have access to the same educational resources as their Anglo counterparts, and they demanded fair practices and pay from employers. In the economic arena, organizations such as the Mexican American Chamber of Commerce built their capitalist visions on networks based on the Spanish language and the market for Mexican cultural goods. Their professional network gave new Mexican-American-owned businesses greater prominence and sought to strengthen economic connections between the Mexican government and Mexican American businesses.[9] Together the members of each organization sought solutions to the challenges of immigrant labor, the place of their Mexican cultural heritage and language in the larger Texas landscape, their personal relations to Mexico, and their treatment of each other.

The urban experiences of migrants, immigrants, and transplants differed greatly in each of three main cities in the Triangle: Houston, Corpus Christi, and San Antonio. By the 1930s, Houston fit the mold of a city with an active Mexican American and Mexican immigrant population. Historian Thomas Kreneck has described Houston as a vortex, a place where newcomers could get lost in the crowd. As he pointed out, San Antonio and Corpus Christi absorbed their migrant and rural populations differently from Houston,[10] with clear social lines drawn between the working class and professional Mexican American residents of San Antonio. Photos of downtown Corpus Christi illustrate the influx of people from the rural areas on the weekends. Due to its smaller size and relationship to the surrounding rural areas, Corpus maintained a small-town feel where neighbors knew each other and were in many of the same organizations. The regular seasonal laborers who went into town for supplies lent continuity to the city's small-town connections.

Evidence also suggests that the Mexican American business community in the larger Texas Triangle used its ties to Mexico to promote a Mexican economic and cultural presence. This marketing strategy marks a third point of this chapter, the use of business and social circles to define the identities and meanings of the term "Texas Mexicans" in response to growing tension between the Mexican social classes that played out around questions of citizenship. This response was particularly visible in the pages of *The Sentinel*, which gave a public voice to those who believed in their patriotic duty as Americans of Mexican extraction. Therein lies one of the contradictions of "becoming American": as the political community sought to sever connections to a national identity rooted in Mexico and deepen a sense of an "American" identity, the business community maintained important financial ties to Mexico.[11] Given this situational dilemma, this chapter discusses how the Texas Mexicans in Corpus Christi responded both in terms of everyday life and economic development. Specifically, by the 1940s, social and political organizations maintained an association stemming from Mexican identity, but business people who had gained social mobility and a political presence saw Mexican culture as a saleable good.

US VERSUS THEM

A heightened awareness of "us" (Americans) versus "them" (Mexicans) emerges in the business, social, and civic conversations that took place in Corpus Christi between 1939 and 1950. Like other cities, Corpus Christi experienced segregation in housing, but those Mexicans with businesses found a way out of their social location. Corpus Christi's entangled past as a site of resistance between the U.S. and Mexican governments offers a picture of the historical legacy in which the Anglo population dominated the economic growth of the city. The emergence of Texas-Mexican-owned businesses led to the economic integration and social mobility of a new entrepreneurial class. The upper echelons of the Texas Mexican population by the late 1940s had two distinct classes: professionals and upwardly mobile entrepreneurs, both committed to ending segregation but not dedicated to a bicultural identity. In a 1974 paper, Diana G. Hernandez outlines the boundaries of "the Hill," which included the "hot spot" of Leopard Street, lined with numerous Mexican American businesses.[12] A reporter for the *Corpus Christi Caller* wrote that at the turn of the century, "Mexicans" totaled approximately 40 percent of the population and that they lived on the Hill.[13]

Because of its proximity to the border, the Triangle functioned as the gateway to trade with Mexico and created new opportunities for Mexican Americans to capitalize on new economic and cultural opportunities. Thus the city was the setting for the emergence of a new class of small business owners whose ventures relied on both their Mexican clientele's need for ethnic goods and the larger public demand for culturally authentic Mexican products. The most obvious point of entry in serving the needs of the surrounding Mexican American and Mexican community was through small markets and newsstands. Their success was also built on family participation as husband-and-wife teams. They built family businesses with their immediate community in mind, but many also believed that their business status gave them access to Euro-American networks built into the business world.

These businesses signaled the growth of Mexican and Mexican Americans as consumers of both luxury goods and basic everyday market necessities. When Alfonso Orea-Velez and his wife bought a small store from C. R. Rodriguez, the value of the store increased five times within the first year. They sold "everything from the usual groceries to unheard of patent medicines . . . He also has dry horned toads, rattlesnakes, humming birds, etc., for sale."[14] Another growing business was MGM Foods, owned by Marcelino G. Medina, which expanded to include a meat department that "would cater to cafes and small grocery stores."[15] And finally, today the Tex-Mex News Stand remains as the last reminder of 1940s Leopard Street–area businesses.[16]

Tex-Mex News Stand, Corpus Christi, Texas, 1950. Rodolfo and Dora Mirabal Papers, Special Collections and Archives, Bell Library, Texas A&M University–Corpus Christi.

THE FORMATION OF MEXICAN AMERICAN
ORGANIZATIONS

The Mexican American Chamber of Commerce in 1940s Corpus Christi emerged from the growing network of businesses catering to the surrounding Mexican American populations. A series of conversations can be discerned by paying close attention to the language of *The Sentinel* and its readers on the topics of identity and place: "What should we call ourselves?" and "Where do we belong?" The letters, articles, and ads reveal developing cultural identities, a fusion of ideals based on U.S. citizenship and Mexican heritage. Political identities drew specifically on notions of citizenship and civil rights; at times they claimed a racial whiteness to separate themselves from the "other." Entrepreneurial ventures created neighborhood spaces that provided for the needs of local residents. These businesses also made economic contributions to local political and cultural organizations that fought against discrimination and segregation.

Business owners in the urban areas of Corpus Christi, Houston, and San Antonio founded organizations or joined social clubs as part of their strategy to create a public picture of authenticity. Unlike earlier *mutualistas*, mutual aid societies that provided financial support and served as a welcoming committee for Mexican nationals, this new strategy created a political and economic structure that paralleled that of their Texas Anglo counterparts. These organizations included the Mexican American Chamber of Commerce and the Order of Sons of America, followed by LULAC and later the American GI Forum. Like LULAC, the Mexican American Chamber of Commerce established itself in the role of a watchdog calling attention to discriminatory racial practices. Discriminatory practices kept Mexican Americans from moving out of ethnic-bound enclaves, hampering social mobility. Members of these organizations thus acted in service to the Mexican American community at large. Moving out of the neighborhood, however remained a priority goal for families because integration into the larger Euro-American residential and business communities signaled a possible end to segregation. Though many of the small-business owners did not have a formal education, they clearly understood the status related to social mobility.

The formation of these early professional class organizations gave rise to the call for Americanization and in the legal arena, a claim to the rights of citizens as "Caucasians." The businesses they comprised offered basic services from beauty salons to printing companies. As the professional class attempted to integrate into predominantly Euro-American networks, they utilized their status as small-business owners to expand their claim to what Jacobson terms their "probationary whiteness,"[17] a whiteness he describes as contingent and partial, revocable in a way that Caucasian whiteness is not.

An unexplored aspect of successful integration on the part of Mexican American entrepreneurs was the concomitant disintegration of neighborhoods, as financial success meant the eventual purchase of property outside of the predominantly Mexican American side of town, the Hill. Politicians targeted the area in the late 1940s with the slogan "As the Hill Goes, so Goes the City," which indicates a voting bloc existed there. Residents refuted the perception of a voting bloc and more specifically, defended themselves against critics who assumed that voters from the Hill were uninformed. An editorial in *The Sentinel* responded, "The so-called Hill vote, perennially accused of following the advice of unscrupulous machine politicians and voting in a bloc, for candidates of unknown quality, Saturday should live up to at least part of those accusations," that being to vote for two candidates who grew up in the Hill.[18] The editorial writer sarcastically responded to allegations that residents of the Hill could be led blindly, when in fact much of the rest of the city often voted against Mexican Americans and thus could be said to vote in a bloc.

As established in earlier chapters, Mexican American and *mexicano* professional middle-class civic organizers, the working class, labor activists, and mutualistas have received much-needed attention from scholars in the last four decades. Their histories on these topics have demonstrated how Mexican Americans have asserted a white racial identity to place themselves higher in the ethno-racial hierarchy. They claimed this privilege through language and citizenship: promoting the English language, pledging allegiance to the United States, and setting legal precedents to overturn segregationist policies. Culturally, they maintained their right to perform and celebrate their Mexican heritage both at home and in public.[19] When questions arose about the work of LULAC to end segregation, an editorial in *The Sentinel* responded, "Should people of Spanish extraction in the future be looked upon as true Americans rather [than] the now popular view of 'just Mesicans,' the citizens who today are taking part in the struggle for equal educational opportunities will be looked upon as heroes and pioneers by posterity."[20]

MEXICAN AMERICAN BUSINESS START-UPS

Mexican American business ownership varied in terms of gender: sole proprietors were most often male; but in family-owned businesses, women contributed significant work, though they remained in the background. Women like Dora Mirabal and her negotiation of physical space operated within traditional models such as the print shop. The special equipment and size determined where they located their businesses. Overall, women recognized existing places that could be renovated into the businesses they sought to own and operate. The business owners cited in this chapter illustrate how Texas Mexicans maneuvered around segregation practices, employing their own family members and neighbors, and building a customer base that sometimes provoked political debate about their presence. The successful growth of these businesses lay in building on a customer base that reflected their customers' segregated place and their aspirations as Texas Mexican Americans.

EL PROGRESO

The businesses in this chapter reflect a traditional model in which women business owners did not have to defend their decisions to be in places considered socially off-limits to women. Although they did not have to justify their place, as with any business, they had to find successful methods of helping it grow. Dora Mirabal's role in the family newspaper, *El Progreso*, is one example of how women moved within race and gender circles. She used her sales skills to increase advertising among English-speaking businesses and thus raise *El Progreso*'s profits. She wrote articles and sold advertising, while her husband did the layout and publishing. Family history has it that

Dora Mirabal reads *El Progreso*, 1945. Rodolfo and Dora Mirabal Papers, Special Collections and Archives, Bell Library, Texas A&M University–Corpus Christi.

Mirabal told her husband, "I have an idea," and he could do little to stop her. The couple opened the first printing press in Corpus Christi and began their Spanish-language newspaper that reached surrounding counties.[21] Though their class status protected them from the everyday discrimination faced by those who worked in the fields or in the homes of Anglos, the Mirabals used their paper as a resource for the Spanish-speaking community and at the same time used their connections to Anglo-owned businesses to expand their advertising sales. Their newspaper continued as the longest-running Spanish-language printed media in the Corpus Christi area.

They began by acquiring a small space, building a clientele, and eventually expanding to larger premises. Like many small businesses of the 1940s, an important component to survival included owning the whole establishment. Leasing or renting left businesses at the mercy of the landlord, as witnessed among other businesses. Rodolfo Mirabal's mother unfortunately knew that lesson and gave her son one of her properties to begin his printing business when he was fourteen years old where he started *El Demócrata*. Together he and Dora opened Mirabal Print Shop in the middle of the local Mexican American community, which is where they printed *El Progreso*. Dora utilized her sales skills to increase readership and paid for the printing cost through ad sales.

Married in 1932, Dora and Rodolfo Mirabal both came from families that had been educated in Mexico and had established businesses in Corpus Christi. Rodolfo's parents had owned a bakery in Corpus Christi that sold a variety of European pastries made from recipes learned from their live-in maid, Josefa. Unfortunately, little is known about Josefa and her family, including their last name. The bakery remained in operation until the 1950s, its ownership having passed to Rodolfo's sister, Ernestina.[22] As is the case with many family-owned businesses, no one in her immediate family wanted to carry on the long hours and skill it took to learn the craft of baking or the operations side of the business. The lack of attention to the bakery resulted in the closing of its doors. Running small businesses required constant attention, particularly those that required a specific skill, like baking. Though by the 1950s, Mexican-owned bakeries and *panaderías* were commonplace, few endured through multiple generations.

Newspaper owner Dora Mirabal instilled a different set of ideals in her children, Rosie Mirabal Garza and Roberto Mirabal. They recall joining their mother on her trips downtown to sell advertising space in *El Progreso*. As a supplement to the newspaper, Mirabal produced *La Calavera* every October. In it, she would write short poems about locals to attract their interest in purchasing the magazine. Her strategies included writing poems about the young women who worked at Lichtenstein's Department Store. She would send her children to the store to let the shopgirls know if there was something written about them, as a way of pushing sales. Competition for prizes for whoever sold the most magazines also served as a free public relations campaign.

Mirabal's fast-growing readership and advertisement sales were the result of working every opportunity presented to her to give a pitch on the economic benefits for businesses taking out an ad and the social benefits for readers buying an issue. What her children considered everyday life, they now see as a calculated decision on their mother's part to introduce them to what they called a "business-minded world." Their childhood included selling the paper, competing for the most sales, and spending countless hours watching their parents work in the print shop. This introduction to business came with *consejos* (advice) and lessons on negotiating with the public. In the 1940s the paper had as many as twenty-two employees, many of whom served their apprenticeship under Rodolfo.

Part of the Mirabals' printing business came from Mexican movie actors' requesting to have flyers printed. The overlap of business and political relations to Mexico continued in post–World War II efforts to end segregation. When Mexican artists traveled throughout the Southwest to raise funds for desegregation efforts, local businesses provided funding for advertisements and offered their business spaces for gatherings. Live events provided money-raising opportunities and built cultural ties. For example, in 1947, less than a decade into its formation, the president of the Mexican American Chamber of Commerce acted as a liaison between the Mexico City YMCA football team and Corpus Christi High School's Buccaneers team.[23] *The Sentinel* helped publicize this international game. This "good neighbor"[24] endorsement by a local paper shows the desire to foster a relationship with Mexico. As a public courtesy highlighting their neighborly relationship, the sports journalist in *The Sentinel* gave credit to the Mexico team after its loss the previous year to the Corpus Christi College-Academy Cavaliers. The article stated, "The YMCA displayed much better game than the Chapingo Military institute who came in 1945 and was outclassed by the Cavaliers."[25]

In contrast to the public displays of the Good Neighbor Commission, LULAC fought to desegregate schools in various legal cases, and the American GI Forum—whose charter defined its membership as Hispanic—was founded. Both organizations had political roots and responded to the segregation and disenfranchisement of Mexican American communities. All the while, Mexican American small-business owners continued to claim space and, by paying close attention to their customers, expand their territory.

Contradictions in Mexican Americans' relationship to their Mexican heritage emerged when political agendas included practices of self-segregation. During the late 1940s, Dr. A. C. Duran and several "businessmen in cities in the Houston–San Antonio–Brownsville area proposed to build the Pan American Hospital which would house seventy-five beds." The proposed hospital was aimed at Mexican American patients and doctors. Most of their funding came in the form of pledges by Mexican artists to make guest appearances.[26] Letters to the editor and articles in *The Sentinel* raised questions about the need to self-segregate. Mexican American organizations in Corpus Christi that had fought to be treated as equals to their Anglo counterparts opposed the building of the hospital out of fear that it would lead to further segregation.

Newcomers to Corpus Christi sometimes had a different reaction to the political progress made by Mexican Americans. Arnoldo A. Lerma, who opened a drugstore on Morgan Street and whose father had lived in Corpus during the 1930s, wrote a letter to the editor exclaiming that although there existed only a "handful" of professional men, they came from well-established families and had done little to fight discrimination. He added, "Latin Americans in Laredo, El Paso, San Antonio, and Brownsville certainly are not in the discrimination status that we are in this town at present; Why?"[27]

The de facto segregation that occurred on the Hill was most apparent in the economic conditions of the area. Oscar Phillips, publisher and editor of *The Sentinel*, noted the disgraceful conditions that continued to exist in the neighborhood of the Hill, though he did not mention it by name. In his editorial of February 13, 1948, Phillips points to the problem of the voting bloc: "The residents in the southwest section of the city know they have gotten a raw deal. They have only to drive or walk in their section and then go across town to notice the difference."[28] The editors at *The Sentinel* should not have been surprised by the overt race discrimination; until the mid-1930s, the Corpus Christi city directory used socially constructed categories of race to mark the business and living patterns for the three main racial and ethnic groups, using "'C' for colored, 'M' for Mexican, and 'EM' for English-speaking Mexican."[29] The continued misleading conceptions of race, or "Mexican" as a race, throughout the 1940s determined where Mexican Americans could live, and while these discriminatory practices opened the door for legal battles, segregation also fostered a need for neighborhood businesses that served Mexican Americans, whether local or rural, English or Spanish speaking. The Hill served as the place where the shifting interplay between socioeconomic status, language, and citizenship would translate into a changing Texas Mexican distinctiveness based on Corpus Christi politics.

Those with professional degrees lent authority to the entrepreneurial class through organizations, combining their efforts with LULAC, the Chamber, and a third club, the Scorpion Club. Those in blue-collar businesses joined other business people in organizations like the Progressive Businessman's Association, including Cipriano "Zip" Gonzalez, who owned an auto service shop.[30]

Corpus Christi organizations served as a watchdog for injustice or discrimination against Mexican Americans in the surrounding towns. When local LULAC officials investigated the conditions of schools in nearby Mathis, they reported back that "Mathis has a scholastic enumeration of 1,676 of which 1,400 are of Mexican extraction, yet the school of the latter consists of one large and two small shacks, all of wood construction, while the school of the Anglo-American is a modern, red-brick building."[31] Corpus Christi's business relationship to its rural communities acted as socially conscious tentacles, as members of organizations, primarily LULAC, often called together all the surrounding towns to meetings. As LULAC looked to better the educational facilities, particularly in Mathis, council members invited the public from Edroy, Odem, Tynan, Skidmore, and Orange Grove to attend a meeting in Mathis: "Se discutirán las razones porqué es que los LULACs están demandando al Estado por separar a los niños de nuestra raza en las escuelas públicas."[32]

The desegregation case in Mathis led to the reinstatement of the Robstown LULAC council in March 1948 after "700 persons, including 100 from Corpus Christi, attended a rally at the Jackson Tent Theatre . . . and listened to top LULAC officials explain the segregation case."[33] A fourth organization, the Progressive Businessman's Association, enlarged its charitable target demographic, working with the Community Settlement House to fund "a young man or woman [who] has a legitimate desire to obtain an education or learn a trade and is financially unable to do so."[34] The award focused on Mexican youth, as the Community Settlement House focused on Mexican and Mexican American families, offering services in both English and Spanish.[35]

POST-WORLD WAR II ENTERTAINMENT BUSINESS

World War II had brought many social clubs to an end and unified their membership under an umbrella organization, but in the late 1940s they reemerged and used their social space to raise money and awareness of the narrow-mindedness of race prejudice. Clubs hosted dances that functioned as major fundraisers. The demand for places to hold dances after the war became evident, as suggested by an editorial of *The Sentinel*. The editors address the problems that social clubs had encountered with the renting of dance halls: "one of the three desirable places where the clubs could hold dances is charging over a hundred dollars for the use of the place. The hall that rates number two is near that price and the third has the reputation of a rowdy 'joint.'"[36] The problems arose not only from the cost or character of the dance halls, but the attitude of the owners. Rumor had it that one hall manager stated that he would not rent the hall to "them" and "if they do insist on using it, they are going to pay a sweet price for it."[37]

Social clubs increased the demand for dance and recreational spaces, as popular orchestras such as the Galvan family performed night after night. The Galvan clan would, over time, make a significant contribution to *la música de orquesta* as well as Corpus Christi's social life when they built Galvan Ballroom. Opened in 1949 at 1632 Agnes Street, the Galvan Ballroom became known as the hot spot for the middle class.[38]

Club owners believed they could count on Mexican American patrons to fill their establishments, as evidenced in the statement made by Riviera Club manager Russell Smith, "We expect a larger house Wednesday . . . they never fail to crowd night clubs on New Year's Eve."[39] During the first six weeks of 1948, six dances were scheduled at Carpenter's Hall, the Legion Center, the Riviera Club, and the Tusugi Club.[40] *The Sentinel* often commented on the high number of dances hosted by social clubs. The clubs' reliance on local business sponsorship came under fire by one merchant, who wrote a letter to the editor to complain of the abuse of dance placards. The original use of the plac- ards was to advertise the dance, but the anonymous writer noted that a change had taken place: "Placards cost no more than $20 or $25. Five or six ads at four or five dollars each would suffice. But now the cardboards are filled with 40 or 50 ads and enough to pay for half the dance expense is derived from that."[41] The writer makes the point that his business did not rely on the patronage of the teenagers or others attending the dances, but rather, that of the neighborhood residents. He suggests that the social clubs not abuse their local support. Such attacks, in this case on the ballroom, as a growing business serving the Mexican American market, were part of the political strife that businesses often faced.

In a perceived effort to reach a wider population that included Spanish speakers, *The Sentinel* published several issues in English and Spanish for two months in 1948. This sudden change occurred with the April 16 issue, when random articles and half of the brief notes found in the "Baker's Dozen" appeared in Spanish without English translation. Oddly enough, it was in the spirit of this short-lived attempt at serving a bilingual population that the contradictions of a claim to "whiteness" were revealed. The editors of *The Sentinel* believed that the American GI Forum could fill a void to assist more servicemen, specifically

Mexican American veterans. They argued that veterans from World War II would know every "Tom, Dick and Juan" in the membership roster, which would foster a sense of belonging. More importantly, they put forth the idea that forum "members will ask for a representative of Mexican descendency at each future draft board; they will ask for repeal of the practice by bigoted real estate dealers who specify 'that this property shall not be sold to or leased by any person other than that of Anglo-Saxon blood'; they will ask for persons whom they can speak to at the Veterans Administration office."[42] The bilingual issues did not make it past May 1948, so what the GI Forum had requested, *The Sentinel* changed, thus ending the bilingual experiment.

Issues of language and representation surfaced against the backdrop of questions of national identity and self-identification. Another letter to the editor of *The Sentinel* the following week requested the republishing of a letter to a San Antonio newspaper in which the writer, Consuelo Almarino, admonishes those who use the term "Latin." Almarino writes, "Unfortunately the general use of Spanish or Latin, referring to those of Mexican birth, is caused by our own Mexican race in the United States. Often, upon questioning one who refers to himself as Spanish, one learns that his parents were born in Mexico." Almarino lashes out sarcastically, "About the closest some of these groups could get to being castillian would be to cover themselves with lather of 'Castile' soap."[43]

As Mexican American communities grew politically and economically and struggled with identity, *The Sentinel* continued to serve as witness to the growing conflict with the Anglo population. A Mexican American parent wrote in to tell of her experience of being treated as though she did not belong at PTA meetings and her children who "often are embarrassed by class mates and teachers because they are not "gringas." This same parent vowed that "When this term ends, I am going back to San Antonio where things are a little better. This is a good town and I am making money in my little business but I don't want my children to grow up with an inferiority complex."[44] Prejudiced stereotypes of Mexicans led to the unjustified shooting of a Mexican man: "Recently, a former serviceman was shot in the arm, while he and his wife walked home from a local movie. The trigger-happy watchman gave out the most childish, feeble alibi. . . . The city police after hearing the watchman say that he thought the victim to be the same individual seen around the place three hours prior to the shooting, uttered 'there's nothing that can be done.'"[45] Other letters to the editor of *The Sentinel* express frustration at the limbo status of Texas Mexicans and condemned police inaction and the department's racially motivated policies. The letter writers look inward for answers on how to better serve each other and outward hoping to show how unjustly they are treated by people they perceive as their equals.

A conflict over who was to be held responsible for discriminatory practices continued to simmer through the letters to the editor. One self-identified U.S. citizen, E. K. Garcia, questioned the use of anti-discriminatory policies when a higher standard of civility needed to be practiced from within the community. He relayed his experience at a local theater "that caters exclusively to the Latin American of this city" and of the filthy state in which he found the men's room. He stated that the theater conditions resulted from economic discrimination and that "Latin Americans" should not be satisfied to receive such treatment from their Anglo counterparts and specifically not from others like themselves, especially those who made it possible for the owner to make a living.[46] A letter the following week looked even closer inward, blaming parents for not having the initiative to teach their children English, alleging that by not doing so, they "lack a[n] amount of Americanism which should be practiced daily." The writer, George J. Galvez, another concerned citizen, suggested that parents should speak "at least 60 percent English to their children."[47] The readers attacked one another and pointed the finger of blame, and in doing so, they contributed to a growing conflict within the politics of identity.

SETTING THE STAGE POST–WORLD WAR II

Back in San Antonio, cantante Rosita Fernández was capitalizing on new business prospects during and after the war. Akin to the way in which a war veteran might use his status to shape his professional identity, Fernández fashioned a new professional look as she built her résumé with local USO opportunities. She gained national attention by marketing herself to San Antonio's military and tourist industries, where she found a healthy following that loved a certain image of Mexican American women in both traditional Mexican costume and American cocktail attire. Both exoticized her presence, one in traditional, demure staging and the other as sexually attractive. When asked about what the singer had done during the war, her husband replied, "During the war, there were quite a number of lyrics for the military because, I think, San Antonio being such a military place . . . they had to keep all of the recruits and all of the soldiers. . . . Rosita would very often sing for hundreds, thousands of troops. Like you see on Bob Hope's." Fernández reasoned, "They would rather we go where they were and we would put on a great show and then dance and play for them too." Fernández's military appearances were tainted with racist overtones, however, and not only against Mexicans. In many cases, Japanese were the brunt of the bigotry as noted in the ad promoting a fundraising social event noting, "and your money will help slap the Japs."[48]

While the war gave Rosita Fernández a new performance arena, the postwar years brought a heightened level of visibility to the discriminatory practices that segregated Mexican Americans. Regardless of overall population, the three major cities in the Texas Triangle all had distinct Mexican American and Spanish-speaking neighborhoods. Mexican Americans did not begin fully integrating into predominantly Euro-American neighborhoods until the 1950s. Mexican Americans had long known that their treatment equaled that of second class citizens, and after the formation of the American GI Forum, World War I veteran Jack Martinez verbalized his hopes that "the Forum can gain the many things we unsuccessfully tried after the first war."[49] Entrepreneurship among Mexican Americans continued to grow at a rapid pace in the post–World War II years, as the demand grew by Mexican Americans still discriminated against in the overall economy. The majority of Corpus Christi and its surrounding towns remained segregated through the postwar years. The refusal of a Three Rivers, Texas, funeral home to perform the services and burial for a fallen war hero, Sergeant Felix Longoria, illustrated the degree to which anti-Mexican sentiment pervaded south Texas. Other World War II veterans in Corpus Christi found themselves coming home to segregated medical facilities, as "Memorial Medical Center . . . segregated in Negro, Mexican-American and Anglo wards. Speaking Spanish in the hospital was forbidden."[50]

EMERGING BUSINESSES

Businesses sprouted in the South Port area of Corpus Christi on the same street as the well-established La Malinche Tortilla Factory. News surfaced in January 1948 that Vicente De Santos, a general contractor, had plans to build a two-story building that would house a furniture and grocery store on the first floor and his office space on the second floor.[51]

Mexican-owned businesses proved important in hosting the meetings of organizations, such as the Mexican Chamber of Commerce, which met at the Shields Club on Leopard Street. The club, established in the 1920s, is now La Terraza Ballroom. "Speaking at a dinner Monday night at the Taxco Cafe[52] before members of LULAC Council No. 1, [Raul] Cortez [LULAC governor]: 'We believe that the case [will] go to the Supreme Court before we can gain a favorable verdict; we must fight until we win."[53] The Shields Club served as another meeting place for LULAC Council No. 1, while the Scorpion Club met at the Triple A Club.

The Progressive Businessmen's Association began a membership drive to enroll new merchants whose stores were located on Agnes and South Port Streets.[54] Locating businesses on these streets highlights a move by Mexican Americans to expand their business sites. Two doors down from La Malinche, Eva Nuncio opened the doors to Eva's Cafe on 704 South Port.[55] While South Port business expanded, advertisements for stores in the area of Agnes, Leopard, and Staples Streets continued to appear through the 1948 issues of *The Sentinel*, including Loa's Shoe Shop, Juan Gonzalez Funeral Home, Estrada Motor Sales, Gomez Pharmacy, a photography studio owned by Mr. and Mrs. M. G. Cortez, and a woman-owned pharmacy, Farmacia Gomez. In a buyout of E. O. Maley's drugstore, Ralph Galvan, Jr., was noted as being part of Corpus Christi's "pioneer" family, a term reserved for Mexican American families with legitimacy; that is, a historical legacy and in good standing. Galvan wielded clout as the leader of his family orchestra and perhaps used that status as an endorsement of his business expertise.[56] Known sports players opened businesses after the war and used their notoriety to promote their openings. One of the top "softballers" before World War II, Arnulfo "Nufo" Barrera, opened a watch repair shop at the end of 1947.[57] Five months later, another softball player, Joe "Pop" Alvarez, bought the Lamar Shoe Store located at 918 Leopard Street.[58]

Downtown property rentals provided some opportunities for interested parties to open new businesses, though purchasing the space proved a better investment. On Morgan Street, 10' × 12' retail spaces rented for $35 a month, with 20' × 50' and 40' × 50' units also advertised as available in the same area.[59] These advertisements in *The Sentinel* imply that owners made the spaces available to everyone, including Mexican Americans, and the location gave access to areas once predominantly Mexican American and largely Spanish-speaking.

Even locals admitted, "For all of Corpus Christi's ambitions to be a big city, it's still a small church-going town."[60] Residents from Corpus Christi and surrounding areas all shared a "kin" network, as illustrated in the Bluebonnet employees' newsletter sent to *The Sentinel*. The Bluebonnet Plant, which produced corn products, hired a number of locals, who often reported on their departure for the training center in Argo, Illinois, or activities there.[61] Both men and women did their training in Argo, Illinois, and lived at the Argo Hotel, where "everybody cooks his own meals so everybody tries to outdo the others in cuisine artistry."[62] Homesickness was the topic of most news from Argo: "Gilbert Trevino paid all of 50 cents to go into a local dance and then spent most of the night in the corner saying: 'It smells! There's nothing like Ralph's orchestra.'"[63]

One factor pushing the emergence of business was a need for basic goods and services, which also led to competition. Raul Garza and his younger brother Gilbert, who owned and operated small grocery stores in the neighborhoods, announced a plan in which their customers could become store members. The plan had been tested and proven successful in other parts of the country, but was a first for Corpus Christi residents. For three dollars a month, customers received a 20 percent discount, after their first fifteen dollars of groceries.[64] For the program to prove cost-effective, Raul "estimated that each store would have to sign up about 400 persons in order to pay the employees and give them a satisfactory investment return."[65] At the time the article was written, the stores had signed up about three hundred people, but with the cost of food increasing, Garza anticipated the plan would meet its minimum quota. The store "would remain open to 'drop-in' customers until enough persons had signed up for the 20 percent discount." Less than a week later an advertisement for Morgan Food Store in the January 16, 1948, issue of *The Sentinel* promoted a similar food club, where customers could purchase a week's membership instead of a whole month. The Morgan store charged a dollar a week, versus the three dollars a month charged by the Garzas.[66]

Long-standing, iconic institutions like La Malinche Tortilla Factory built their customer base on both surrounding retail stores and local customers. Alejandro Cortina "A. C." Chapa opened La Malinche Tortilla Factory in 1939 during a time when eating tortillas marked Mexican Americans as "different."[67] The tortilla factory sold retail items for a short time in the 1940s but focused on wholesale commerce throughout its lifetime. When A. C. Chapa left to serve overseas in World War II, his wife, Dolores, took over the business. On his return, she continued working as his partner. Like Dora of *El Progreso*, Dolores always looked for a sales opportunity. In one favorite family story, while she was in the hospital, the person in the room next door was the Corpus Christi School District's director of food services. Dolores paid her a visit and asked why the school district did not buy La Malinche tortillas to serve to the students. Her former son-in-law, Rafael Carrizo, said that she never missed a sales opportunity, including her evenings at the bingo hall. A. C. Chapa's obituary emphasized his perseverance as a young business owner:

> Chapa founded La Malinche Mexican Food Co. in 1940. His small plant turned out about 100 packages of tortillas a day, which were sold to local grocery stores. Chapa himself made deliveries on a bicycle. The business today is a tortilla retail-wholesale industry with a factory on South Port that turns out about 25,000 tortilla packages daily. . . . Chapa learned the tortilla manufacturing business from his father, Wenseslado Chapa, who, after moving his family to this country from

Monterrey, Mexico, set up a tortilla business in Harlingen in 1917. He invented much of the machinery used in making tortillas today. The Harlingen factory is still operated by the Chapa family.[68]

Like the Mirabals, Chapa had business experience and training in a specific area, and he capitalized on the exclusion of Mexican foods in commercial markets and the discriminatory cultural practices that set Mexican Americans apart from Euro-Americans. Both the Mirabals and Chapas built their public relations image not solely on their product, but on their equipment. La Malinche advertised itself as "The Best-Equipped Plant in the Southwest," suggesting timeliness and production ability as well as quality. The tortilla factory hit its peak in the 1960s and 1970s, after which the advent of commercial tortilla suppliers as well as city codes made it almost impossible for the business to expand.[69]

At the time of Chapa's death, his sons A.C., Jr., and Abel co-owned the factory, but their mother took it over during the next six years.[70] His daughter Rosario, who lived in Panama at the time, bought the factory from her mother in 1980 and operated it until her own death in 2005.[71] Rosario Carrizo, after a divorce, played the common double role of primary caretaker and businesswoman, as she cared for her mother and ran the family business.[72] Though the business did not increase its market share and eventually lost the bulk of its business to the competition of chain grocery stores such as H.E.B., Chapa maintained the business on its reputation for quality and relationship to the Mexican American and larger Corpus Christi community.

As discussed in the next chapter, the conventional small role of women was integral to the growth of family businesses and sole-proprietorship-operated establishments and in challenging narrowly defined gendered work and other domestic activities relegated to the home. Examples include businesses that served as social spaces and that survived for decades under the same ownership in the wake of numerous changes in alcohol laws, music styles, and business costs.

❀ 4 ❀

FIGURING SPACE
THE TEXAS TRIANGLE

"A theme is a point that connects all the dots,
ties up all the stories." "That's funny. Tying up all
the stories. Why somebody want to do that?"

Between 1910 and 1935, the south Texas social and cultural landscape
changed drastically. The growth of a Mexican-American- and Tejano-
identified urban middle class, coupled with an influx of a Mexican
immigrant population and an emerging agricultural migrant working-
class set in motion identities informed by class, region, work status,
and eventually citizenship.[1] The onset of the Great Depression simultaneously cut deeply into already existing impoverished conditions
among working-class Mexicans and fostered a new entrepreneurial
base tied to ethnic goods and services. Mexican repatriation in the
1930s resulted in the loss of whole communities, as out-of-work farm-
hands sought assistance to keep their families fed. The repatriation
program was an agreement between the Mexican government and the
Hoover administration to send Mexican nationals back to Mexico in an
effort to create more jobs for U.S. citizens. In a period of job decline,
the long-standing notion of who was American, and therefore eligible
for the rights of citizenship and work, targeted more than two million
Mexicans and Mexican-Americans in a forced deportation. An educated and civic-minded population of Mexican-born and U.S.-born
Mexican Americans looked inward as they supported their *patria* but
also sought ways to demonstrate and invest in their rights of citizenship. Across parts of Texas, the new movements, propelled in part by
the Great Depression as well as by larger racial and ethnic relations,
gave rise to social and economic communities, both rural and urban.

"Space" in this chapter conceptually defines the fluidity of where people, in particular Texas Mexicans, called home or created room for socializing. "Place" defines the physical or structural claim to where people lived, worked, and socialized. South Texas as a space embraced constant movement as families followed seasonal labor needs, and south Texas as a place became home to numerous small-business owners who catered to Spanish-speaking populations. I focus on the "Texas Triangle," a geographic space connected today by interstates and Texas highways. The triangle shape is evident when lines are drawn on the map between Corpus Christi, San Antonio, and Houston, establishing a place home to urban and rural communities; permanent migrant-worker settlements; and Texas Mexicans, Texans, and Mexicans. This chapter explores the making of those ethnically or racially defined communities over time and the layers of cultural definitions and economic opportunities that influenced the making of Mexican-American-owned businesses. Those layers, I argue, do not connect in a straight line nor do they depict a simple chronological timeline of "women were there, too." What they do is reveal a landscape that, when looked at as a whole, is made dynamic by movement and constant negotiation of gendered, class, and racialized identities. These developments in the Texas Triangle emerged from the convergence of race, nationality, culture, and ethnicity in pockets throughout the region. The fragments of this kaleidoscope reveal reflections of the production of a cultural identity, significant in the making of Texas Mexican culture and shaped both by everyday living and proximity to Mexico.

On their own, the points of the Texas Triangle and the areas in between paint a picture of economies controlled by whites, and lands that produced riches from oil, cattle, and agriculture. Prominent Mexican American activists and business owners emerge who made an impact on Texas histories. In fact, women like Rosita Fernández, Dora Mirabal, and Ventura Alonzo were vibrant actors in their local communities and represent a specific narrative about each of their home bases. In widening the lens of Rosita's sixty-year career and using it to look at the role of music performance and business, and the gendered negotiation of those spaces, the south Texas landscape reveals a map of concentric circles. Each circle connects a space and a time that was ripe for launching new businesses and developing community infrastructures dedicated to Mexican American and Spanish-speaking residents.

A new map of the performance spaces, travels, and connections between communities in the Texas Triangle can be traced by following the movement of women cantantes and pinpointing women-owned bars, nightclubs, and dance halls. These entertainment-oriented businesses and sites of cantantes' performances served as centers of communities and as cores of economic and social activity. They were the places that everyone knew as a spot to gather on a weeknight or to host a *pachanga*, a big party, on the weekend. With towns providing the majority of the audience for cantantes, the social spaces created gave meaning to the activities in individual communities, thereby forming a regional Texas Mexican identity bounded by the Texas Triangle.

Across the Triangle, Mexican and Texas Mexican communities arose, developed, flourished, and eventually died down and disappeared. This development and disintegration give rise to this chapter. I seek to understand the formation and development of racial and ethnic identity and community among entrepreneurial Texas Mexicans. More specifically, I explore the role of business, and in particular, of women- and family-owned businesses, in the growth and decline of Texas Mexican space and place. The businesses examined in this study illustrate a complex set of ethnic, professional, class, and gender relations unique to the creation of public, private, and cultural spaces in this region.

Since the 1930s, the mapping of historic sites, such as the Alamo, and the tracing of race and ethnicity in urban areas have provided the public with a list of official pieces of the past, places considered relevant to the narrative of U.S. history. Unfortunately, these places have not always included sites within ethnic communities whose experiences of displacement do not lend themselves to the traditional qualifications of historically significant sites, because many of them no longer exist, or their stories do not fit into a constructed "American experience." Exclusion is inherent in the criteria by which official historic sites are identified. Focusing on the Alamo as a source of

Mexican-American Texas history, for instance, negates the importance of cities like Alice, Robstown, and Kingsville, where cultural and social spaces central to rural communities developed informally and disappeared once the needs of agricultural production changed and small towns became virtually nonexistent.[2] Bars and dance halls, part of a larger social and economic network, contributed to the growth of an informal economic infrastructure of Mexican American communities. While the carpas (tent shows) no longer exist and La Villita seems like a modest bar, both locations provide a new focal point here for examining how families and women survived these difficult times, in part via their emphasis on music and performance.

Certainly, significant work already exists on the making of Mexican and Texas Mexican identity and communities. Tejano scholars, for instance, have examined how Texas Mexican political organizations in the 1930s and 1940s grappled with questions of how to handle social and political disparities. Much attention has been directed toward social and political organization, the rise of political figures and groups, and questions of whiteness. I extend this research based on the experiences of women already discussed to this point, as a way to explore how business communities navigated race and class obstacles in order to participate in the open market of capitalism. As highlighted throughout the preceding chapters, gender sits at the center of this book, via the exploration of women's stories and of family businesses, as a means to complete a history that has more typically emphasized men's work. As seen through oral histories and archives, the women reframed the meanings and expectations of mother, wife, and daughter, but they never say it directly. They do not connect the dots but leave the dots in wide open spaces, the spaces between the memories of their personal obligations and their professional demands.

In telling the story of Mabel McKay, Greg Sarris beautifully narrates a story of when author meets storyteller. What we learn is that as author and novelist, Sarris's model of making meaning of a story is challenged by McKay's resistance to the idea that narrative creates meaning. It just happens. Sarris's response to McKay's nonchalant disregard of his insistence to move in a straight line and finish a story resonated with my own perplexed reaction when the women I interviewed seemingly refused to buy the idea that their story fit into the bigger story of Texas. Unlike McKay, they did not represent the last of a magical and powerful group of people. However, they do represent a group of women who, for a short time, used a cultural window to respond to an economic opportunity. They did what they had to do to make ends meet. They identified a need, a demand for social spaces, and they met it. That space was marked by passersby, laborers on their way home or moving to the next farm, and later, performers traveling between one Spanish-speaking community and another.

Following Sarris, I argue that oral histories—especially of these women—contain great knowledge about Mexican American families and women in public space, the formation of business communities, and the solidification of a Texas Mexican identity rooted in place and shaped by cultural configurations associated with being Mexican. Oral histories reveal that, at the heart of new fortunes and growing tensions over discriminatory practices, women cantantes and business owners engaged in a constant negotiation of a Texas Mexican identity tied to citizenship, cultural capital, and social status in reaction to these changes. These oral histories also demonstrate that, faced with limited choices and resources, mexicanos working in the fields either trekked thousands of miles following seasonal work or made the decision to find new work in the cities. The families who lived as sharecroppers faced limited financial resources and were forced to endure the Great Depression wherever they had settled. Building community and neighborly networks came second to economic sustainability, thus giving weight to the development of informal networks and word-of-mouth advice about where one should live.

In piecing together their travels, remembering the scars of seeing their neighbors repatriated to Mexico, and the long-term impact of increased segregation and discrimination, the view is much like what is seen in the twist of a kaleidoscope. Fragments of time, experiences, and community-building scattered the landscape. The words of Mabel McKay ring in my head: "That's funny. . . . Why somebody want to do that?" Her concern and mine is that the tying-up process overly neatens a messy story. Though academic conventions often require a clearly coherent narrative, racial and ethnic negotiations often defy such order. Arguably the variances in time, population, and economic development across the region, namely Corpus Christi, San Antonio, and Houston, provoke doubt about the possibilities of finding workable parallel comparisons among them. But the heart of this analysis targets the growth of small family-owned businesses fundamental to the making of political, social, and cultural identities. Thus, at best, perhaps, I offer in this chapter a loose tying together of the stories of the business activities of Texas Mexicans in the Texas Triangle, collected in oral histories, told through newspapers, and found in archival collections.

TRIANGULATING THE SPACE

Living in the Texas Triangle did not change the status of Texas Mexicans, nor did it result in drastically different opportunities for wealth as compared with their counterparts in the border region. Whether having fled Mexico during the Revolution or having left for the idea of greater economic opportunities, Mexican immigrants in Texas faced numerous questions about where they belonged in the ethnic and racial hierarchy, and how to negotiate unspoken class lines created by Texas Anglos and shaped by the response of Texas Mexicans. The major difference between the two geographical areas lay in the density of the Mexican populations in each region: the Texas Triangle had pockets of Mexican communities, while in the border region Mexicans made up the majority, though perhaps not always in power.

For many in the Triangle area, the border Mexicans' proximity to Mexico guaranteed that those living there could never assimilate into Anglo society unless they increased their geographical distance from Mexico. Madsen's example of small business owner "Alberto" as "an upper-middle-class Latin" reveals the complexities of the class divisions and the ways class ideals shaped ethnic identities. He describes Alberto's restaurant as segregated: his wife actively participates in the daily operations, and his son has no desire to continue the family business. The restaurant serves a range of customers, from tourists to local Anglos, which makes it possible for Alberto and his wife to continue their business.[3] Madsen's ethnographic research into the lives of Texas

Mexicans and immigrants produced insider information about how people saw themselves as occupying the spaces of the border region, and the development of regional identities. Less fully explored are the daily practices that also served to contest such inequities.

At the same time, expanding industries in the Triangle cities of San Antonio and Houston opened new opportunities for Mexicans already established in those areas. These settlement patterns are worthy of mapping and weaving into the narrative of other states' histories because they highlight the stories of Mexican Americans.[4] But more important, the patterns of travel, work, and struggle between metropolitan areas like Corpus Christi, San Antonio, and Houston link small towns and communities located en route within the region.

Thus, by framing the boundaries of the Texas Triangle and the communities that developed within it, I argue that Texas Mexicans' sense of place shifted as their identity was influenced by interracial relations and the enforcement of segregated spaces, movement between cities and rural towns, and the development of an informal secondary market made up of Mexican-owned businesses. This space did not embody just one Tejano identity; instead, it displays evidence of various groups of Mexican and Mexican American small businesses that shared a regional identity and economic strategies even as significant differences emerged among them. This Triangle region experienced high traffic and circular migration patterns among Mexican Americans. For instance, although families traveled west toward El Paso, Lubbock, and San Angelo, often they first made their way through the southern part of the Triangle via Robstown, Corpus Christi, and Taft. Moving northwest, migrants had to go through Houston, San Antonio, Lockhart, and Austin. As they made their way through towns and cities, stories of their encounters followed them for others to learn the lessons of the terrain and the people they would meet.

The Triangle is bounded, in part, by the three main south Texas cities that, both then and now, were home to large numbers of Texas Mexicans. Though similarly positioned as urban, rather than rural, Corpus Christi, San Antonio, and Houston gave rise to differently situated and negotiated Texas Mexican communities. Houston, in particular, looked different from San Antonio or Corpus Christi.[5] For Houstonian Texas Mexicans, Arnoldo De León writes, "the economic downturn became an unfortunate reversal which exacerbated already dismal conditions."[6] Hardest hit were the unskilled labor population: they were the first to lose their jobs when companies responded to the economic crisis by letting go of their Mexican workers. Citing local newspapers and collections, De León argues that in fact, of those living in Houston, over 15 percent left the city due to deportation and repatriation efforts between 1930 and 1932.[7] As De León points out, such efforts highlight the line drawn between those with and without citizenship, regardless of their time in the United States. The Depression thus marked a change in the cultural and physical landscape for Texas Mexicans, in particular for those who had to decide where they would make their home permanently.

As the destination for tourists seeking a taste of Mexican culture, San Antonio provided a celebration of its Mexican and Spanish heritage that overshadowed the smaller towns, where la música tejana influenced the building of communities. In making a sizable financial investment in its identity as distinctly Mexican American with a refined Spanish past, San Antonio has enjoyed an advantage: the presence and preservation of the infamous Alamo along with the emphasis on Old Mexico. The Texas Mexican community that emerged here would be crucial to the success of Rosita Fernández. Fernández became best known, immediately following the Depression, as the cultural icon for San Antonio's connection to Old Mexico, as she asserted the idea of a physical location in Texas but a cultural connection to Mexico. Prior to the naming of her bridge and her numerous performances on the bridge that also served to join Texas Anglos and Texas Mexicans through music, Rosita built a bridge between the countries through dance and performance.

The Texas Triangle is much more than just the three cities that define it. Indeed, the emergence of Texas Mexican communities happened as much, if not more, in the spaces and places in between. The rural nature of the land situated between the three cities and the distance between these urban hubs made the small-town areas important places through which people—in particular, Mexican

Americans—journeyed, labored, and rested. As laborers, residents, and entertainers traveled along these same informal routes, they contributed to the building of informal economic structures that served as the foundations of urban and rural Mexican American and Spanish-speaking communities. Too often, migrant laborers, working classes, and emerging professional classes appear as separate populations with distinct histories; in reality, their paths often overlapped—from the services they sought to the resources they relied on in the making of community life. Tracking migrant populations and understanding their relationships is difficult because there is limited written evidence of their lives and their struggles. Thus we need to look at other means of understanding the movement, economic structures, and relationships that defined the Texas Triangle as significantly as its geographic boundaries did.

MUSIC, MOVEMENT, AND COMMUNITY

Music and movement are two of the many strategies through which Texas Mexicans created communities and networks and through which we, today, can recover their lives. Often lacking access to more formal modes of communication and interaction, migrant laborers forged community through song and travel. Before the Depression, Mexican American communities depended on carpas and traveling performances for social opportunities. Before the emergence of permanent establishments, carpas hosted itinerant troupes of families and groups who performed vaudeville or other live music shows. These tent shows paved the way for enormously important community formation and subsistence, at the heart of which were Mexican American women. Carpas provided the first stage for a number of well-known musicians, including Lydia Mendoza and Rosita Fernández, "La Rosa de San Antonio."

Along with carpas, Texas Mexicans wrote and distributed *corridos*, which served as forms of shared entertainment, but also as means of communication. Corridos provide a different, and strangely neglected, access point to the worlds of work and leisure in the Triangle and the Southwest more generally. As Américo Paredes notes, corridos were a central Mexican and Texas Mexican cultural tradition. He argues that corridos met two significant needs: one, they attested to the survival of Mexican Americans, and two, they were a popular-culture form of information. Often corridos detailed people's experiences in a particular town or with specific individuals. The songs made their way along routes of migrant labor travel, and some were eventually recorded as singles or albums.[8]

Both then and now, corridos supplied a means to learn about and follow migration patterns and relationships to townspeople in places like rural Texas. The lyrics of corridos—and music in general—provided cautionary tales for other travelers, sent wishes of farewell, or described places of sentiment left only in a singer's memory. Revealing details of workers' lives that historians will not find in newspapers or local documents, these corridos fill a void when oral histories of people living, working, and driving through the Texas Triangle remain absent. In the "Corrido de Robestown" [Robstown], for instance, many of Eusebio González's verses address why laborers traveled to Robstown, a small town twenty-five miles west of Corpus Christi whose popularity as a destination might otherwise remain unclear:

> *Del Norte se bienen [sic] muchos*   Many come from the north
> *de San Antonio tambien*   and from San Antonio too
> *a piscar el algodon*   in order to pick cotton
> *para bolverse [sic] otra vez*   and so return again.[9]

This simple verse suggests that migrant laborers may have traveled long distances to work in the fields of Robstown, and perhaps that work was not so bad, for they returned again. Indeed, the town's high school mascot arose as the "Cotton Picker," which further underscores the significance of cotton and migrant workers to this area. Yet, the corrido reveals something more: it tells of an existing network of laborers who relied on the experiences of others to inform them of what to expect. The suggestion that people returned suggests that perhaps the pay made the trip worth one's while in time and money, or perhaps workers chose work by the way they were treated. Or perhaps it was that they could find social events in Robstown to make their stay more pleasant. Regardless, the "Corrido de Robestown" begins to reveal the ways in which movement and music were and are connected.

Beyond their historical impact, music such as corridos remains a central part of the formation of community and business. In my conversation with my grandmother, Mary F. Villarreal, the owner of the Pecan Lounge in Tivoli, she recalled a customer coming through in 1997 and asking if he could play a personal record on the jukebox, so she put the record in and played it once. At that time the Pecan Lounge still used a 45-rpm jukebox. The record was the "Corrido de Robestown." Mary stated, "at that time teníamos puro mexicanos and they thought the song was great." While her quote about having "nothing but Mexicans" at the bar hints at the various ways that people positioned their identities, the fact that the customer traveled with his 45 says more about the meaning of his music. His stop in the small town of Tivoli illustrates an existing link between music and what it meant to be part of this Mexican space and place. In many such mundane and often forgotten ways, music and movement helped shape Texas Mexican identity and community.

ECONOMICS IN UNFAMILIAR TERRITORY

Starting in the 1930s and continuing for decades, entertainers and performers moved from town to town and gave rise to a unique economy and sense of community. The circuits they traveled, propelled by economic opportunities, were central to their success. The Depression, for instance, sent families like the Mendozas home to San Antonio. They had found an audience for their Cuarteto Carta Blanca in late-1920s Detroit, but they returned to look for work and finally found a place in San Antonio's Market Square.[10] Having designed their travels out of necessity for survival, the Mendozas then followed the trail of Mexican American workers who both welcomed and needed their presence.

In the 1940s, the Marroquins, Armando and Carmen (Hernández), also followed similar pathways of Mexican American workers, but for different reasons. After Armando had partnered with Paco Betancourt to start Ideal Records, the husband-and-wife business team (she was also half of the sister dueto of Carmen y Laura), set out to promote their records. Carmen Marroquin recalled, "At the end of the war we decided that in order to sell more, the artist had to make appearances.

So Mr. Marroquin and I got in the car and we went west."[11] By this time, Lydia Mendoza also had a solo career and was traveling throughout the United States performing live and on the radio.

During their tours, musicians and performers acted as a small part of a larger business venture that served a need in Mexican American communities scattered throughout the Southwest. That need became apparent for many who started their careers by joining carpas and who eventually established permanent spaces in "Mexican districts" or found new venues that allowed Mexican Americans. Both audiences and musicians had to travel for an evening of entertainment, driving distances to places as close as the town next door or as far as one hundred miles away.

Though travel and movement were key to the success of many cantantes and business people I examine here, it was also often difficult and taxing. Imagine south Texas in 1928, when Lydia Mendoza's family drove from Kingsville to San Antonio to record for the Okeh Record Company. After discovering an advertisement in *La Prensa* for a recording opportunity with Okeh Records, Mendoza's father, Francisco, insisted that the family head immediately to San Antonio. Getting there was not an easy task. Their "ride" in an old Dodge truck took more than two days with more than twenty flat tires along the 150-mile stretch. After their arrival in San Antonio, the Mendoza family group, the Cuarteto Carta Blanca, with lead singer Lydia Mendoza, recorded twenty songs with Okeh over a three-day period, March 8–10, 1928.[12] This recording marks the beginning of one of the longest documented careers among Mexican American women singers and suggests that perhaps the Mendozas' willingness to endure such a trip was instrumental to her career success. Though she recorded hundreds of records in her solo career, Lydia Mendoza developed a large following partly through her live performances throughout the country. Radio gave listeners more access to Mendoza, but live performances allowed her to travel to Spanish-speaking communities for her shows. Along with other performers and business people, the Mendozas played a key role in maintaining a sense of place for the Spanish-speaking communities across the Texas Triangle in which the Mendozas performed, moved, and lived. The hidden histories of cantantes such as Lydia Mendoza, as well as of the laborers who constituted her audience, have remained outside of the official Texas history narrative. But in their stories, we begin to see the many interconnections that fostered the rise and sometimes fall of Texas Mexican identity and community. Economics, music, and movement emerge as clearly interrelated.

For many Texas Mexicans, the Depression became the cause for seeking different kinds of entertainment spaces, particularly since patterns of migration slowed for purposes other than work. Regardless of the specific decisions driving migration, the result of the simultaneous movement and yet a desire for stability in the geographical area located between Corpus Christi, San Antonio, and Houston, produced unintended routes of travel, novel opportunities for work, and connections between rural and city services. Though laborers did not generate new monies, they did redirect money into local businesses that catered to Spanish speakers and those of "Latin extraction."[13] In turn, the emergence of Texas-Mexican-owned businesses allowed for the stability and growth of self-sustaining neighborhoods in the three cities. These increasingly popular networks of travel, which created new job possibilities and a fortuitous reliance on migrating populations, gave rise to new economies and relationships—including music—between and among Mexican American communities. The circuits traveled by the cantantes helped build a larger sense of community through the music itself, as well as growth in the concomitant businesses and economy of the Texas Triangle.

The Triangle area offered a variety of opportunities to create entertainment for migrant, rural, and urban populations. Depending on the place and time, traveling artists found ways to set up entertainment spaces to meet the social and cultural needs of migrant labor communities. Stopping in small towns on the way to larger cities, as performers still do today, entertainers found that they could make enough money to continue to their next venue. After completing a south Texas tour, for example, the Mendoza family headed out on a western tour. On the way, they stopped in small towns to earn money for the rest of the trip.[14] The early days of an emerging Spanish-language music market meant that singers might perform live on a radio station with little or no notice, or set up an impromptu stage for a live performance. Such venues contributed to the Mendozas' popularity and highlighted a need for venues open to hosting Spanish-language entertainment.

The contradictions of the cultural landscape during the Depression put some families in danger of deportation, left others with the challenge of making financial ends meet, and allowed a few in urban areas to find financial stability. The communities, networks, and identities that emerged and grew differed across the Triangle. Families living in rural areas or small towns, for instance, depended on their ability to acquire jobs during the various seasons. In the case of the Mendoza family, Rosita and her uncles, and other carpa performers, success depended on those families who found seasonal work and desired entertainment.

These places, the bars and dance halls, provide the sites significant to my analysis of working-class, entrepreneurial Mexican American lives. For instance, beneath the layer of Corpus Christi's fame as the "Home of Selena" (Quintanilla) lies the layer of a place that catered to Mexican Americans long before the superstar was born.[15] These places included the Galvan Ballroom and Sofie's Place. In Alice, Texas, La Villita became the site of community meetings. Victoria, Texas, known for its poor treatment of Mexicans, did not have inclusive dance halls until the 1960s, and even then, those that emerged were placed on the outskirts of town. Still, despite the racism they faced there, Texas Mexicans in Victoria and elsewhere managed to create places and spaces of their own. Similar to other rural social events that relied on surrounding communities for support, these establishments built their clientele on locals who stopped by after work or residents from outlying communities who traveled into town for an evening of dancing. Many of these places closed by the late 1990s due to the dislocation of Mexican enclaves, the decreasing demand for Spanish-language live-music venues, and the owners' age and health. Their temporal impact, though, reinforced a place on the Texas landscape for their cultural- and language-driven needs for social entertainment.

The loss of rural small businesses must be treated as part of what geographer Peirce Lewis calls for in the exchange of culture in terms of the "whole," and not just the "part." He makes the case that "the landscape is not something to be admired or denounced. Instead it is like one vast archaeological dig—a layered accumulation of artifacts created by the disorderly accumulation of people we call our ancestors."[16] He continues that most people have been "conditioned" to look right past what they believe are ordinary landscapes, creating this false idea that some places have more historical meaning than others. Lewis argues, "If we do not know that these places were won through struggle, and must be retained through struggle, it becomes much easier for us to lose them."[17] In some cases, the passerby must look beyond the overgrown yard and the fallen trees. The boarded windows indicate that the physical structure is off-limits, yet the emptiness inside might conceal, for example, the story of the *dueto*, sisters Carmen y Laura, making one of their hit records for Ideal. Carmen Marroquin's dance hall, La Villita, in Alice, Texas, provides an example of the rare popular space that has survived its community's economic downturn.

Although many of these early bars came into business after World War II, they were built on existing communities that had established themselves during the 1930s and 1940s in spite of the economic and social discrimination the communities faced. To date, most of what we know of Mexican American and Texas Mexican businesses comes from the work of sociologists and geographers who have addressed a range of largely urban spaces. My turn to the south Texas landscape, with its predominantly Mexican and Mexican American population, identifies the intersections of critical changes in agricultural communities, development of Mexican districts in and around urban areas, migrant labor patterns between these urban areas, and racial segregation as key factors in the development of Texas Mexican communities.

The story of the Chairez Family, who traveled from San Antonio to Houston in 1919, offers a glimpse into the kinds of non-urban communities that emerged and the role of bar halls and music in those communities. De León notes, in his discussion of what he names a Mexicanist identity in Houston, the significance of the family patriarch, Feliciano Chairez, and his participation in the Sociedad Mutualista Benito Juarez (Benito Juarez Mutual Aid Society).[18] In contrast, I turn to Chairez's son and his commitment to music. Chairez's son performed with his orquesta at Teatro Salon del Campo in Baytown,

Texas.[19] Located approximately a half-hour outside of Houston, Baytown seemingly served a large-enough Mexican American population for the establishment of a Mexican or Spanish-speaking performance space. The event points to the small-town populations that helped support musical groups. While mutualistas were certainly vital to many Texas Mexicans, for others, especially those located outside of urban centers, the everyday practices of participating in music, whether as performer or audience, were central to their formation of community and identity.[20]

Baytown is not unique as a small town that became home to Texas Mexicans. In the city of Premont, Texas,[21] thirty-six miles south of Alice (home of La Villita), a burgeoning Texas Mexican community emerged as early as 1909 through 1922. The editor of *El Mesteño*, Homero Vera of Premont, found through county records that one of the early founders of the town, Charles Premont, doubled as a ranch foreman and real estate agent to Texas Mexicans, primarily due to his Spanish-speaking skills. Premont's willingness to learn enough Spanish to promote the sale of land to Texas Mexicans on the margins of town offers one example of the way in which segregated neighborhoods arose. His ability to capitalize on the desire of Texas Mexicans to settle their families was key to the growth of a Texas Mexican neighborhood and community. The cost of the lots initially ranged from twenty-five to thirty dollars; they eventually sold for as much as eighty dollars. The Mexican tract lay east of the railroad tracks and contained a plaza named after Father Miguel Hidalgo, home to a dry-goods store, a blacksmith shop, a hotel, and a healer. Vera found that many of the new landowners were also sharecroppers on Rancho La Cabra, which belonged to Andrés Canales.[22] That they were both sharecroppers *and* landowners suggests that either they fared well in production or that Canales proved to be a fair employer who paid wages high enough to purchase land and make workers aspire to stay.

The Premont community also illustrates the importance of services in the growth and strength of the community. The plaza in Premont continued to serve the community, possibly through the late 1960s. The local residents had all the services, such as a barbershop and movie theater, conveniently located around *la plaza de Hidalgo*.

Through oral history interviews conducted by Vera, many of the older residents recalled the theater, "El Tropico," hosting traveling Mexican movie stars. The only evidence that now exists of the Texas Mexican side of town is dilapidated buildings and photos of businesses now neglected and falling down.

The link in Premont between place—Hidalgo plaza—and music brings to light how Texas Mexican laborers, performers, and businesses created community economies in both rural and urban centers. Because these communities operated informally and lack accounting records, they have often gone unexamined as significant economic players in business histories. When we look carefully, however, new stories emerge. For instance, the Alameda Theater in Premont hosted carpa troupes in the mid-1940s. Vera writes, "The Alameda was an important theater as this was the gathering place for the Mexican-American population of the area to gather and be entertained. . . . Homero Canales of Premont recalls, as a young boy living in Falfurrias, that an automobile with the actress Maria Antonieta Pons stopped at a gas station where he was at to ask directions to the Alameda. Canales' mother, Apolonia Peña Canales, worked at the Alameda part time as a ticket seller, concession vendor, and helping out as a projectionist. . . . Sadly the Alameda will be demolished in the near future but the memories of the good times will live on with the people of the area."[23]

Evidence of the need for local spaces can be discerned in stories such as those found in Lydia Mendoza's biography. Traveling west through small towns, the Mendoza family often used already-established travel routes to determine impromptu performance locations that would generate revenues to help finance the rest of their trip. They would follow what might have been considered the "beaten path," posting flyers to advertise their shows. Mendoza recollects one instance when the family cleaned up a makeshift stage, waited for an audience, and then, "at about six o'clock that afternoon, we saw what looked like a religious procession coming toward us through the streets of the town. Each person or group was carrying their own lantern. . . . And they were all carrying something to sit on."[24] Mendoza's experience alludes to the existence of an informal network of performers following their audiences and in turn how the audiences came to the performers, a reminder, again, of the connection between music, travel, and community.

While the cultural landscapes of Texas Mexican communities change from region to region, traveling for the purpose of providing entertainment is one thing that remains constant. An easy way of coming together often happened through pachangas, because they could be held in someone's backyard and there was always music involved.[25] Given the many difficulties of travel for Mexican Americans, including limited financial resources and the pervasiveness of racism across much of the Triangle region, evidence that Mexican American performers and audiences were willing to travel suggests the importance of music to community. Despite the difficulties, Texas Mexicans would often "make do" and get where they could with the resources available. Indeed, for performers, community and music may have been more important than money. Carmen Marroquin, for instance, when asked about the pay, replied, "We were not making a living out of that. We didn't do it to make a living . . . We didn't depend on music."[26] Instead, she explained that she and her family were willing to travel because people wanted to hear the music.

Although travel was important to both performers and audiences, such travel, as I indicated earlier, was often difficult. During the 1920s to 1940s when the cantantes traveled, they constantly encountered racial hostility toward Mexicans and Mexican Americans. As racial conditions changed throughout south Texas, the travel topography changed for the cantantes. These changes ran the gamut from where they could travel to how and when they should end their careers. For Rosita Fernández, traveling as a child often meant that she was away from her family. When her father asked if she was happy traveling, she told him, "not so much," and he eventually put a stop to her touring. Though she did not offer a description of the distances or the places to which she traveled, or the exhaustion she experienced, she often told the reporters the same story of her early experiences with segregation: "It was very hard in the beginning with my uncles. I remember one time, not one time, several times, going to the little towns. My Uncle Sotero would ask if we could be served. If they said 'yes,' fine. If not, they would say 'in the kitchen.' My uncle would say, 'No, just give me the food; we know where we can eat it.'"[27] Her uncles continued to travel despite the treatment they received, for their musical talents supported their families.

Along with race and racism, gender complicated travel for many women cantantes. They understood "cultural codes," or the parameters of behavior expected of them. By performing as part of family groups, cantantes maintained their image as "good women." Although audiences may have seen the cantantes as unusual in terms of their livelihood and perceived freedom of movement, their performances never transgressed cultural codes of propriety.[28] The Mendozas, for example, traveled as a family, and Rosita Fernández traveled with her uncles. After Rosita left the company of her uncles, she traveled extensively with her husband. On the other hand, Chelo Silva, refusing to abide by such cultural norms, paid the price in terms of community perceptions of her life, as she was often seen as the "bad girl" who overindulged in the social life of the entertainment world.[29]

The practical difficulties of access to transportation in the early 1900s gave way to opportunities with the advent of the automobile. The automobile made it possible for people to travel long distances faster, and to places not served by rail. The building of major highways and interstates has created a false sense of direct travel and easy access. Today the 150-mile trip from Kingsville to San Antonio takes a mere two hours in an air-conditioned vehicle—a trip that also, coincidentally, bypasses Alice, Texas, the birthplace of Tejano music. For the Mendozas and other traveling troupes, it was a more complicated two-day journey by train. By the 1920s, the automobile facilitated the cantantes' travels as well, making it possible for them to perform at unscheduled stops. Performers could set their own pace for travel, thereby further establishing the complex network of the Texas Triangle. Even when it would benefit the family to have immediate transportation, however, they could not always afford such luxuries. Migrant families often purchased affordable used vehicles or paid a driver per head and rode cramped in the back of a pickup for hundreds of miles. Before leaving Michigan for Texas, the Mendoza family bought a small truck, saving them from having to sign another labor contract or increase their debt to an individual party for their transportation costs. Records of travel expenses offer some concrete evidence of the real cost to procure personal transportation for families like the Mendozas, who worked both as laborers and entertainers.

Just as the automobile and travel expenses affected those in the music industry, they also had an impact on sectors of marginalized communities, such as migrant farm laborers and women. The going rate for passage by truck from south Texas to work in the Michigan beet fields, for example, averaged $10 per adult and $5 per child.[30] The Crystal City study found a total of 188 families employed in the beet fields from April through December. They had an average annual income of $400, with individuals earning an average of $6.33 weekly when working approximately forty-nine hours a week.[31] Workers from Crystal City packed into the back of a truck, occasionally stopping for gas and other vehicle needs, and the riders were cramped together for the duration of the trek. And while middle-class white women took advantage of the opportunity to "hit the road" in newly bought cars, either with their children or with other women, Mexican women did not enjoy the same privileges.[32] Travel was not always easy for them, for they were often unwelcome in the auto camps.[33] While some of the cantantes discuss the segregation they sometimes encountered, the experiences of the audiences who traveled outside of their neighborhoods remain unknown.

Through this brief window of time, we can see how the constant shift in populations resulted in an ongoing re-creation of places as they were used to create a sense of home. The three cities that comprise the Triangle actually "gave birth" to home bases and crossroads where constant travel and movement impacted the construction of various Texas Mexican identities, both urban and rural. An exchange took place between travelers and residents in the region, where musicians and performers identified pockets of Mexican American populations, both established and emergent. Travel occurred in ways that might have seemed non-uniform and unregulated, because performers and audiences followed word of mouth.

The rural nature of south Texas meant that people sometimes traveled from one town to the other for a dance or special performance.

Following their trail provides evidence of the many communities—
some now gone—that then flourished. A week's travel is represented
by a July 1954 flyer announcing several scheduled engagements for
Los Alegres de Teran. Their shows ran through south Texas towns
starting at Jesse's Place in Elsa (near Harlingen), and then moving
north to La Villita in San Benito (different from the one in Alice), El
Patio Deans in Kenedy, and El Casino in Raymondville. Today that
trip would include driving on U.S. Highway 77, U.S. Highway 181,
and several other Texas highways, covering more than two hundred
miles if followed in linear south-to-north sequence. Indeed, today that
trip might not make sense, as the routes taken and towns visited are no
longer home to significant Texas Mexican communities.

Although not referencing travel in the Triangle, Lydia Mendoza
also emphasized the significance of touring to cantantes' success: "All that territory—beginning from Mission all the way to
Brownsville—is full of small towns like Donna, Weslaco, La Feria."[34]
All of these town contributed to the ability of musicians and their
families to stay financially afloat and continue to tour. Though there
is a limited paper trail today documenting the centrality of music to
Texas Mexican communities, the evidence, although scarce, emerges
from the narratives of oral history interviewees who attended performances and patronized bars, or from the cantantes themselves.
By pointing to specific sites important to Mexican American communities, I go beyond the simple marking of place. Place, I argue, is
tied to a community's sentiment, its geographical space, its cultural
production, and its temporal space.

Place in the Texas Triangle, then, is more than geography. It
includes the exchanges that occurred when the itinerant cantante left
a part of her culture behind and took a part of the community with
her. For cantantes who sang in Spanish and attracted predominantly
Mexican crowds, these exchanges took the form of the cantante giving them her music, and the audience giving her their hospitality and
appreciation. These performances kept alive the social practice of
informal performance spaces that radio and records had displaced.
Such exchanges helped foster the bonds established through travel in
the Texas Triangle.

THE RACE RECORD INDUSTRY

Though music was clearly central to the emergence of Texas Mexican identities and communities, its status was often tenuous, in part because of the larger politics of race that intersected with the music industry as well as with community. The incongruities of economic opportunity and reality come to the fore in in the matter of consumption. The rise of interest in women singers and their music was part of a larger music industry interest in so-called "race" records. Race records emerged in the recording industry after a representative from Okeh Records made a recording in 1920.[35] It was not surprising that his company was the first to discover other non-Anglo artists, as it was one of the few companies dedicated to recording ethnic music.[36] Having also joined the race record market, Columbia issued blues recordings and other race music. The Brunswick record label began its own jazz and dance series with all-white orchestras.[37] The new Spanish-language music industry not only shaped musical artists' travel but also created a product available for purchase. But, a contradiction of the industry lay in the politics of representation and production. Despite growing interest in race music, the status of Spanish-language music as a category remained unclear nationally. Though corporate record companies had identified their star singers and musicians, the onset of the Depression led to the termination of cutting records of Spanish-language artists.

Despite the Depression-related demise of recording opportunities for Spanish-language performers, their music continued, in large part via the efforts of Texas Mexican communities. Communities continued to want this music, and individuals such as Eleuterio Escobar in San Antonio made it available. Escobar, an active businessman, tapped into the growing demand for Spanish-language recordings. Archival materials reveal that after paying musical groups a set amount for a selected number of songs, which he then owned, he went on to contract the services of record companies to cut the singles. Throughout the 1930s, Escobar sold records out of his store, the Escobar Furniture Company. Though not a producer himself, he managed the business performers such that by the beginning of the 1930s, Escobar had established a relationship with the Columbia Phonograph Company.[38] A letter from Columbia's assistant manager, H. A. Schmiedeke, indicates that by the end of 1929 Escobar had a credit line with Columbia for the purchase of records. He also earned a 2 percent discount on records by groups he recruited, and he charged the groups a fee for signing them to Columbia. A contract from 1930 obligated the recording artists to sing solo or in a duet at Escobar's request. Individuals were paid anywhere from one dollar to ten dollars per double-sided record and had to agree to at least a one-year contract. Escobar also negotiated with Columbia for him to maintain exclusive rights and receive royalties from the recordings. Escobar's example shows how managers and talent scouts made money from both sides of the industry.[39] Though such practices may have exploited the cantantes, they also helped keep the Spanish-language music industry alive.

The 1940s brought a new level of demand in Spanish-language Texas communities for both records and dance space, as local Mexican American communities gathered at *terrazas*—open-air dance floors that replicated entertainment venues in Mexico—that became increasingly popular after World War II. La Villita in Alice, Texas, began as a terraza, but the weather eventually forced the owners, the Marroquins, to add a roof. Arnaldo Ramírez, founder and owner of Falcon Records, used the Falcon house band at his terraza-style dance floor. During this time cantantes like Rosita Fernández regularly performed before predominantly white audiences, a development that indicates the increasing acceptance and consumption of Mexican music by white audiences and the gradual desegregation of entertainment spaces.

LIVING IN THE RURAL AND URBAN LANDSCAPES

Not surprisingly, the racial climate of Texas and the Texas Triangle shaped the economic lives and communities of Texas Mexicans. The political picture that emerges in this triangle of travel, private places, and public spaces also reveals much about the changing nature of neighborhoods and cultures in the collective memory. As public historian Jo Blatti writes, "There are, in fact, many stories to be told if we are to understand the truths of past times with any complexity."[40] Many of these stories reveal the complexities and contradictions of Texas Mexican identity and community. For instance, Texas Mexican children born during the late 1920s would see no improvement in their standard of living over the course of their lives. Sofia Flores Gonzalez's story offers one example of the intersection of race, economics, and rural life in the Triangle. Born in Nursery, Texas, on September 18, 1928, to sharecropper parents Alfredo and San Juanita Flores, Sofia Gonzalez was the oldest of six living children. She made it to the third grade, "but you could graduate from that school. It went all the way to the twelfth grade."[41] When asked about her educational background, Gonzalez responded, "We were all together [with Euro-American children], but I knew I could never compete [with them]. I couldn't speak English my first two years."[42] Although she was not in a segregated school, Gonzalez knew that being Mexican made her different because of her language skills. The reality for the majority of south Texas was that separate schools for Mexicans were in effect. Perhaps administrators in the region did not worry about integration since, like Gonzalez, few Mexican children made it past the primary grades. Indeed, Gonzalez spent much of her time helping her mother, father, and brother pick cotton, grow peanuts and watermelons, and sell corn. They would go into town and sell the remaining third share of the crop (two shares went to the landowners).

Families in rural areas often supported themselves through sharecropping, with a family's success dependent on the number of workers in a family, and difficulties such as a parent's illness made it harder for the family to sustain itself. When opportunities arose or rumors were heard about the possibility of earning more money elsewhere, families often moved. In 1940 at age twelve, Gonzalez moved to Victoria, Texas, eleven miles down the road, to help care for her grandmother after her uncle had left for the Armed Forces. During this time, she began her first job at a bakery, earning twenty-five dollars a week. Within the next few years, her father's poor health required that the family move because they could not support themselves. When a family friend, Maggie Ramirez, told Gonzalez's parents that in Austwell, Texas, they could *"barrer el dinero con una escoba"* [sweep up the money with a broom], the family relocated forty miles southeast where the main crops harvested included onions and cotton. However, their lack of experience pulling and cutting onions posed a problem. Gonzalez recalls, "The onions, you had to pull, and they would pay for the basket. We never did it, we just never did that."[43] Thus, Gonzalez and her family had to look for other means of support. She soon acquired a job in a general store, and her mother, Señora Flores, went to work in a café. When Gonzalez's father died in 1946, her mother raised the last four children on her own. Gonzalez's mother sometimes worked fifteen to twenty hours a day to raise her family and support herself.[44] She recalled that her mother was a cook at a café-turned-dance hall, El Ranchito.[45] She opened the café at 4 A.M. and worked until closing at 10 P.M. On nights that there were dances, she worked until 1 A.M.

Families who followed other community members in search of better pay often found themselves facing a variety of obstacles. For instance, outsiders not familiar with beet harvesting soon found out that this work also required experience.[46] Lydia Mendoza recalls her father signing a beet contract, but the family did not know how to pick them. She recalls, "Those little plants—we had never seen anything like that before."[47] Though given directions on how to work the plant out of the soil, Mendoza told of how they instead butchered the beets: "Well, we'd tug on the leaves . . . and we'd yank out the whole plant . . . It was hard work and we weren't very good at it."[48] Like the Floreses, who encountered difficulties when they moved to an area dominated by onion crops, the Mendozas found that the backbreaking work of pulling beets required them to learn new skills quickly because their wages depended on weight and number of bags picked. It is doubtful that the Mendoza or Flores families lacked the ability to acquire new skills; rather, it seems that the learning process would have been a waste of time and money. Given the opportunity to do other, more enjoyable work for better pay, they did so. While the Flores family migrated only once, a 1938 WPA study of three hundred families in Crystal City, a little more than a hundred miles southwest of San Antonio, illustrates the complexity of following migrant workers' travels throughout Texas. The study recorded that "19 out of 20 families migrated north or east to work."[49] In addition, over 60 percent migrated to areas between Michigan and Montana to work the sugar beet fields. Another group picked cotton from July to October, and half of those chopped cotton before the picking season.

Just as Mexicans faced difficulties in rural areas, they struggled in urban areas as well. Mirroring the poor living conditions of rural areas, Mexican neighborhoods in urban centers featured "old, dilapidated housing, rough and dusty roads, and lack of sanitary facilities."[50] The WPA project *Houston Housing, 1939,* showed that 36,934 groups (family and non-family) lived in substandard housing. "Latin Americans" occupied 8.7 percent of the dwellings, with a majority having two parents with children. Within the Latin American population, over 90 percent were tenants and fewer than 10 percent owned their homes.[51]

Historian Arnoldo De León points out that mutual aid societies spread nationally, providing much-needed support for transplants in urban areas.[52] Mutualistas and the development of Mexican-owned businesses such as *tienditas* (Mom-and-Pop stores) and restaurants encouraged growth as well as the ongoing participation of Mexican Americans in their neighborhoods. Social and political organizations also challenged existing practices that negatively impacted Texas Mexicans. Women working in factories had to fight for their rights through strikes, pushing the front lines of union organizing, as best illustrated in the Pecan Shellers Strike.[53] And when the Texas government continued to fail Mexican Americans in the area of education by allowing a racially segregated system that remained in dire need of adequate facilities and financial support, Texas Mexican organizations fought back. Headed by LULAC member Eleuterio Escobar, Mexican professionals in San Antonio formed La Liga Pro-Defensa Escolar (The School Defense League), an organization concerned with inequities in school funding.[54] Acting as an umbrella organization that sought separate-but-equal schools rather than integration, La Liga created a coalition of eighty-three organizations to address the situation described by one of the organization's founders, María L. de Hernández: "The Mexican schools were in a bad state and our children were suffering. Clearly, the children were bearing the effects of racial discrimination."[55]

The cultural and economic context also affected the formation of Mexican American communities in the Texas Triangle. For instance, while cotton had been the number one cash crop in Nueces County (southeast Texas coastal area) through the 1920s, new industries had a continued impact on Mexican American labor and migration. In 1926, the city of Nueces built a deep-water port, expanding the shipping market to include petroleum. The growth of natural gas fields in the early 1920s and the discovery of oil in 1930 increased the financial earnings of Nueces County and of the farmers who owned the mineral rights to the land.[56] Laborers still followed the work, moving through Nueces County both north and south depending on the time of the year. More than seventy thousand migratory workers from the Lower Rio Grande Valley harvested crops in Texas and the rest of the United States.

Along with new industry, changes in agriculture also affected the development of Texas Mexican communities in the Triangle. By the 1930s, mechanization had started to displace agriculture workers, primarily rural, who permanently relocated to the cities.[57] Families and single men, the core audience of the cantantes, now resided in cities where they had access to various social spaces such as church halls and Spanish-language theaters. This new round of migration then had a significant impact on musicians, who were no longer one of the main means of entertainment. Unfortunately, rural labor across many of the rural areas of the Triangle was directly correlated with the ability of traveling musical groups to sustain themselves financially. Manager and radio station owner Ramiro Cortés recalled that he used to take the family on tour to north and west Texas "during the cotton-picking season; there were a lot of people, a lot of money. Not now, because now they pick cotton with machines."[58] While travel had provided some assurance of finding a fan base and new paying audiences, ultimately the decreasing agricultural labor force meant a shortfall in earnings for traveling performers such as Lydia Mendoza. Determining the overall economic impact on musicians and other forms of entertainment is difficult; however, the upshot was that as the populations dispersed, musicians had to find other audiences outside rural listeners.

After the Depression, the implementation of new farming machinery continued to have negative effects on the livelihood of rural Mexican families and where they chose to live. In 1938, the Texas State Employment Service (TSES) agency produced the *Survey of Farm Placement in Texas, 1936 and 1937.* As with most government documents published during this time, the TSES focused its energies on the expected change in employment patterns. While cotton farmers continued to employ large numbers of laborers, the agricultural industry overall began losing pace in comparison with the manufacturing-mechanical industry, of which oil was "the leading Texas industry in value of products."[59] These changing agricultural conditions, coupled with the discrimination that Mexican American agricultural laborers encountered, suggest that they had to negotiate available work opportunities by retooling and moving into new industries. This point is further evidenced by the fact that conditions had not improved ten years later in 1948, when Congress cut funding for the U.S. Extension Service after Mexico banned the use of Mexican labor on Texas farms.[60] The ban's effect on the Triangle region varied, as continued racially biased practices raised the ire of political organizations over Mexico's perception that Texas was still not behaving like a "good neighbor" and thus not deserving of Mexican labor, and the ban also impacted the labor available for local farms in the dwindling rural communities. The growing distinction between Mexican national workers and Mexican American workers also added to the tension residents faced in the Texas political climate.

These changes were also informed by and occurred on the landscape of social and economic realities. For instance, both Mexican Americans and Mexican immigrants struggled for political, economic, and labor justice throughout the Southwest during the Great Depression. The Triangle region, Francisco Balderrama and Raymond Rodríguez write, "was primarily inhabited by destitute tenant farmers and agricultural workers," some of whom saw no other option than to return to Mexico, which left the Mexican consulate scrambling to offer assistance to those facing repatriation.[61] Mexican repatriation during the Depression made it most difficult for poor working Mexicans and Mexican Americans to establish financial security. U.S. census numbers report that in a ten-year period from 1929 to 1939, over half of those deported under repatriation efforts came from Texas.[62] Those not deported or repatriated continued to work as seasonal laborers, "although apparently at a reduced rate."[63] This combination of repatriation and poverty shaped the kinds of communities that emerged and dwindled.

The demand for cheap agricultural labor also impacted Texas Mexican communities. It increased the number of migrant laborers who traveled from town to town following the seasonal crops in hopes of making ends meet. Representatives from the TSES found that farmers frequently overstated the need for workers, for an influx of workers would help drive wages down. For example, in 1936 a "desperate" request was made by farmers for two thousand cotton pickers. After assessing the situation, the field representative found that eighty-five cotton pickers would suffice.[64] After a labor surplus disaster in 1935, The office of TSES attempted to monitor the number of laborers going to the same job site. The field officer stated that "reports had been exaggerated as to the cotton yield. Truck after truck of Mexican laborers poured into Lubbock from every direction."[65] In addition to being subject to practices that kept wages low, Texas Mexican migrant communities were also subject to health risks. Housing, food, and medical facilities were often poor. In Lubbock, following that large influx of laborers, for instance, the combination of too few and inadequate facilities, coupled with rainfall, led to a number of cases of sickness with no medical aid available. The Survey of Farm Placement report emphasizes the difficulty of placing an accurate number on mortality rates: "It was never known . . . how many children died from exposure and sickness."[66] Not only did backbreaking labor take a toll on workers, but also the system failed to provide care for families moving from field to field.

By the 1940s, mexicanos working in the fields either trekked thousands of miles following seasonal work or made the decision to find new work in the cities.[67] Although Texas had lost 40 percent of its Mexican population between 1930 and 1940, the activities of political and social organizations kept the issues of Mexican Americans at the forefront.[68] The signing of agreements for the Bracero Program in 1943 initially resulted in a small increase in the Mexican agricultural labor force, though many journeyed outside of Texas. Regardless of their assistance in supplying labor due to the shortage caused by World War II, Mexican agricultural workers did not receive any benefits such as sanitary living conditions or fair wages, and they were not protected from discrimination. In fact, Texas growers, in particular, mistreated Mexican workers both in the fields and through segregationist practices in social spaces. Their unjust practices led to the Mexican government denying Texas any new workers until the Texas government resolved to punish any discriminatory practices against Mexicans, regardless of citizenship.[69]

CONCLUSION

Historians have demonstrated the significant impact of Mexican American political organizing on the development of Texas Mexican cites. Its importance is unquestioned. Still, while political organizations such as LULAC fought in court for rights of citizenship, individuals also played an important role as the development of communities and small businesses defined a particular identity of Texas Mexicans. The Triangle, though heavily populated by Euro-Americans who also owned the natural resources, was a place where Texas Mexicans laid claim to their immediate surroundings through social events and called on nearby towns and communities to participate in the making of a new Tejano identity. The distances journeyed by workers, musicians, and audience members served to create and maintain social ties and develop unique market needs. While some journeyed only as migrant workers, others participated as musicians and entertainers. In both cases, their mobility played an additional important role in the development of an economic infrastructure and community in the form of consumers, performers, audiences, small business owners, and entrepreneurs.

Ultimately, the layers of the Texas Triangle reveal how Texas Mexicans created a sense of community in the midst of redefining their place and identity, how the state highway and federal interstate system physically changed communities, and how the development of an informal economic infrastructure dependent on travelers, Spanish language speakers, and Mexican culture defined the area. Rosita Fernández, for example, found success in her travels through much of her career before settling in San Antonio. Throughout the 1950s and 1960s, she spent short periods on the road. In 1958 she and the Conquistadores, a mariachi group, participated in a four-day tour accompanying a Palm Springs group led by Phil Harris.[70] In January 1962, Fernández traveled to Corpus Christi and performed at the Petroleum Club for three weeks. Her daughter, Diana Rosa Almaguer, also a talented dancer, accompanied Fernández much of the time prior to her own marriage. Later, in 1968, Fernández spent six days as one of four headliners doing two performances a day at the Famous-Barr department store in St. Louis. Others who performed with her include Felipe de la Rosa, Willy "El Curro" Champion, and her daughter, Diana.[71] Although the Famous-Barr store traditionally used a festival theme, a member of its promotion staff had attended Fiesta Noche del Rio and decided to focus on Texas and hire the San Antonio performers. Even in this capacity Fernández represented the city, traveling as part of a team led by Walt Warner, manager of the San Antonio Chamber of Commerce's tourist department. He told a reporter, "the project is important in the promotion of tourism, since St. Louis has long been considered the very heart of San Antonio's tourist industry."[72] Amtrak's "Texas Eagle," which started in 1941, provided service between St. Louis and San Antonio, serving as a direct tourist rail line between the two cities.

Although Fernández successfully positioned herself as part of the San Antonio tourism industry, she still built her career on the various networks made available to her through the work of many entertainers over decades. Her success reveals her ability to capitalize on tourist and audience demand for music that represented the cultural life of Mexico. Other women—some of them singers—not privy to the limelight of cultural tourism found themselves tending bar as owners and operators of cantinas and dance halls, meeting the demand for social spaces created by Spanish-speaking populations and those affected by segregation.

These places are etched into people's memories, absent from the historical narrative or the county or state museum, but memories that shed light on how people steered their careers through a politically and socially hostile terrain. The next chapter examines the movement of workers, cantantes, and travelers on the roads and highways of south and central Texas. Their mobility was facilitated by changing demographics and new market sectors. I argue that attention to this geographically defined space uncovers a rich view of how Mexican Americans negotiated their place inside and outside of their immediate communities by operating through a new cultural identity of "Texas Mexican," one based on notions of citizenship and the right to access space and develop economic opportunities.

❖ 5 ❖

MAPPING COMMUNITIES
RACE, GENDER, AND PLACE

EL PROGRESO en el día de la Independencia de los Estados
Unidos, rinde pleitesía como un tributo a los cincuenta y
tres patriotas que unánimemente firmaron la Declaración
de la Independencia el memorable 4 de Julio de 1776. Loor
eterno a aquellos caudillos que se ofrecieron en holocausto
en defensa de la Justicia, la Libertad y el Derecho. Loor
eterno al Gran Patricio, Libertador y primer Presidente de
los Estados Unidos, George Washington, Jefe del ejército
insurgente que puso de manifiesto su valor a toda prueba en
las serranías de Lexington. Por lo que con justicia se le llama:
"El primero en la Guerra; el primero en la Paz; el primero en
el corazón de sus Conciudadanos."

In this piece, in the issue published on July 4, 1939, Rodolfo and
Dora Mirabal, editors of the Spanish-language daily *El Progreso*,
highlighted Independence Day to their readers as a day to celebrate
justice, liberty, and patriotism. Ironically, Mexican Americans in the
south Texas region had experienced few moments of justice and
liberty; discrimination and segregation in housing and public spaces
marked their daily lives. The Mirabals made their community aware
of the difficulties their *compatriotas* faced, reporting in the same
year on *los repatriados* and the deported, the scapegoats of the Great
Depression's unemployment rate, who were targeted as a burden on
resources.[1] Informational in nature, the news articles hinted at but did
not fully explore immigrant experiences, the day-to-day consequences
confronted by those without citizenship, and what life was like for
those inhabiting the bottom rungs of unskilled labor.

A broad view of these stories indicates the larger climate surrounding Mexican nationals, Mexican Americans, identity, and

citizenship. What the news did not relay was the long-standing struggle for economic security and stability in an era of anti-Mexican sentiment. The selective story of Mexican Americans that appeared in *El Progreso* belies, or at least does not fully account for, a larger and more complex picture of the lives and circumstances of Mexican nationals and Mexican Americans. Over the preceding thirty years, the rising number of Mexican immigrants and Mexican American laborers had increasingly faced economic anxiety and changing migration patterns.[2] In addition, in the two decades prior to the Depression, south Texas experienced significant changes in its social and cultural landscape as some Mexican Americans, both English- and Spanish-speaking, created permanent communities through the purchase of land in rural areas and urban barrios. At the same time, Mexican immigrants and Mexican Americans also faced increasing poverty during the Great Depression due to the segregated economy.[3] These economic, migratory, and sociocultural patterns, alongside the struggles that appeared in the pages of *El Progreso*, were all woven into the negotiation of identity on the part of Mexican Americans and Mexican nationals.

This chapter further examines the Texas Triangle, a region rich in layers of migration, discrimination, political activism, and urban-rural relationships that have not yet been explained in other scholarship.[4] Cultural identity is transformed by movement and interaction. By tracking the development of the Texas Triangle through various markers—immigration patterns, labor migration, entertainment travel, and the emergence of small Mexican-American-owned businesses discussed in the preceding chapters—I attempt to locate and identify these transformations. In the midst of segregation, each marker is dependent on the others.

Another set of factors and issues centers on the connectedness of the urban and rural. In particular, I examine the economic and social relationships that exist between those who reside in the urban centers and those in the rural communities. Three major cities mark the parameters of analysis: Corpus Christi, San Antonio, and Houston. For example, the small towns Nursery and Austwell segregated Mexican Americans along unofficial, unspoken boundary lines, while other communities created ordinances that determined where Mexicans could live. Just over one hundred miles from Austwell, Kingsville had implemented "separate quarters for Mexicans" since the early 1900s.[5] Through instructions given by Henrietta King to set aside and sell a portion of the King Ranch, Robert Kleberg established the Kleberg Town and Improvement Company to oversee the selling of parcels of land in 1903.[6] David Montejano argues that these segregated living spaces for Mexican Americans and African Americans resulted from company policy, which reflected the changing class structure of rural areas where Euro-American landowners kept Mexicans indebted to them as tenants. Given the historic geopolitical complexity of the Texas Triangle, I argue that attention to this geographically defined space uncovers a rich view of how Mexican Americans negotiated their place within and outside of their immediate communities by operating through a new cultural identity of "Texas Mexican," an identity based on notions of citizenship and the right to equal access and opportunities.

For many Mexican Americans across the Texas Triangle, gaining admission to extant spaces or creating new spaces absent of hostility to Mexican Americans—spaces for political gatherings, social events, and shopping—was articulated as a right. In earlier chapters I explored how the migration of Mexican American laborers and the movement of entertainers who followed their audiences, often comprising those laborers, brought new opportunities for local musicians and families interested in opening small businesses. As Mexican Americans, whether laborers or entertainers, sought to build their lives across the Triangle, they also helped create spaces—such as bars and dance halls—in which they could come together, free of the racism that they faced among Anglo Texas communities. Unspoken lines of ethnic division between Texas Anglos and Texas Mexicans also drove the demand for the making of new social spaces. Defined and shaped by national and class status, these new spaces ultimately produced a new web of power relations. These Mexican American businesses had their own clientele who sought places to eat lunch and have a beer, working-class joints for a drink after work and dancing on the weekends, and larger dance hall spaces for social and political organizations to hold benefits and dances. An entertainment industry grew up in these new social spaces.

Not all spaces are created equal, however. The region examined in this study, though heavily urban-centered, encompasses mainly rural areas, and rural entertainment spaces tended to be makeshift. They often hosted open and informal gatherings, sometimes in churchyards or abandoned lots. Traveling shows with their own tents could easily set up in these spaces and then move on to the next rural town. In contrast, urban areas usually provided formal open spaces, such as parks, church halls, and venues used by political organizations. These spaces, both urban and rural, were crucial sites in which Mexican Americans and Mexican nationals negotiated their place and their identity.

Many Mexican Americans living in the Triangle region experienced and created their own cultural identity as Texas Mexicans or Tejanos (middle-class-identified Texas Mexicans), which sets them apart from what De León identifies as a decidedly Mexicanist culture.[7] Not all mexicanos living in the region identified themselves as Texas Mexican, but the business world across much of the Triangle was indeed often informed by an ingrained sense of citizenship (Texan) and cultural pride (Mexican). Texas Mexicans served to bridge the gulf that existed in periods of anti-Mexican sentiment, particularly during times of economic scarcity. In other parts of the country, and especially at the end of the 1920s, the larger question for and about Mexican immigrants was whether they would align themselves with the United States or maintain their connection to Mexico.[8] Non-Mexicans often expected that the choice would be one or the other; however, as immigration studies over the last two decades have illustrated, the process of back-and-forth border crossing actually led to a more fluid identity. Writing about Mexican immigrants in Los Angeles, George Sánchez asserts that "ethnicity arose not only from interaction with fellow Mexicans and Mexican Americans but also through dialogue and debate with the larger cultural world encountered in Los Angeles. . . . For over time, as Mexican immigrants acclimated themselves to life north of the border, they did not remain Mexicans simply living in the United States, they became Mexican Americans."[9] Indeed, a dual allegiance—a desire to maintain cultural heritage and also display loyalty to the United States—emerged as Mexican Americans shed nationalistic ties to their Mexican homeland or their "Mexicanist" identity.[10] The added element of Texas regional identity influenced how Mexicans claimed their cultural identity, specifically in terms of language and labels (that is, mexicano, Tejano, or Mexican American).

Regional experiences varied by class and location, and even within the Texas Triangle, loyalties played themselves out differently, particularly in newly developing urban neighborhoods. For example, Corpus Christi and San Antonio remained tied to surrounding towns and their populations, and the emergence of LULAC signified the growth of a middle class ready to participate in the American cultural and political process. LULAC's commitment to social justice pointed to the economic and social disparity that existed between Anglos and Mexican Americans. In early scholarship on Tejanos and segregation, assessments of class and status remain male-focused. In contrast, I argue that the conversation is gendered by space. Often women's experiences remain obscured by scholarly attention to the male workers, whose migration patterns have served as the focus of several studies.

Attempts to locate Texas Mexican women in 1930s work life remain constrained by a lack of primary documentation. Published manuscripts on Texas Mexicans in Houston and San Antonio concentrate on factory workers and unskilled labor. Historian Barbara Rozek writes that by the end of the 1930s, Mexican women workers stayed in the city while their husbands or other male family members followed the seasonal crops.[11] Rozek's observations aptly characterize some cases in Houston where women may have stuck around to work in factories.

Alongside such patterns are others that reveal a very different gendered negotiation of space, identity, business, and community. Cantantes provide one example of how women reshaped family expectations and larger cultural negotiations with their public appearances and their career decisions. Women in the entertainment industry, like Rosita Fernández and Lydia Mendoza, pursued their singing careers.[12] In doing so, they not only offer different insight into the making of Texas Mexicans across the Triangle, but they also reveal quite clearly the salience of gender. Currently, little is known about their lives and careers, for stage performers remain marginal to labor studies, perhaps because data is inconsistent and tells little about the larger population of women workers. The absence of records and the relative invisibility of Mexican Americans in rural communities make it difficult to ascertain any number of things, including how many businesses faded when their clientele moved on, as has continued to be the case through much of the twentieth century, or how language and citizenship intersected. What can be traced through existing records and oral histories, though, is that in the midst of racial hostility and the reinforcement of gendered expectations, Tejana cantantes found numerous routes of travel and performance. Their careers, businesses, and work open new doors to locating historical sites destroyed by time or neglected by maps that seek only to plot points "significant" to the male-biased Texas meta-narrative.

Mapping travel circuits through the movements of the cantantes identifies places where they performed and offers some insight into how those places fit spatially into the regional politics of race and segregation. Historical guides like WPA, *Texas: A Guide to the Lone Star State* and the later *Hispanic Texas: A Historical Guide* offer two views of early Texas: Euro-American Texas and Spanish Texas. A mining of WPA's *Texas* yields travel routes available to cantantes and provides some idea of what they saw on the road.[13] However, the WPA *Texas* guide is obviously framed around travels relevant to Euro-American identities: "Naturally, the State's population is predominantly Anglo-American; Texas' history, culture, character, and progress have been shaped primarily by this group."[14] The second guide, *Hispanic Texas*, published in 1992, emphasizes sites relevant to Spanish explorers and communities built in the nineteenth century and highlights contemporary points of interest, mainly churches and festivals relevant to communities up to the 1920s. The WPA guide illustrates the roads available for travel, while the Hispanic guide widens the lens to include Hispanic people and places. Lacking in both is the explicit presence of Mexican American and mexicano populations—not a surprising observation, but one that again points to their erasure from the official narratives of the Texas Triangle during this period. That Mexican Americans and mexicanos were present in great numbers is undeniable; how they secured space for business, entertainment, and residential purposes is the story that remains to be told, and those are the spaces still to be mapped.

Identifying spaces on maps targeting the leisure traveler does give some details about the places important to this work. The WPA guide, written during the Depression by unemployed writers, details a total of thirty-two tours along Texas highways. The WPA guide has limitations since it largely ignores travel related to Mexican residents, but it does highlight places that were impacted by people's movement, for those who traveled by car. Each numbered tour gives a description of the towns and route to follow, in particular offering impressions of road conditions and accommodations along the highways that connected the major cities of the Texas Triangle. In Tour 25, for instance, a 311-mile route between Rosenberg and Laredo is noted as having "alternating concrete and asphalt paving," whereas the 149-mile excursion between San Antonio and Corpus Christi can be made entirely on asphalt paving.[15]

Such maps provide glimpses into the historical imagination of travel experiences in the Texas Triangle for those who were neither white nor traveling for recreation. Descriptions of towns along the Rosenberg–Victoria road indicate that a large African American population resided in small pockets around the Rosenberg area, which was dominated by the oil and cattle industries. The San Antonio–Corpus route offers a wider range of possibilities for finding Mexican communities along the way, for the area depended heavily on cotton, with Mexican Americans working the farms and fields.[16] This account of travel corresponds with the popular carpas located in the area between Alice, Robstown, and Falfurrias. Lydia Mendoza recalls staying in New Gulf, located between Wharton and Bay City, Texas, where a community of Mexican Americans took her family in and set up a place for them to play a concert. Traveling through New Gulf today, a visitor will find few remnants of the thriving community that Mendoza and her family once recognized as a stopping point to play music for the evening.[17]

Women on stage reveal more about the communities in which they performed, from the money they spent to the spaces they found or created in response to social demands. Women persevered in performance spaces, knowing that they often did not walk through wide-open doors. At the same time, when reflecting on what women singers faced in the late twentieth century, Rosita Fernández felt that her path was easier to negotiate than some. When asked about the difficulty women had in the music business, Fernández replied "que la negocia era diferente pero no era muy difícil. Hasta cierto punto, claro, pero había oportunidades." [The negotiation was different [in the past], but not difficult. To a certain extent, yes, but there were opportunities.][18] The opportunities for Fernández, who started her career in San Antonio, rested on her ability to market a "Spanish Mexican" identity acceptable to tourists.

What emerges then, when we add gender and music, via cantantes, to the study of Mexican American and Mexican national communities and identities, is a more nuanced construction of both community and identity. Across the careers of cantantes we can see the growth of a Texas Mexican cultural identity through the negotiations that their careers as performers required. Music and performances gave cantantes and other Mexican Americans a way of "becoming Tejana" or Texas Mexican. Historian Vicki L. Ruiz describes this process as "cultural coalescence" in which "immigrants and their children pick, borrow, retain, and create distinctive cultural forms."[19] Ventura Alonzo and Rosita Fernández best exemplify the merging of these national identities, American and Mexican, among Tejana singers. Although both women were born in Mexico, over time they began to identify themselves as belonging north of the border. These cantantes represent the formative expression of la música tejana, the process of blending, choosing, and fashioning a style that fit their singing talents and personalities. Their place as citizens did not come into question or debate, though they both lived through the turbulent times of repatriation and deportation, even if they did not personally experience them.

Early in their careers, most cantantes specifically sought Spanish-speaking people as their audience—the same population that was forced into uninhabitable living quarters and separate eating and recreational spaces. With their individual achievements marked by the necessary negotiations of segregation and discrimination, the individual stories of these cantantes reveal a sense of triumph, of quietly and successfully becoming Texas citizens with a Mexican heritage. Nevertheless, this process of becoming Tejana was one of the only experiences that cantantes shared. Across their lives, the differences in their negotiations also become clear. Consider, for instance, Lydia Mendoza. With her experiences reflecting the cultural coalescence that took place in the lives of Mexicans throughout the Southwest, Mendoza felt a closer attachment to Mexico than did other cantantes who moved from Mexico to the United States as children. Mendoza's frequent migration as a child throughout south Texas and Mexico reinforced her dual identity, while others strove to create a permanent tie to the United States. These different perceptions of cultural place translate into a fluid Texas Mexican identity filled with varying connections to citizenship, language, space, and culture. At any given time, one of these pieces acted as the driving force in determining how a cantante would satisfy audience and customer reasons for paying for their entertainment.

In part, the significance of women cantantes lies in their specifically gendered negotiations. What also emerges when we look at cantantes is the centrality of the growing demand for established social spaces that catered to the Spanish-speaking population. Cantantes were significant here for their link to performance spaces. But looking beyond the participation of cantantes points to the making of other businesses directly related to that demand. Mapping the Texas Triangle also allows one to map the cantantes' travels—travels that correspond to the emergence of many small businesses with lifespans of thirty years and more. These businesses, including print shops, dry-goods stores, and furniture stores, met everyday needs; others, such as bars and dance halls, met the need for recreation.

In the world of small business, nothing guarantees success. A mapping of emergent Texas Triangle businesses between 1930 and 1955 demonstrates, however, that their location and accessibility to a primary customer base ensured continuity. In some cases the enterprises lasted beyond a generation. The case of *El Progreso* provides insight here. Printed out of Corpus Christi, Texas, by Rodolfo and Dora Mirabal, *El Progreso* was placed squarely in the middle of the political, entertainment, social, and sports activities taking place not only in Corpus Christi but also nationally and internationally. Focusing on their readers, the Mirabals marketed goods and services across language barriers, thereby highlighting that the Spanish-speaking community had a consumer voice. In a similar vein, *La Prensa* in San Antonio ensured that its readers saw themselves as part of a national narrative, and created a discourse that participated in the emerging Texas Mexican identity. Mirabal called on her readers to be active participants in political and social networks. Moreover, these and other newspapers were crucial to the success of surrounding Mexican American and Texas Mexican businesses. Their simple practice of identifying resources and places through ads and stories increased the visibility of businesses that catered to Spanish speakers and helped guide consumers to those stores. For musicians and entertainers in particular, newspapers such as *El Progreso* helped to promote Spanish-language entertainment, in part by naming the venues for both men and women. News stories often highlighted upcoming events for the men's organizations, the women's auxiliaries, the youth, or for all family members, which enabled a social event such as a dance sponsored by the youth of one of the social clubs to succeed financially.

Small businesses helped shape the formation of a new Texas-Mexican identity in part by offering discursive spaces in which conversations about topics of citizenship, ethnicity, and even gender could occur. Arguments over these topics were hashed out in the editorial pages of *El Progreso*. With Dora Mirabal's entrepreneurial vision framing her role in *El Progreso*, the paper did not leave women out of the picture. From advertisements to editorials, Mirabal ensured that women remained present in the public discourse. Though *El Progreso* hosted a section on the social life of women and their families, Mirabal's editorials and other news coverage made men accountable for the success of women as well.

Those businesses that stayed out of the fray of controversial public battles over gender politics, government policies, or civic responsibility still had to play within an economic structure that often dismissed Mexican Americans as largely ignorant politically, socially, and financially. The entrepreneurial spirit of Texas Mexicans signaled a willingness to the entire community to engage both their immediate community, and at times, the larger Texas Anglo community for the survival of their family business. Businessmen and women had to choose a location carefully as they considered who their customer base would comprise and where those customers would be best served. Women faced various conditions as the intersections of race, space, economy, gender, and language played out differently across time and place. Fernández, as we have seen, responded by promoting herself as a San Antonio attraction, while some women found an opportunity to open their own businesses and others turned to family operations as a way of entering the public arena.

For the Mirabals, the location of their paper in Corpus Christi, beginning in the late 1930s, meant that they served populations in and around the city. The Mirabals reached a large readership both locally and in surrounding towns, taking advantage of the Spanish-language population that did not take the major local newspaper printed in English. Circulation peaked at approximately twenty-two thousand copies, and articles covered stories from surrounding cities like Alice and as far north as San Antonio and south to the valley of south Texas. News items included reporting on softball games in Taft, the drowning death of a sheriff's deputy in Rockport, and a tornado sighting near San Antonio. News also covered the entertainment industry—such as the arrival of actors and actresses, specifically entertainers from Mexico who made special appearances to promote their movies. The inclusion of small-town news and news from as far away as San Antonio suggests three key observations about the people of Corpus Christi. One, Corpus Christi residents had a working or personal relationship with townspeople from the surrounding towns; two, circulation reached outside of the Corpus Christi city limits, and three, readers were interested in knowing what was happening beyond their backyard.

A wide range of businesses emerged across the Triangle. Some Mexican-American-owned businesses eventually vanished when mechanization replaced farm labor and the customer base moved to find other agricultural jobs or to work in cities. Still, the performance and gathering spaces highlighted throughout this book paint a picture of thriving Mexican American communities that hosted people from surrounding towns as well as local neighborhoods. Such spaces provided relief from the social, labor, and economic practices that placed Mexican Americans in a category of "Other," apart from their Texas Anglo counterparts.

The formation of this newly emerging Texas Mexican identity occurred against the backdrop of a racial climate that positioned Mexican nationals and Mexican Americans as Other, virtually regardless of citizenship status, class, and even gender. For much of the first half of the twentieth century, Mexican behavior and cultural practices intrigued anthropologists, who viewed Texas Mexicans, particularly laborers, as an entirely different breed of people. Anthropologist William Madsen, for instance, though genuine in his interest in Mexican and Mexican American agricultural laborers, described the male laborers' choices of migration and settlement as an inherent characteristic: "Working the land seems to him to be a natural and noble labor."[20] Limited and largely blind to women's roles, scholarly conclusions missed a lot of what was happening in migrant communities. Historian Sara Evans argues that the division of wage labor in agriculture also fostered the segregation of spaces that was gendered.[21] Citing the work of sociologist Ruth Allen, Evans goes on to suggest that by paying the men for women's work, Mexican women's presence in workplaces was ignored. Although Evans and Allen point to a critical distinction between private and public spheres, they both overlook Texas Mexican women's whole sense of community and the ways they transformed their living quarters into public gathering spaces. The obvious exclusion from early historiography of women like Rosita Fernández, Ventura Alonzo, and Dora Mirabal, as well as dismissive attitudes toward their work, has resulted in the overlooking of their role as consumers, or financial decision makers. All of these women have been identified in recent years as bold and significant in their specific realm of expertise, but not in the whole of their contributions to the larger Texas history narrative.

More significantly, their roles had a social, cultural, and economic impact on how Mexican Americans and mexicanos viewed themselves vis-à-vis their rapidly changing landscape. As the number of Mexican ranch owners in Texas decreased, some had to work the land they once owned but ultimately lost to white ranchers. Segregation continued to be a factor in how Mexican Americans conducted business and where they purchased property. In addition to suffering the loss of land, they lost access to existing public spaces. De jure segregation led to the establishment of separate eating places, schools, swimming pools, and seating sections for Mexicans and Euro-Americans.[22] Historian David Montejano further documents this segregation by noting that, "separate quarters for Mexican and Anglo were to be found in the farm towns."[23] Although Texas Mexicans and Spanish speakers were "marked" by body type as Other and hence as outsiders to Texas, it was mostly impossible to differentiate between citizens and immigrants.

In his 1929 book *An American-Mexican Frontier*, Paul Taylor asked Texas Mexicans in Nueces County how they viewed themselves. In examining the different self-perceptions of Mexican immigrants, Texas Mexicans, and Mexican Americans, Taylor learned that being an American citizen did not play as strong a role in self-perception as did class standing or loyalty to an American identity.[24] Scholarly work such as Taylor's also offered early insights into how Mexicans were viewed by one another and by outsiders. Unfortunately, these studies also reinforced stereotypes of Mexicans.

Taylor also identified a process of becoming Tejano similar to that of the cantantes, a cultural identity formed by long-term residents of Texas. The cantantes' roles as public figures—even as representatives of Texas—bolstered the making of their distinct Texas Mexican identity. Simultaneously, a process of "amalgamation" occurred in Mexican communities, as illustrated by Montejano, who provides a survey of Kingsville to demonstrate the process by which a perception on the part of Anglo Texans blurred the ethnic lines between native Texas Mexicans and Mexican nationals.[25] Only the elite who did not have to work in the fields were exempt from the racist thinking that "all Mexicans look alike." On the Texas landscape, labor signified a type of Mexican for Texas Anglos, specifically a sense of recent arrival to the United States and an attachment to Mexico.

Texas Mexicans experienced continued discrimination based on biological assumptions of race. Montejano uses Taylor's field notes to support his argument that "race-thinking" developed parallel to commercial farming, perpetuating old stereotypes and creating new notions about Mexicans. These racial ideas sustained the practice of segregation in housing, education, and business. "Race-thinking" politics also influenced middle-class Mexican Americans, encouraging them to dissociate themselves from any possibility that they were Mexican. Historian Benjamin Márquez quotes an explanation from an early LULAC member: "at that time we didn't want to say we were Mexican-American, not because we were ashamed—but we wanted to get away from the Mexican because everywhere you could see signs saying 'No Mexicans Allowed.'"[26] This dissociation seemed a prerequisite for economic mobility and integration into Texas Anglo venues.

Economic security was less attainable for agricultural laborers. Andrés Tijerina's history of Lubbock County in north Texas reiterates the significance of the migration and settlement patterns of mexicanos and Mexican Americans. He describes Mexican tenant farmers in the 1920s as "different from the old nineteenth-century type of tenants or sharecroppers, who were bound by their livelihood to a given plot of land. These [Mexican] tenants were actually day laborers, only some of whom actually resided on the farms."[27] Various discriminatory practices of hiring farm hands and laborers, coupled with sharecropping systems that favored landowners, perpetuated economic segregation throughout south Texas. Taylor's study of agricultural laborers in Nueces County reveals that many systems kept Mexican agricultural workers in debt. He best illustrates his point through the sharecropping system, where each family received ten acres to work, while the farmer provided the tools and divided the cost for ginning and seed. Taylor writes, "Farmers usually plan to have one Mexican family on halves for each 160 acres which they farm."[28] Some farmers tried other tactics to keep Mexican families indebted to them before the start of the cotton season. Tijerina writes of the pre-Depression era when Mexican populations in small towns operated their own businesses. He compares the population growth and activity to that of the predominantly Mexican south Texas areas: "It looked as if Southeast Texas might become as much Mexican as the Rio Grande Valley had always been."[29] However, as the Depression destroyed the local economy, many of the migrant workers began moving to find other jobs.

Rural Mexican American communities continued to experience tumultuous times as the Great Depression took its toll on the agricultural economy and increased poverty levels among laborers. "Farming out" children became a common practice in rural towns as parents who could not afford to feed or clothe all of their children would send a child to live and work on a ranch. The ranch family would then provide housing and food, and in return the child would work for the family.[30] The children who remained at home with their parents helped by chopping cotton, picking onions, growing watermelons, and watching younger siblings. Facing limited financial resources, Mexican families endured the Depression by simply reducing their costs of living and settling in one area for the duration.

Despite these many differences rooted in class and location, by the end of the 1930s, newspapers and city directories were documenting the existence of a new sector of small businesses. The emergence of an entrepreneurial class created a splinter group among Texas Mexicans, particularly among a growing, socially mobile Texas Mexican population who worked to maintain their businesses and political interests. Tensions surrounding the claiming of space within the Texas Anglo community were complicated by questions of who belonged, who deserved access to economic resources, and who participated in the political system. The differences translated into disagreements about ethnic identity, a dangerous line drawn on an already racially hostile landscape.

The growing distance between Mexican Americans and Mexican nationals became public in a 1940s Cinco de Mayo talk given before two different audiences by the Corpus Christi Mexican consul, Augusto Moheno. He announced, "I have never heard of a country named Latin-America and I do not understand what these people mean when they say they are Latin Americans."[31] Moheno later clarified that he was speaking only of Mexican nationals who ought to claim their nationality, and did not mean to direct his comments toward "American" citizens.

A public exchange between the Mexican consul and a reader of *The Sentinel* signaled the continued demarcation between citizenship and cultural pride. Since the repatriation and deportation efforts of the 1930s, Texas Mexicans had embraced legal citizenship as a signal of who belonged in the United States and who was to be sent back, but the language of their cultural citizenship incorporated a geographical sentiment rooted in Latin America. Such an affiliation with the broader Spanish-speaking world blurred the lines for Mexicans who did not have U.S. citizenship but allowed them the unspoken claim of belonging in the U.S. while seeking citizenship. In other words, though foreigners, Latin Americans had significant leverage over Mexicans in the United States, and yet, Mexicans distanced themselves from being seen as foreigners. Moheno's editorial statement thus reflected his frustration with Texas Mexicans who wanted a cultural tie with Mexico but overlooked the needs of the larger population who did not have citizenship. The idea of having to rebuff one's claim to Mexican citizenship by replacing it with a Latin American status seems to have troubled him. In the broader state context, Moheno must have been aware of the treatment of Texas Mexicans by Texas Anglos, regardless of their citizenship.[32]

Obtaining U.S. citizenship was a way to claim a Texas identity, which seemingly made it easier for artists to cross the international border for performances. But cantantes created a different strategy: their music style could shift according to the language of their audience, and to a lesser extent, their audience's national identity. The Alonzo and Fernández families fled the Mexican Revolution and eventually settled in urban areas of the Texas Triangle to find employment. During my 1999 visit with Ventura Alonzo, she showed off her citizenship certificate, which still hung on her wall. Alonzo maintained her sense of Mexican roots both in language and community, while raising her children to live up to the American Dream, as did many families in the 1940s and 1950s. Her children's loyalty to the United States was evident from her sons' military service during the Korean War.

Rosita Fernández traveled from Monterrey to San Antonio, where her family eventually settled.[33] Fernández remembers, "At the time that we came here to San Antonio it was the WPA . . . but that's how my uncles and my father would work. That's how the river was built, because they were asked to work there. Not only my uncles and my father, but a lot of us people [Mexicans], our people, and of course, the American people."[34] The identification with "our people" and the language used by Fernández to acknowledge her ethnic heritage imply that becoming Mexican American did not mean becoming "white."

The construction of national allegiance did not appear problematic for Lydia Mendoza, who was born in the United States and did not have to go through the process of obtaining citizenship. She instead made a conscious decision to associate her roots with the working classes of Mexico, often drawing attention to the influence that Mexican styles and music genres had on her childhood and eventually on her music: "When I was growing up, I felt very Mexican [laughs] of course. Although I would have liked to live in Mexico, well, I was born here, and my parents brought me here. . . . It put the environment of here on me. Although I was born here, and my parents were from Mexico, well . . . for me it would have been the same if I had stayed, or if I were to have stayed in Mexico."[35] Perhaps most people simply assumed that musicians in the Spanish-language music industry were Mexican.

Kathleen May Gonzalas's thesis examining the San Antonio Mexican community in the 1920s provides insight into the class distinctions that locals placed on one another. Her self-designation as having "been born and reared among the Mexican people, and having their interests at heart which compelled her to try to reveal the home life of these people," also gave her a sense of authority as one speaking from the inside.[36] Although her thesis is more a personal testament than a theoretical study, she credits the strength of Mexican American organizations to their being rooted in the early years of mutualistas (mutual aid societies), which provided medical benefits, life insurance, and other charitable benefits to their membership. Her stereotypical descriptions of Mexican American men, women, youth, and families in general offer a glimpse into the personal responses of those who thought of themselves as "white" Mexicans and yet who shared a cultural heritage with all Mexican Americans. Gonzalas's work details class distinctions between "white" Mexicans and Mexican Americans who had cultural, familial, and economic ties to Mexico that kept them from assimilating into American values.

The Works Progress Administration conducted several studies on race in the late 1930s, establishing patterns of work and wages in southwestern agricultural communities and paying particular attention to the cotton industry. The study raised questions about the effects of displacement, but only with regard to farmers and economic projections.[37] One study focused on the prospects for agricultural laborers facing the introduction of new farm machinery. The direct impact of the Depression on Mexican laborers remained unknown to the authors, though they determined that seasonal labor families averaged an annual cash income ranging from two hundred to five hundred dollars. Unfortunately, the authors did not address the larger picture of labor migration, such as the communities that would be most affected by the new farm machinery or the scope of people involved. By ignoring these people and basing their study only on the experiences of Texas Mexicans, they missed an important element in regard to how Mexican migrant workers were perceived, for they were now forming into two distinct groups. The WPA authors came to the conclusion that Mexicans from Texas were a different cultural and racial entity and held a different work ethic from that of Mexicans in other states. The report states, "Texas Mexicans have proved to be a more stable group of migratory workers than the various racial minorities—Chinese, Japanese, Hindus, Mexicans—who have been employed in California agriculture."[38] Unlike Taylor, the WPA authors did not talk extensively to farmers or laborers. Instead, they relied on statistical data to report income and forecast future income for laborers. In doing so they contributed to the growing separation between mexicanos and Texas Mexicans.

The contradictions between Tejanos and Mexican nationals did not manifest themselves uniformly across the region. Mexican middle-class people responded differently to the new communities of immigrants depending on the area's development and demographics. Conflict, contradiction, and compromise had long characterized Texas Mexicans as to their Mexican American identity. Historian Richard Garcia writes that by the mid-1800s, there existed a "dual consciousness of being *mexicano* and *tejano*" in San Antonio.[39]

Mutualista organizations in Texas, grounded in mutual aid societies from Mexico, pursued what historian Emilio Zamora calls a "Mexicanist sense of community."[40] Mutual aid societies played a vital role in offering financial support to both their members and new immigrants. The societies rebuilt networks that they had left behind and helped people settle with whatever resources they had. Zamora writes that new arrivals joined an organization as soon as they acquired a job, and that the societies sought to reinforce a sense of community. As an example, la Sociedad Mutualista Protectora Benito Juárez from San Benito, Texas, declared that they sought "progress and unity among the entire Mexican working class in this country, as well as of the U.S.-born."[41]

At the same time as newcomers continued to join mutualistas in support of their *paisanos* (compatriots), an emerging class of professional service workers in the late 1920s gained new economic footholds and began separating themselves both physically and geographically from working-class Mexican Americans. Historian Garcia argues that the distinction between the classes occurred "when they [lower middle-class workers] spoke of moving to a better section of town, joining their own clubs, and playing sports only with their friends and others like them." The middle-class Mexican Americans, however, removed themselves from the association with cantinas and the Latin Quarter though they lived in the area.[42] The contradiction of such an attitude reveals itself in the relationship that Texas Mexican small-business owners had with their customers, particularly when their businesses relied on Spanish-speaking populations. An evident example of that contradiction was the early members of LULAC who also owned restaurants and markets that served Spanish-speaking laborers and were filled with low-paid or undocumented populations. Such inconsistencies reflect the politics of resources and citizenship through an ideological framework of deserving and undeserving.

The emergence of organizations like LULAC and the Orden Caballeros de America (Order of Knights of America) in 1929 points to the efforts of Tejanos to address the racial discrimination they faced as a people of Mexican descent. Before the 1930s, Mexican

Americans occupied the racial categories of "Colored" or "Other," despite their claim to the rights of "Caucasian." The political activities of the 1930s attempted to broaden the Caucasian "race" to include Mexican Americans. While new scholarship has critiqued this practice as building on inherently racist ideas, I argue that instead of claiming "whiteness," the strategies used were actually built on specific socioeconomic ideals, reinforced by a notion on the part of Mexican Americans that Texas was their home, even though their cultural identity was "Mexican."

These middle-class Tejanos created a separation between themselves and working-class Mexican Americans and Mexican immigrants. They saw themselves as distinct from Mexicans who were new to the United States or who sustained ties to Mexico. Historian Benjamin Marquez writes, "LULAC members rejected any suggestion that their people were innately inferior to the Anglo-Saxon and proclaimed an unshakable faith in the potentials of their people and their ability to succeed in American society."[43] Historian Neil Foley adds that "beginning around 1930 [Mexican Americans] sought to overcome the stigma of being 'Mexican' by asserting their 'Americanness.'"[44] The underlying implication of the decision to emphasize Americanness meant also asserting one's "whiteness." Foley argues that whiteness brought more privileges than citizenship, and that Mexican Americans' later claims of "Caucasian" rights in the 1940s did indeed include a demand for fair treatment of all regardless of citizenship status. Their actions reflected their beliefs as they fought for the same privileges and access to education, housing, and the political franchise that Euro-Americans enjoyed.[45]

LULAC promoted an agenda that proclaimed Mexicans as "the other white race" and required members to be U.S. citizens and to speak English.[46] LULAC members questioned how Euro-Americans could keep them from entering "white only" establishments when they considered themselves white Americans as well. Thus, while LULAC participants upheld class lines, they brought Mexicans under the racial umbrella of "white." Foley writes, "Indeed, middle-class, mostly urban Mexican Americans would invent themselves as a separate group after 1930. . . . They would come to insist that all Mexicans, citizens or non-citizens, were full-fledged members of the 'Caucasian' race."[47] Even though LULAC members categorized all Mexicans as white, they did not, however, afford all of them the same privileges. This was especially true of Mexican nationals. Marquez contends, "Adverse political and social conditions compelled Mexican Americans to work together, but not to reach out to Mexican nationals."[48] Such attitudes evidence ideas about separate classes of Mexicans.

The argument for integration often hinged on the idea that Anglo Texans had failed to recognize that Mexican Americans had assimilated, although not everyone was in agreement about the progress of Mexican Americans. As Army recruiter Oscar G. Garza pointed out, the American GI Forum and LULAC had a greater language problem to deal with than they realized. Although he did not cite the source of his statistics, he told a crowd in 1948 that "very few, lamentably few, persons of Mexican descent make an effort to speak English . . . I am sure you would be surprised to know that four out of every five persons of Mexican descent who apply for active duty in the Army have little practice in the use of the English language and consequently have little chance of holding down a responsible and desirable position in the Army."[49]

The success of Mexican American organizations often depended on how well they negotiated obstacles created by Euro-Americans uncomfortable with sharing resources. Euro-American residents' opposition to public events hosted by Mexican Americans remained high, even when Mexican Americans were serving their country on the battlefields of World War II. In May 1942, the Mexican consulate had occasion to support the request for a beer license by San Antonio resident Frederico Garza "and others"[50] to sell beer at San Pedro Park for a Cinco de Mayo celebration on May 2, 3, 4, and 5. A committee of Euro-American residents of San Antonio protested the granting of the application on the basis that the permit would "lower the public morale."[51] The committee, consisting of representatives from the Co-ordinating Council for Youth Welfare, the Y.W.C.A., and the P.T.A., used the war support workers' schedules as the premise for their petition. "Mrs. Troutman . . . told the judge the park is filled with children in the evenings because so many parents are working in defense plants."[52] The response from the consul indicates that the Mexican government perceived that the petition was grounded in racist attitudes. D. M. Macías, chancellor of the Mexican consulate in San Antonio, spoke on behalf of the Cinco de Mayo board. While a newspaper journalist called the beer request a means to "enliven the Mexican holiday," the chancellor did not couch his request in such terms. He simply pointed out the legalities of the issue: "Beer is not illegal in Texas."[53] The presiding judge determined that based on the laws in place, he could not deny the beer license request. The citizens' committee moved one step further and secured a temporary injunction on the second of May. Two days later, the injunction was lifted and the permit granted, but the injunction prevented beer from being sold on Saturday and Sunday, two of the busiest days.

Throughout the first half of the twentieth century, regardless of individuals' class and citizenship status, both rural and urban Mexican communities encountered difficulties. Mexicanos experienced a backlash across the state from Texans of Euro-American descent, who blamed them for the lack of available jobs. While Tejanos sometimes felt the repercussions of the hostility toward "alien" Mexican immigrants, they attempted to create separate communities to shield themselves from being lumped in with them. But regardless of the efforts of the middle class to be part of the mainstream while simultaneously holding on to cultural attributes, discrimination continued to permeate every aspect of life for them and mexicanos alike, leading to segregated entertainment venues. As noted earlier, the "Mexican" sections of town, which included movie theaters and dance halls, signified the development of a Tejano cultural community. In Corpus Christi and surrounding areas on the Gulf Coast, audiences had the opportunity to meet Mexican movie stars and dance at clubs with live music.

Major moves toward desegregation came after World War II, when ordinary Mexican American men demonstrated their loyalty to the United States and emphasized their identity as U.S. citizens. The formation of the American GI Forum created a new vehicle to test the legalities of overt discrimination against Mexican American veterans. The well-known incident in which a funeral home in Three Rivers, Texas, refused to accept the body of Mexican American war hero Felix Longoria and hold services for him gave rise to protest by the GI Forum.[54] In the end, Longoria was buried at Arlington National Cemetery through the intervention of then senator Lyndon B. Johnson, and though a commission was sent to investigate the incident, the funeral director was not cited for discriminatory practices. The result gave the American GI Forum leaders the momentum to mobilize around voter registration, hoping to give weight and meaning to their voting power.[55]

Middle-class Tejanos based their power over mexicanos in terms of citizenship. They discovered that they carried more political leverage when they boosted their socioeconomic status; thus, entrepreneurial ventures made sense as in some cases it tied Mexican Americans to the larger community development. Their play on "whiteness" not only buttressed their claim to resources like equal education and the integration of spaces, but their capitalization on a demand for market goods. The purchasing power of Mexican workers, though limited, allowed them to purchase simple products as well as luxury items like furniture. Eleuterio Escobar's furniture store in San Antonio and Felix and Janie Tijerina's restaurant in Houston catered to fellow Tejanos or Mexican Americans, while also establishing their owners as potential political allies for the city's larger population. Cities like Austin, San Antonio, Houston, and Corpus Christi had an active population of Mexican Americans who sought to change the discriminatory practices of their Euro-American counterparts. Their civic engagement reflected the dual consciousness referred to by Sánchez and Garcia: they were split in their tie to a Mexican cultural identity and their claim to the rights of U.S. citizenship. However, after the 1930s with the rise of LULAC's influence, Texas Mexicans were encouraged to shift their alliances to an "American" identity. This transformation in their cultural identity created new possibilities for connecting to Anglo communities through business transactions. By the 1940s a handful of Texas-Mexican-owned businesses, ranging from flower shops to dance halls, had registered their names with the appropriate county seats.

Despite the political and cultural conflict that emerged between Mexican Americans and Mexican immigrants, the demand for Spanish-language entertainment created new opportunities for businesses. During the continued migration of workers, entertainers, and travelers passing through the Triangle region of the 1930s and 1940s, the establishment of cultural and economic institutions, resulting from the demand for social spaces reinforced segregation in language and culture. Simultaneously, hard-fought court cases and the work of the Mexican Chamber of Commerce highlighted new possibilities for integration into the wider Euro-American economic and residential infrastructure. Ventura Alonzo, Carmen Marroquin, and Sofia Rodriguez all arrived on the music scene at varying times, but they knew that their style of music would be well received due to a growing demand for singers who could deliver both Spanish and English performances. Historian Arturo Rosales offers an example of a company-designed musical group. He writes that music had become so popular that the Southern Pacific Railroad "organized a company band made up mostly of Mexican workers."[56] The creation of these bands affirms the social demands by laborers and their willingness to build a sense of community around music. While not every musician or performer found a stage, families increasingly saw new opportunities to earn money. Mendoza's family history reflects a similar situation, as when the family abandoned the beet fields to provide entertainment for laborers in Michigan.

Following this period of increased demand for entertainment, early cantantes began their careers; more specifically, Rosita Fernández and Lydia Mendoza found new stages and sang before various audiences. Fernández and Mendoza continued touring, marking spaces of Mexican American social life. Their oral histories alone outline their travels from remote areas to city parks and auditorium-style venues. In the face of discrimination, cantantes continued to emphasize the importance of acknowledging their fans for their support over the years.[57] Music was their art and their passion regardless of the racial and gender borders they confronted; they traversed between multiple worlds, public and private, as well as over lines of segregation.

While rural areas rarely face the same destruction of historic Mexican American venues caused by urban renewal and gentrification, years of neglect have led to the rotting of structures significant to Mexican American communities. As the women in this study go into retirement, their businesses remain vacant and without regular upkeep, slowly deteriorating. There exist numerous sites throughout south Texas that tell a story of Mexican social life, yet these spaces continue to be left out of Texas public history sites because they occupy a marginal role in the informal sector and have few concrete connections to political history or civil rights. Rather, they represent places created as a result of social struggle but where those struggles and personal troubles were left at the door.

Despite the number of places that excluded Mexicans and Mexican Americans, their careers demonstrate that they found places and communities open to them. Numerous Texas Mexican businesses associated with the music industry simultaneously gave refuge to and built a market on those excluded and discriminated against by segregationist practices. Doors opened particularly in the period after World War II, when women built up enough savings to invest in the purchase of lots and buildings. Sofía Rodriguez, for example, started in the beer business in San Antonio following her stint in the defense industry, later moving to Corpus Christi to open a café and eventually a club at a central location accessible to working people looking for a place to relax.

The Alonzos' performances tell of the many spaces open to Mexican Americans in Houston. The list of venues includes "The American Legion Hall on 75th Street, The Union Hall on Houston Ave[nue], The Acapulco on Washington Ave[nue], El Tropical on Smith Street, The Log Cabin on Old Galveston Road, Salon Juarez on Navigation, The Azteca Theatre on Congress Street, The Palladium on South Main, and The Blossom Heath on Airline Drive."[58] In the 1960s, the Alonzos opened a dance hall in one of the most populated sections of Houston. Though distinct in its roots in growth and development through the early part of the twentieth century, an emerging Spanish-language and Mexican-owned business infrastructure developed in the spirit of entrepreneurship and a growing desire to move into the middle class.

Whether political, economic, or social mobility served as the driving force behind new business opportunities, the reality was that in many cases businesses provided a community anchor, a sense of place necessary during a span of time that created uncertainties about who belonged and who did not belong. Scholars of Mexican American history have repeatedly situated community at the center of their studies and from that point have drawn a picture of activism embedded in labor, politics, or social justice movements. Place mattered, and once established it could be leveraged for visibility and stability.

The Texas Triangle never had permanent or official boundaries, but its shifting landscape viewed through numerous lenses, whether from the Pecan Lounge or Rosita's Bridge, uncovers a vibrant story of evolving identities and cultural relationships. Navigating racial, ethnic, gendered, and economically situated realities, the women of this narrative never stopped pushing the boundaries that tied them to a sometimes hostile environment. Nor did they take credit for doing anything extraordinary, when in their minds it was all a part of what needed to be done to take care of their families.

CONCLUSION

This narrative started at the jukebox with my simple question about the women singers who made the cut, in my grandfather's version of the show "The Voice." I asked, was it because women singers just didn't exist? Did the men and women putting coins in the jukebox, as they sat and drank their beer, not think twice about hearing mostly men singing? Would they have been surprised to learn that so few women existed on popular records? As I widened my view and watched the daily happenings in the bar, I had to wonder, how did a bar with only four brands of beer, a jukebox, and two off-balance pool tables continue to stay in business? Stepping back and looking at the landscape of Tivoli, Texas, the questions turned to exploring the lives of women who ran their own business, the mobility of customers, and the impact of regulars who regularly drove in from out of town, and what it meant to be Mexican American in a space fraught with tension over citizenship and who belonged. In this book I sought to put those pieces on the table and watch various pictures emerge. It is a historical kaleidoscope that follows the same people, roads, and community over time and illustrates a moment where women took seemingly ordinary risks to create their own spaces.

Through oral histories, newspapers, and archival materials, two major points emerged. First, the "Triangle" offered a valuable cultural and geographic landscape for marketing the Spanish-language music industry, as it provided both a live audience and record-buying consumers. Second, though the industry was predominantly male in social arenas—therefore making the space available to majority-male *orquestas*—there existed a need for women singers to accompany them. Lacking the social freedom to travel without their families, women like Rosita Fernández, Carmen Marroquin, Lydia Mendoza, and Ventura Alonzo nevertheless found ways to make themselves known.

This study makes clear that particular moments in time opened new doors to women willing to invest in an idea that required a negotiation of boundaries. Regardless of their urban or small-town setting, women took advantage of opportunities to use their skills in new territory. Turning the kaleidoscope in the slightest way reveals how they built on a vision, a talent, or a business aperture. Fernández seized on a moment when the San Antonio market needed a "Rosita" to build its international marketing. Marroquin and her husband built a Spanish-language record company in the absence of one. Rodriguez opened a bar where railroad workers could stop right after work. Alonzo built a dance club around her family's orquesta. Villarreal saved the bar from being used as a cantina by her husband and his friends rather than a business.

Rosita Fernández's career trajectory sheds light on what it meant to be a woman and a professional at the same time. Like Mary F. Villarreal and Sofia Rodriguez, Fernández negotiated this gendered boundary in creative ways. Though perhaps, like Villarreal, disavowing or at least not claiming the label "feminist," Fernández made an impact as a woman. Willingly performing the ideal image of the Mexican señorita and doing so in a way that led to becoming "La Rosa de San Antonio," she took gender and cultural ideals and turned them into a business strategy.

Over a twenty-five-year period and situated in different places, these women created access to opportunity. What has made this study unique is that none of these women responded to the demand for Spanish-language entertainment in the same style, with the same negotiating power, or with the same support. Watching my grandmother get up at four every morning to make and sell breakfast taquitos until 8 A.M. and then return to the bar from 5 P.M. until midnight suggested that her decision was not always a choice. She had a financial responsibility to raise me, and selling breakfast tacos and beer gave her the financial means to do so. The constellation of these women's business decisions points to a moment of access to creating new businesses and opening a pathway regardless of the social constraints that limited their access to capital.

Women took advantage of unique business opportunities that accompanied the growth of informal economies within Mexican American enclaves. Beyond the music industry, women and their families took advantage of community needs as a chance to build an informal economic exchange. Texas-Mexican-American women pursued businesses that catered to a social network of Mexican Americans whose love for music and dancing demanded venues. With limited access to public resources, locals went to great lengths to take ownership of their community life. These women stepped in to fill existing cultural yearnings for space, newspapers to read, and celebrations.

When Villarreal retired from the bar business in the year 2000, it was a surprise to many. She had not made any big announcement of plans to close down the Pecan Lounge. She just said she was done. The Pecan Lounge survived her husband, Raymond, by ten years and had provided a site for camaraderie, grief counseling, and showing off new dates by customers who had lost their spouses over the years. Villarreal didn't anticipate that the bar would be missed; it was just a business, after all. The only three remaining gathering places were church, Canales Cafe (formerly Reyna's Cafe), and the Dairy Queen, where Villarreal had spent her early weekday mornings drinking coffee and Sunday mornings after church as part of her ritual. Unlike Fernández, who intentionally designed her legacy, Villarreal gave little consideration to how she might be remembered or how much "The Place" would be missed. Today, Wal-Mart in Port Lavaca serves as a place for connections while people pause from their shopping to drink a cup of coffee in the retailer's café. Ironically, Villarreal must travel twenty miles now to see familiar faces, the people who work there or others who might also be stopping for coffee or lunch. If touring at one point connected people, their mobility now disconnects them, as bigger and cheaper options for socializing appear. My grandmother rented the bar out for a short while, but it was clear that the twenty-hour-a-day commitment to a small business that pulled in only small profits was not an investment anyone else wanted to make. As my grandmother learned from a former regular customer one day while browsing through Wal-Mart, her new social space, the bar just wasn't the same without her in charge.

The Pecan Lounge now houses carpentry tools, as Villarreal passed on the building to her son Raymond, Jr., who has turned the bar into his workspace. Sofie's Lounge also sat decaying after a long period of inattention when Sofia Rodriguez retired. She, too, rented out a small part of her Corpus Christi club to serve the lesbian community, a clientele that visibly emerged in the 1990s with a similar need for social gathering spaces. Recognizing the business opportunity to maintain a small income, Rodriguez also understood that such spaces were necessary. Where she stood politically on the matter was irrelevant to her, as she recognized the social constraints that locked people out of their communities.

Two places remain as a reminder of the meaning of space and the ability to create a legacy. Rosita's Bridge has perpetual visibility on San Antonio's Riverwalk, a reminder for those who saw Fernández perform or perhaps learned about her after eating at Mi Tierra restaurant and seeing the "American Dream" mural. After being closed for a number of years, La Villita was brought back to life by Rachel and Jason Ramirez in May 2013. This time, as the city of Alice confronted the realities of increased gang violence, the Ramirezes saw La Villita as a place to introduce Christian bands to the Alice community. Rachel Ramirez told a reporter for the *Alice Echo*, "Alice really needs to hear the lyrics, to get inspired and change their lives."[1] Thus space, recreated and reimagined, serves to rebuild community in times of need and opportunity. The introduction of the Sidewalk Prophets to a dance hall where the biggest names in Tex-Mex and Tejano music were once billed raises questions about how Mexican American identities have shifted over time, and reflects the expanding social identities that they choose. The need for both lesbian and Christian spaces, as two of many possible spaces, speaks to the changing landscape. Therein lies the promise of the kaleidoscope. In its endless movement it seemingly creates a new sense of community, and possibly distorts the real moment.

NOTES

INTRODUCTION

1. José L. Limón, *Dancing with the Devil: Society and Cultural Poetics in Mexican-American South Texas* (Madison: University of Wisconsin Press, 1994), 173. Limón's search for the devil reveals how women moved in and around spaces that required them to fend off unwanted attention, particularly from men who had had a few drinks, when what the women sought was only a night of dancing and a good time for the evening.
2. James Clifford, *Routes: Travel and Translation in the Late Twentieth Century* (Cambridge, Mass.: Harvard University Press, 1997), 39.
3. For a more expansive study on the meaning and making of Tejano identity, see Raúl A. Ramos, *Beyond the Alamo: Forging Mexican Ethnicity in San Antonio, 1821–1961* (Chapel Hill: University of North Carolina Press, 2008).
4. George Lipsitz, "Land of a Thousand Dances: Youth Minorities and the Rise of Rock-n-Roll," in *Recasting America*, ed. Larry May (Chicago: University of Chicago Press, 1989), 269. Lipsitz, a historian, describes a lingering nostalgia surrounding the 1950s, and specifically rock and roll, where "much of this memory involves rock-n-roll music as the core icon linking the present with the past." Using Lipsitz's argument that rock and roll music "reveals important connections among music, memory, class, ethnicity, and race, and it illuminates the enduring usefulness of rock and roll as a vehicle for collective popular memory," I locate those same five intersections in a region where small businesses arose to meet the need for social entertainment spaces.
5. Vicki L. Ruiz, "Situating Stories: The Surprising Consequences of Oral History," *Oral History Review* 25 (Summer–Fall 1998), 72–73.
6. Greg Sarris emphasizes his early frustration as he attempts to get Mabel McKay to talk about her life in the order he has in mind. Her responses highlight how she is amused by his aggravation because he cannot get her to tie her stories together. In the end, his oral history interviews with her result in the book *Mabel McKay: Weaving the Dream* (Berkeley: University of California Press, 1994), in which he draws together multiple voices through the stories of Mabel McKay.
7. Chapter 4 focuses extensively on the making of the Texas Triangle.

8. Karen Sacks discusses some of her difficulties in the participant-observer methodology in her work *Caring by the Hour*, where she participated in a unionization drive by clerical, technical, and service workers. She writes that her approach allowed her to focus on the process rather than the conditions. What she found was difficult to record on paper: "that everyday people doing ordinary tasks in more or less the same way, day in and day out, made things change." Karen Sacks, *Caring by the Hour* (Chicago: University of Illinois Press, 1988), 3. In analyzing the narration of everyday activities and encounters with friends and neighbors, I borrow from communication scholar Archana Pathak. In her examination of South Asian-American populations, she writes, "hybridity is rooted in the narratives we tell and in our ways of telling them or not telling them. Who we are is how we tell or don't tell our story." Archana Pathak, "Being Indian in the U.S.: Exploring the Hyphen as an Ethnographic Frame," *International and Intercultural Communication Annual* 31 (2009): 176.

9. A review of San Antonio city government documents shows that various forms of "Riverwalk," including RiverWalk and River Walk, are used by different departments. I chose the spelling "Riverwalk" because it is the one used by the San Antonio Convention and Visitors Bureau.

10. Interview with Rosita Fernández, courtesy KSAT 12, Mario Orellana, San Antonio, Texas. http://medialibrary.utsa.edu/Play/159.

11. Sample works covering politics and labor include: Cynthia E. Orozco, *No Mexicans, Women, or Dogs Allowed: The Rise of the Mexican American Civil Rights Movement* (Austin: University of Texas Press, 2009); Henry A. J. Ramos, *The American GI Forum: In Pursuit of the Dream, 1948–1983* (Houston, Tex.: Arte Público Press, 1998); Ignacio M. García, *Hector García: In Relentless Pursuit of Justice* (Houston: Arte Público Press, 2002); Zaragosa Vargas, *Labor Rights Are Civil Rights: Mexican American Workers in Twentieth-Century America* (Princeton, N.J.: Princeton University Press, 2005); Craig A. Kaplowitz, *LULAC, Mexican Americans, and National Policy* (College Station: Texas A&M University Press, 2005); Michelle Hall Kells, *Héctor P. García: Everyday Rhetoric and Mexican American Civil Rights* (Carbondale: Southern Illinois University Press, 2006).

12. The layers of Texas Mexican community start to become visible with the emergence of the Spanish-language music industry in the 1920s. As communities created social venues for entertainment, the related businesses that emerged over the next three decades shaped the informal economy of ethnic enclaves and neighborhoods in cities and rural areas. The Spanish-language music industry provides a new dimension to the regional character of the Triangle area, particularly because race politics affected the recordings (interracial recordings were not encouraged, for example, in the 1930s). The emphasis on language as opposed to skin color gave Texas Mexicans access to an otherwise closed industry. There existed rigid distinctions in the operations of the rural black (blues) and rural white (hillbilly) music industries in Texas. The third category, that

of rural Texas Mexican, is rarely, if ever discussed. Historian William Kenney argues that record companies like Blue Bird, which started in the mid-1930s, did not give African Americans a role in the business of making and selling records until World War II. The debate, six decades later, over the cultural boundaries of south Texas and the birthplace of *la música tejana* reveals a fundamental layer of connectedness between Houston, San Antonio, and Corpus Christi.

13. Perhaps best known in the literature of la música tejana as a member of one of the first female duets, Carmen Marroquin also co-owned and operated a long-standing dance hall, La Villita, in Alice, Texas. Her business practices reveal how she negotiated within the entertainment industry to sustain her small venture.

14. "Tejano South Texas" maintained a dominant population of Mexican Americans.

15. Daniel D. Arreola, *Tejano South Texas* (Austin: University of Texas Press, 2002), 2.

16. Employees of the Bluebonnet Plant who came from Corpus Christi, Robstown, and Alice considered themselves "South Texans." "The Readers Forum," *The Sentinel*, February 13, 1948. La Verdad, Special Collections and Archives, Bell Library, Texas A&M University–Corpus Christi (hereinafter Texas A&M Archives).

17. Richard H. Schein, "Race and Landscape in the United States," in *Landscape and Race in the United States*, ed. Richard H. Schein (New York: Routledge, 2006), 13.

18. Matt García, *A World of Its Own: Race, Labor, and Citrus in the Making of Greater Los Angeles, 1900–1970* (Chapel Hill: University of North Carolina Press, 2001), 4.

19. Alberto López Pulido, *The Sacred World of the Penitentes* (Washington, D.C. : Smithsonian Institution Press, 2000).

20. Frances R. Aparicio, "U.S. Expressive Cultures," in *The Columbia History of Latinos in the United States since 1960*, ed. David G. Gutierrez (New York: Columbia University Press, 2004), 356.

21. Unlike middle-class African American women, who at the turn of the century engaged in the "politics of respectability," a term coined by Evelyn Brooks-Higginbotham, the women in this research did not respond to what they perceived as racial violence. They served their own communities and sought to keep them in line. They posted signs that they had the right to refuse service to anyone, a reminder that the customer did not have ultimate decision-making rights.

22. Eileen Boris, "On the Importance of Naming: Gender, Race, and the Writing of Policy History," *Journal of Policy History* 17 (2005): 72–92.

23. Interview with Mary F. Villarreal by author, March 2001.

24. Interview with Ventura Alonzo by author, May 2000.

25. Susan Drucker and Gary Gumpert, *Voices in the Street: Explorations in Gender, Media, and Public Space* (New York: Hampton Press Communication Series, 1996), 4.

26. Although this work draws comparisons between the social and economic development of Mexicanos (Mexican immigrants, both nationals and undocumented

peoples) and Mexican Americans. I tend to avoid the use of two existing terms, "Latin American" and "Tejano." Professional Mexican Americans use the term "Latin American" to describe themselves, hinting at their class status and distancing themselves from working-class and immigrant Mexicans. "Tejano" also denotes middle-class identified Texas Mexicans. "Tejano" disappears as a political identity after the Depression. The term "la música tejana" eventually transforms into the "Tejano" music explosion with a profound regional impact.

27. Pre-interview documentation between Sofia Rodriguez and Mary Ann Villarreal.

28. Maria Eva Flores, "The Good Life the Hard Way: The Mexican American Community of Fort Stockton, Texas, 1930–1945" (Ph.D. diss., Arizona State University, 2000), 5.

29. Sarah Deutsch, *Women and the City: Gender, Space, and Power in Boston, 1870–1940* (New York: Oxford University Press, 2000), 6.

30. Ibid., 5.

31. Orozco, *No Mexicans*, 11. Orozco outlines the inadequacies of previous studies' accounts of LULAC's individual members and the larger LULAC organization.

1. BUSINESS FIRST

Epigraph. KCOR Radio flyer, December 1967. Rosita Fernández Papers, 1925–97, MS 18, UTSA Archives Library, University of Texas at San Antonio (hereinafter UTSA).

1. I use "Rosita" in reference to her entertainer name and "Fernández" when talking about her personal life or her role as a businesswoman.

2. KCOR was for numerous decades San Antonio's main Spanish-language radio station.

3. By 1963 the Fiesta was attracting more than 100,000 attendees.

4. San Antonio Convention and Visitors Bureau.

5. Published by Sandoval News Service, El Paso, Texas. Fernández Papers, MS 18, UTSA.

6. I elaborate on the geography and meaning of the Texas Triangle in chapter 4.

7. Fernández recalled in an oral history interview that her husband composed the lines she sang for a Fritos commercial on WOAI Radio. She sang the first few lines: *"Fritos / Muy ricos / Si usted quiere. . . ."* but then her voice faded as the words escaped her.

8. Interview with Rosita Fernández and Raul Almaguer by Deborah Vargas, August 18, 1999.

9. Matt Garcia, *A World of Its Own: Race, Labor, and Citrus in the Making of Greater Los Angeles, 1900–1970* (Chapel Hill: University of North Carolina, 2001), 125.

10. Garcia, *A World of Its Own*, 124.

11. Jean Del Castillo, "Fernandez Chose Family Over Fame, Fortune," n.d., box 1, folder 19, Fernández Papers, MS 18, UTSA.

12. Newspaper clippings. Fernández Papers, MS 18, UTSA.

13. Biographical flyer. Fernández Papers, MS 18, UTSA.

14. Newspaper clippings. Fernández Papers, MS 18, UTSA. *The Indianapolis Star*, Sunday, March 3, 1963. The article was sent to Fernández from someone in Indianapolis, as indicated by a handwritten note on the article copy: "We get all the news from S.A."

15. As historian Alicia Rodríguez-Estrada points out, the "study of ethnic stars' experiences can illuminate the way in which real and imagined identities were reflected within shifting cultural contexts." Alicia Rodríguez-Estrada, "Dolores Del Rio and Lupe Velez: Images on and off the Screen, 1925–1944," in *Writing the Range: Race, Class, and Culture in the Women's West*, ed. Elizabeth Jameson and Susan Armitage (Norman: University of Oklahoma, 1997), 475.

16. Interview with Rosita Fernández by author, March 29, 2001.

17. Scrapbook clippings. Fernández Papers, MS 18, UTSA.

18. Fernández Papers, MS 18, UTSA.

19. The record's subtitle is "The City of Many Charms." The black-and-white version sold for $1, while the full-color souvenir edition sold for $1.35.

20. "Singer Marks Six Decades in Spotlight." Fernández Papers, MS 18, UTSA.

21. Interview with Rosita Fernández by author, March 29, 2001.

22. The three murals, respectively, are the series "Mujeres de San Antonio," South Presa Street and South St. Mary's corridor, by Theresa A. Ybáñez; "La Musica de San Anto" Mural Project, 1303 W. Commerce Street, by David Blancas; and "American Dream" at Mi Tierra restaurant, San Antonio. Additionally, artist Jesse Trevino painted a 2006 portrait, "Rosita," Museo Alameda, San Antonio.

23. Newspaper clippings. Fernández Papers, MS 18, UTSA. "Her Career Just Happened, She Never Took A Lesson," *The Indianapolis Star*, March 3, 1963.

24. Interview with Rosita Fernández by author, March 29, 2001.

25. Ibid.

26. According to a letter sent by Jacob Hamburger, Rosita appeared on the Arthur Godfrey program on Monday evening, June 22, 1953. Fernández Papers, MS 18, UTSA.

27. Interview with Rosita Fernández and Raul Almaguer by Deborah Vargas, August 19, 1999.

28. Ibid.

29. Interview with Rosita Fernández and Raul Almaguer by Deborah Vargas, August 24, 1999.

30. Ibid.

31. Interview with Rosita Fernández by the author, March 2001.

32. Interview with Deborah Vargas, August 19, 1999.

33. Ibid.

34. Interview with Rosita Fernández and Raul Almaguer by Deborah Vargas, August 24, 1999.

35. The Colonial Country Club was located at 3735 Country Club Circle. There was no charge for members, $3.50 for guests.

36. Fernández Papers, MS 18, UTSA. There is no date on the newspaper ad; however, it can be deduced that the ad was placed in the early 1970s, because Walter Jurmann, songwriter of "San Antonio," died in 1971.

37. Interview with Rosita Fernández by author, March 29, 2001.

38. In her children's book *Rosita's Bridge*, Mary Macmillan Fisher relates the role of Fernández's father in the construction of the bridge. The story is narrated through the voice of Rosita's granddaughter Carla Maria. Mary Macmillan Fisher, *Rosita's Bridge* (San Antonio, Tex.: Maverick, 2001).

39. Scrapbook, p. 3, Fernández Papers, MS 18, UTSA. In the Metro section of the *San Antonio Express-News*, December 10, 1992, a caption under Fernández's photo refers to her as the "original San Antonio Rose."

40. KSAT 12 interview.

41. Carmina Danini, *San Antonio Express-News*, "First Lady of Song," May 4, 2006, Metro section; program from Fernández's retirement party.

42. Her 90-year-old mother, Petra, was also in attendance.

43. She first performed for Lyndon Johnson in 1959 and continued to do so throughout his political career, as illustrated in a photo in *Texas Magazine*, May 4, 1967. More recent examples of her performances at political rallies at the Arneson River Theatre or La Villita include appearances for San Antonio mayoral candidate Henry Cisneros and George W. Bush during his 1994 gubernatorial campaign.

44. KSAT 12 interview.

45. In an interview with Deborah Vargas, Raul Almaguer stated that they raised over $800,000 for the Arneson River Theatre.

46. Newspaper clippings. Fernández Papers, MS 18, UTSA.

47. Interview with Rosita Fernández by author, March 2001.

48. Correspondence. Fernández Papers, MS 18, UTSA. Scrapbook, p. 2.

49. Fernández considered retiring in 1976, but did not officially do so until 1982, at the age of 64.

50. Newspaper clippings. Fernández Papers, MS 18, UTSA. Rodolfo Resendez, "Romantic Rosita Honored by Council," *San Antonio Express*, September 3, 1982.

51. Fernández Papers, MS 18, UTSA.

52. Interview with Rosita Fernández and Raul Almaguer by Deborah Vargas, August 18, 1999.

53. Newspaper clippings. Fernández Papers, MS 18, UTSA.

54. Ibid.; *San Antonio News*, December 18, 1972. Even though Almaguer had rigid definitions of husband-wife roles, he took an active part in setting up her singing engagements. He encouraged and even started traditions in the Fernández-Almaguer family. In 1941, Almaguer was asked to play Santa Claus for the Guadalupe Church parish. He was trying on the costume at home when their two-year-old son, Raul, Jr., walked in and thought he really was Santa Claus. "The happiness that enveloped Raul, Jr., had such an impact on his dad that, then and there, it was decided he would play Santa for the family every year." San Antonio Express News, December 18, 1977. The tradition soon expanded

to include close relatives, and in 1969, twenty-eight years later, with Mamá Fernández, Rosita's mother, as the matriarch, the ninety-member family had to move their festivities to San Antonio's La Villita. The mission built in the 1800s as one of the original settlements next to the Alamo, is currently located downtown. It sits on the east bank of the San Antonio River. The rest of the year La Villita and its neighboring stage, the Arneson Theatre, put the spotlight on Rosita; however, at this party, Almaguer was the center of attention for Fernández's mother, Mamá Fernández, and her thirty-four great-grandchildren.

55. Newspaper clippings. Fernández Papers, MS 18, UTSA. *San Antonio Express-News.*

56. Ibid.

57. Diana was also considered a talented performer, making appearances at Fiesta Noche del Rio. Some thought she would follow in her mother's footsteps.

58. KSAT 12 interview, courtesy of Mario Orellano, grandson of Rosita Fernández.

59. Ibid.

60. Ramiro Burr, "Singer's Husband Dies at age 83," *San Antonio Express-News,* August 26, 2000, Metro section.

61. Ibid.

62. Fernández Papers, MS 18, UTSA. Newspaper clipping, ca. 1990–91.

63. Identifying the specific beginning and end of her career is difficult, as Rosita's early travels were varied and not all documented, and her multiple retirements were followed by continued public appearances.

64. Newspaper clippings. Fernández Papers, MS 18, UTSA. Elizabeth McIlhaney, *San Antonio Light,* Friday, May 30, 1980, weekend edition.

65. Ibid.

66. Carmina Danini, *San Antonio Express-News,* "First Lady of Song," May 4, 2006, Metro section.

67. Ibid.

2. A "PROPER, FITTING OR MORAL OCCUPATION" FOR WOMEN

Epigraph. U.S. Supreme Court, *Goesaert v. Cleary,* 335 U.S. 464 (1948). A female tavern owner and her daughter challenged a Michigan law denying bartender licenses to females, except for wives and daughters of male tavern owners.

1. "La música tejana" from the 1930s through the 1950s describes a region more than a genre. The term Tejano music reflects a shift in style in the late 1960s to such bands as Little Joe y La Familia.

2. Fernández Papers, MS 18, UTSA. Elizabeth McIlhaney, "Rosita Celebrates 50th Anniversary as a Performer," *San Antonio Light,* 1980.

3. See Cynthia Orozco, "Regionalism," where she argues that the women of LULAC who participated in both chapters and auxiliaries expanded those boundaries in the political and social arenas. Vicki L. Ruiz in *From Out of the Shadows* offers numerous examples of women's political participation as both Spanish- and English-language speakers. In contrast to places considered

off-limits, there existed a number of conventional businesses in which Mexican women also participated. they opened flower shops, operated restaurants and markets with their husbands, or started Spanish-language newspapers.

4. In her groundbreaking work *Incorporating Women: A History of Women and Business in the United States*, business historian Angel Kwolek-Folland argues that family responsibilities and the uncertain and overwhelming burdens of family-run businesses ensured that many women managed businesses even when they did not have the legal right to do so. Kwolek-Folland, 134. *Goesaert v. Cleary*, 335 U.S. 464 (1948).

5. *Cronin v. Adams*, 192 U.S. 108 (1904). The court affirmed sections 745 and 746 of article 15 of the Denver ordinance, which fined the entrance of women into locations that sold liquor.

6. Ibid.

7. *Crowley v. Christensen*, 137 U.S. 86 (1890) and *Cronin v. Adams*, 192 U.S. 108 (1904).

8. For more literature on *la música tejana* see Manuel Peña, *The Texas-Mexican Conjunto: History of a Working-Class Music* (Austin: University of Texas Press, 1985) and *Música Tejana: The Cultural Economy of Artistic Transformation*, University of Houston Series in Mexican American Studies (College Station: Texas A&M Press, 1999).

9. If we apply the term "cultural citizenship" used by William Flores and Rina Benmayor, in their edited volume *Latino Cultural Citizenship: Claiming Identity, Space, and Rights,* to bars and dance halls, then arguably these places also created "a sense of cultural belonging."

10. La Malinche, known as Doña Marina by the Spaniards, originally served as an example that betrayal by a Mexican woman can lead to the demise of an entire civilization. Numerous books have focused on her role as the mother of the Mexican people at the cost of the Aztec empire. Chicana feminists have reclaimed La Malinche as symbolic of their agency of determination and survival.

11. Lydia Mendoza, Chris Strachwitz, and James Nicolopulos, *Lydia Mendoza: A Family Autobiography* (Houston, Tex.: Arte Público Press, 1993), 149. Note in bracket mine.

12. Richard A. Garcia, *Rise of the Mexican American Middle Class: San Antonio, 1929–1941* (College Station: Texas A&M University Press, 1991), 210.

13. Interview with Sofia Rodriguez by author, March 28, 2001.

14. Fernández Papers, MS 18, UTSA.

15. Vicente Carranza, "Las Hermanas Góngora," *La Voz Latina: The Paper for KSAB-FM and KUNO-AM* (April 1994): 1.

16. Mendoza, Strachwitz, and Nicolopulos, 127.

17. Yolanda Broyles-González, *Lydia Mendoza's Life in Music / La Historia de Lydia Mendoza: Norteño Tejano Legacies* (New York: Oxford University Press, 2001), 74.

18. Clifford Edge, Bicentennial Heritage Profiles, Texas A&M Corpus Christi Special Collections. Edge writes that one of Jackson's carpas had a capacity of 3,000 seats. The cost of attendance was ten cents per person and would increase slightly over the next two decades.

19. I had the privilege of interviewing Señora Alonzo in May 2000, six months before her death on December 14, 2000. She and her daughter welcomed us into their home and allowed us to shoot video and photos of her during the interview, and to hear her play the piano. I thank sociologist Deborah Vargas for working with me to locate and interview Ventura Alonzo.

20. Frank and Ventura Alonzo Collection, Houston Metropolitan Research Center, Houston Public Library (hereinafter Alonzo Coll., Houston Publ. Lib.). According to a family history paper written by her granddaughter, Rosa Linda Alonzo Saenz, Frank and Ventura married in 1931.

21. Alonzo Coll., Houston Publ. Lib. Rosa Linda Alonzo Saenz, "Frank and Ventura Alonzo: Houston Big Band Leaders," family history paper written April 1982.

22. Alonzo Coll., Houston Publ. Lib.

23. La Terraza opened in 1956 at 1515 McCarty Drive in Houston. The Venturas went into a partnership with two other friends, a Señor Torres and a Señor Lombraña.

24. Alonzo Coll., Houston Publ. Lib. Rosa Linda Alonzo Saenz, "Frank and Ventura Alonzo: Houston Big Band Leaders," family history paper written April 1982.

25. Interview with Ventura Alonzo by author, May 2000.

26. A mural dedicated to Alonzo was painted by local art teacher Teodoro Estrada in 1996. The mural is located on the side of a Houston Firestone store at 6901 Harrisburg. In retirement, she dedicated her time to playing the piano for senior citizens of the Denver Harbor community every Friday at the Centro Alegre.

27. The lack of documentation on Laura Cantú sets her apart as the "other" sister. Yet her participation must be noted as part of a historical era of female *duetos*, although she chose to leave her career to raise a family. Las Hermanas Góngora also married and went on to raise families. María Luisa has since passed away, and Lupe lives in the Corpus Christi area, where in 2002 she was still singing with her church choir.

28. Other singers disappear, like Eva Garza, who found success outside of the United States. Both Fernández and Mendoza named Garza as one of the women who found success during the 1930s and 1940s. Garza recorded for Blue Bird records, but after marrying Felipe "El Charro" Gil of the Caporales, she left for New York. While Garza's husband achieved international success, it seems unclear what became of Eva Garza's own career. Her disappearance from the Texas music scene illustrates the difficulty of finding cantantes who chose to leave the profession. Sociologist Deborah Vargas's current research includes interviews with Garza's family members.

29. Vicente Carranza, "Las Hermanas Góngora," *La Voz Latina* 4, no. 40 (April 1999).

30. Interview with Carmen Marroquin by author, July 7, 2000.

31. Dance hall owners Armando and Carmen Marroquin started their own Spanish-language record label as co-owners of Ideal Records.
32. Interview with Carmen Marroquin by author, July 7, 2000.
33. Peña, *La música tejana*, 95.
34. Interview with Carmen Marroquin by author, July 7, 2000.
35. Ibid.
36. Interview with Sofia Rodriguez by author, March 28, 2001.
37. Ibid.
38. Ibid.
39. Ibid.
40. In her oral history interview Sofia Rodriguez again reinforced her commitment to women as good, law-abiding patrons, noting that a lesbian bar was not illegal and her renters were good tenants. While she may have relied on some stereotypes about women, such as the idea that women did not bring the same trouble as men patrons, forty years of business gave her some reliable information about women customers.
41. In her ethnographic study, *The Mexican American Family: Tradition and Change* (New York: Rowman and Littlefield, 1990), Norma Williams argues that the exclusion of Mexican Americans from Anglo society and the development of Mexican Americans apart from Mexican society resulted in families shaping their own traditions and family patterns.
42. Interview with Sofia Rodriguez by author, March 28, 2001.
43. Ibid.
44. Interview with Mary F. Villarreal by author, March 29, 2001.
45. Villarreal taught herself how to drive around town but did not actually get her driver's license until after her husband's death.
46. Interview with Mary F. Villarreal by author, March 29, 2001.
47. Ibid.
48. The term "nicle" refers to the phrase "not worth a nickel" or in this case, nickels spent.
49. Interview with Mary F. Villarreal by author, March 29, 2001
50. Interview with Sofia Rodriguez by author, March 28, 2001.
51. Mary Jo O'Rear, *Storm over the Bay: The People of Corpus Christi and Their Port* (Corpus Christi, Tex.: Gulf Coast Books, 2009), 34.

3. THE BUSINESS OF CULTURE

Epigraph. Advertisement in *The Sentinel* [Corpus Christi].

1. Photos and oral histories highlight the emergence by the late 1930s of businesses owned and operated by Mexican Americans in Corpus Christi's predominantly Mexican neighborhood called "the Hill."
2. *The Sentinel*, Editorial, January 16, 1948 (vol. 1, no. 7). Dr. Hector Garcia Papers, Special Collections and Archives, Bell Library, Texas A&M University–Corpus Christi (hereinafter Texas A&M–CC). Frustration grew when the Good

Neighbor Commission's executive secretary, Thomas E. Sutherland, declared that while the GNC was against all segregation, the commission held no "police powers" over specific departments such as the Health Department, which was investigating labor camps in Mathis, Texas.

3. Pete Carroll offers an excellent example of how the Good Neighbor Commission stepped in on behalf of LULAC when they challenged the denial of a proper funeral of Felix Longoria at a Three Rivers, Texas, funeral home.

4. *The Sentinel*, "Dr. J. A. Garcia Interviene en Clasificación de la Raza," April 23, 1948 (vol. 1, no. 21). Garcia Papers, Texas A&M–CC.

5. In 1916 the decision to separate Mexicans and Americans in the U.S. census left many Mexican Americans angry and resentful. Mario T. Garcia gives a detailed account of the challenge to the separate census categories in "Mexican Americans and the Politics of Citizenship: The Case of El Paso, 1936," *New Mexico Historical Review* 2 (April 1984): 187–204.

6. *The Sentinel* was originally published in English. The editors tried a semi-bilingual run of the paper starting with its twentieth issue in 1948, when the editors began including news and local gossip in Spanish, without English translation. The editorial column was the only section in both languages. In the twenty-first issue, a note to the readers pointed out the difference in print between the English and Spanish editorial text, solicited notes, and offered advertising space for a cost. All mail was to be sent to *El Sentinel*, 2624 Segrest.

7. The eldest son, Rodolfo, Jr., took over the original Mirabal Printing Company. After he sold it in the mid-1970s, the other children, Rosie and Roberto, carried on the tradition of the printing business.

8. Joe G. Rodriguez, *The Sentinel*, "The Sentinel Observes First Anniversary of Publication," November 26, 1948 (vol. 2, no. 1). Garcia Papers, Texas A&M–CC.

9. It could be argued that the growth of Mexican American chambers of commerce and their shift to being called Hispanic chambers of commerce moved the focus from the small business owner's economic ties to corporate social relations and a role as liaisons to Latin American consulates.

10. Thomas Kreneck, personal communication.

11. In their groundbreaking scholarship on Mexican American identity, historians Vicki L. Ruiz, George Sánchez, and David Gutierrez examine the generational transformation in the early 1990s, focusing on the Southwest and the Los Angeles area and the impact of popular culture on newer generations of Mexican American youth.

12. Diana G. Hernandez, "'The Hill': Mexican Americans in Corpus Christi, 1900–1950," unpublished paper, July 1974. Hernandez conducted interviews with former residents to map and collect her evidence. Texas A&M–CC.

13. Mary Alice Davis, "City Had a 'Minority,'" Garcia Papers, Texas A&M–CC.

14. *The Sentinel*, "Railroader Retires to 'General Store' Business," March 26, 1948 (vol. 1, no. 17). Garcia Papers, Texas A&M–CC.

15. The store was located at 3104 Morgan Street. Ibid.

16. The Tex-Mex News Stand, which advertised itself as "Little Mexico in Corpus Christi," is located at 316 N. Staples.

17. Matthew Frye Jacobson, *Whiteness of a Different Color: European Immigrants and the Alchemy of Race* (Cambridge, Mass.: Harvard University Press), 1998.

18. *The Sentinel*, Editorial, July 23, 1948 (vol. 1, no. 34). Garcia Papers, Texas A&M–CC.

19. The historiography of LULAC includes Benjamin Marquez, *LULAC: The Evolution of a Mexican American Political Organization* (Austin: University of Texas Press, 1993).

20. *The Sentinel*, Editorial, March 12, 1948 (vol. 1, no. 15). Garcia Papers, Texas A&M–CC.

21. Interview with Rosie Mirabal Garza by the author, March 2001.

22. The exact year the Mirabal Bakery went out of business is unknown, but an advertisement in the November 1949 issue of *La Calavera*, annual supplement to *El Progreso*, indicates that it was still in business. I found further documentation of its existence in Diana G. Hernandez's 1974 paper, "'The Hill,'" which indicates that the Mirabal Bakery occupied the space formerly belonging to Campos Bakery. This raises the question of when it moved from its original site on Sam Rankin Street.

23. Corpus Christi High School was renamed Miller High School in 1950.

24. For more reflections on the Good Neighbor policy from the perspective of Mexican American professionals at the time, see Alonso Perales. *Are We Good Neighbors?* (San Antonio, Tex.: Artes Gráficas, 1948).

25. *The Sentinel*, December 26, 1947 (vol. 1, no. 4). Garcia Papers, Texas A&M–CC.

26. Articles appeared in two issues of *The Sentinel*, January 16, 1948 (vol. 1, no. 7) and April 2, 1948 (vol. 1, no. 18). A later report, "$5,000 Plus in Proposed Hospital Fund, Report" (vol. 1, no. 19) showed that the committee was seeking $150,000 for a tuberculosis ward. More than $12,000 had been raised, but almost $8,000 had already been spent.

27. *The Sentinel*, "The Readers Forum" (vol. 1, no. 17). Garcia Papers, Texas A&M–CC. Lerma also placed his ad in Spanish, "Botánica y Farmacia Lerma, Servicio de Recetas y Medicinas de Patente."

28. *The Sentinel*, Editorial, February 13, 1948 (vol. 1, no. 11). Garcia Papers, Texas A&M–CC.

29. Davis, "City Had a 'Minority.'"

30. "Zip" advertised in *The Sentinel* in the January 16, 1948, issue. A photo caption in *The Sentinel* dated October 22, 1948, reads: "An eight man delegation represented the local chamber of commerce at the Mexican Chambers of Commerce convention at Dallas last week. The above pic was snapped shortly before they left. Shown are, back row, standing, left to right. Reymundo Longoria, Doroteo Benavides, Juan Gonzalez, N. Cipriano (Zip) Gonzalez, and Lee H. Scott. Kneeling, left to right: Manuel Maldonado, J. B. Mascorro and A. C. Chapa."

31. "LULAC Group Demands 'Clean-Up' In Mathis," *The Sentinel*, April 16, 1948 (vol. 1, no. 20). Garcia Papers, Texas A&M–CC.

32. *The Sentinel*, "Gran Junta Pro-Fondo Escolar en Mathis" (vol. 1, no. 21). Garcia Papers, Texas A&M–CC.

33. *The Sentinel*, "Robstown Council to be Reactivated in Meet Tonight," March 12, 1948 (vol. 1, no. 15). Garcia Papers, Texas A&M–CC. Councils in Kingsville, Alice, and Falfurrias also moved to reactivate their membership.

34. *The Sentinel*, "Progressivemen Open Fund for Needy Youth," December 26, 1947 (vol. 1, no. 4). Garcia Papers, Texas A&M–CC.

35. For more information on the Community Settlement House, see Joanne Rao Sanchez, "From Familial Shelter to Expanding Horizons," in *Beyond the Latino World War II Hero: The Social and Political Legacy of a Generation*, ed. Maggie Rivas-Rodríguez and Emilio Zamora (Austin: University of Texas Press, 2009).

36. *The Sentinel*, Editorial, May 14, 1948 (vol. 1, no. 24). Garcia Papers, Texas A&M–CC.

37. Ibid.

38. San Antonio's Rosedale Park has played a central role in providing a gathering place for political rallies and live entertainment. It is one of the last known venues where Corpus Christi songstress Chelo Silva performed for a KCOR event. Most recently the Tejano Conjunto Festival makes Rosedale Park its home base.

39. *The Sentinel*, "Crowds Jam Night Spots," December 26, 1947 (vol. 1, no. 4). Garcia Papers, Texas A&M–CC.

40. *The Sentinel*, "Six Dances Listed for Current, Next Month," January 16, 1948 (vol. 1, no. 7). Garcia Papers, Texas A&M–CC. The Riviera Club was considered high-end, described as "swank."

41. *The Sentinel*, "The Readers Forum," May 14, 1948 (vol. 1, no. 24). Garcia Papers, Texas A&M–CC.

42. *The Sentinel*, Editorial, April 2, 1948 (vol. 1, no. 18). Garcia Papers, Texas A&M–CC.

43. *The Sentinel*, "The Readers Forum," March 19, 1948 (vol. 1, no. 16). Garcia Papers, Texas A&M–CC.

44. *The Sentinel*, "The Readers Forum," March 12, 1948 (vol. 1, no. 15). Garcia Papers, Texas A&M–CC.

45. *The Sentinel*, "The Readers Forum," April 23, 1948 (vol. 1, no. 21). Garcia Papers, Texas A&M–CC.

46. *The Sentinel*, "The Readers Forum," April 2, 1948 (vol. 1, no. 18). Garcia Papers, Texas A&M–CC.

47. *The Sentinel*, "The Readers Forum," April 9, 1948 (vol. 1, no. 19). Garcia Papers, Texas A&M–CC.

48. *San Antonio Express*, "Stars of the 'Fiesta Noche' to St. Louis," October 16, 1968. Fernández Papers, MS 18, UTSA.

49. *The Sentinel*, "World War I Vets Welcome GI Forum," April 2, 1948 (vol. 1, no. 18). Garcia Papers, Texas A&M–CC.

50. Davis, "City Had a 'Minority,'"

51. De Santos to Build on Port," *The Sentinel*, January 2, 1948 (vol. 1, no. 5). Garcia Papers, Texas A&M–CC.

52. The Taxco Mexican Restaurant advertised in *The Sentinel* and was located at 1120 Agnes Street, near Staples Street.

53. *The Sentinel*, "LULAC Attorney Sees Segregation Case on Way to Chief Court," January 16, 1948. Garcia Papers, Texas A&M–CC.

54. "Agnes–S. Port Merchants Aim of PBA," *The Sentinel*, January 9, 1948 (vol. 1, no. 6). Garcia Papers, Texas A&M–CC. The president, A. R. Falcon, was an income tax consultant and moved his business operations to 1904 Agnes, as reported in the January 16, 1948 issue of *The Sentinel*.

55. Advertisement in *The Sentinel*, April 2, 1948 (vol. 1, no. 18). Garcia Papers, Texas A&M–CC.

56. "R. Galvan Jr. Operator of Agnes Drugs," *The Sentinel*, January 9, 1948 (vol. 1, no. 6). Garcia Papers, Texas A&M–CC.

57. "Sports Views," *The Sentinel*, December 26, 1947 (vol. 1, no. 4). Garcia Papers, Texas A&M–CC.

58. *The Sentinel*, January 9, 1948 (vol. 1, no. 14). Garcia Papers, Texas A&M–CC.

59. Advertisement in *The Sentinel*, December 26, 1947 (vol. 1, no. 4) and April 2, 1948 (vol. 1, no. 18). Garcia Papers, Texas A&M–CC.

60. *The Sentinel*, "Sports Views" (vol. 1, no. 8). Garcia Papers, Texas A&M–CC. The reference was made specifically about attempts to enter into a formal baseball league and move the games to a field outside of the city limits.

61. "Baker's Dozen," *The Sentinel*, January 9, 1948 (vol. 1, no. 6). Garcia Papers, Texas A&M–CC.

62. *The Sentinel*, "The Readers Forum" (vol. 1, no. 11). Garcia Papers, Texas A&M–CC.

63. Ibid.

64. "Cost-Price Groceries Plan to be Offered by Garzas," *The Sentinel*, January 2, 1948 (vol. 1, no. 5). Garcia Papers, Texas A&M–CC.

65. Ibid. The stores were located at 502 S. Brownlee and 2217 Agnes.

66. Ibid. The owners of the Morgan Food Store were Charles A. and I. R. Phillips. The Phillips family were active members of LULAC.

67. A. C. Chapa's obituary dated February 24, 1970, in the *Corpus Christi Caller-Times* stated, "He was 57 years old and lived at 2502 Cloyde." It also claims that the tortilla factory opened in 1940, which conflicts with other accounts of its opening in 1939. In Vicki L. Ruiz's article "'La Malinche Tortilla Factory': Negotiating the Iconography of Americanization, 1920–1950," *Privileging Positions: The Sites of Asian American Studies*, ed. Gary Y. Okihiro, et al. (Pullman: Washington State University Press, 1995), she examines the "images of an American life filtered into the barrios of the Southwest."

68. Alejandro Chapa Family / Mexican. Chamber of Commerce Papers, Texas A&M–CC.

69. In the 1940s there was a second tortilla factory, Monita Corn Products, but little information exists about it. Its owner, a Mr. Maldonado, sponsored a local softball team.

70. Chapa was survived by his wife, Dolores, and two daughters, Rosario Carrizo of Panama and Laura Ann Chapa of Corpus Christi.

71. Kathryn Garcia, "Owner of Tortilla Factory Dies at 65. Her family plans to continue with running the store," *Corpus Christi Caller-Times*, August 15, 2005.

72. Jaime Powell, "Planned Parenthood clinic named after women's rights activist," *Corpus Christi Caller-Times*, January 5, 2006. "For more than 30 years, local businesswoman Rosario Carrizo was on the front lines in Planned Parenthood's struggle to educate local women and provide birth control, said Amanda Stukenberg, the executive director of Planned Parenthood. Wednesday, Planned Parenthood renamed its Dillon Street clinic, the Planned Parenthood Carrizo Clinic in honor of Carrizo, who died last year at age 65 of breast cancer. In the early 1970s, when Carrizo started volunteering for Planned Parenthood, it was tough for a woman, much less a Hispanic woman, to come out in favor of birth control and family planning, said Carrizo's longtime friend and fellow Planned Parenthood advocate Vicki Garza."

4. FIGURING SPACE

Epigraph. Greg Sarris, *Mabel McKay: Weaving the Dream* (Berkeley: University of California Press, 1994), 5.

1. In *The White Scourge*, historian Neil Foley locates his study in the "ethnoracial borderlands of central Texas" which includes the region I identify as the "Texas Triangle" and extends northward to Dallas. *The White Scourge: Mexicans, Blacks, and Poor Whites in Texas Cotton Culture* (Berkeley: University of California Press, 1997), 15.

2. An exception is the Arneson River Theatre and Rosita's Bridge along San Antonio's Riverwalk. Though the two sites are linked, the theater's presence eclipses the bridge that connected Rosita to her fans. San Antonio serves as a way to theorize space but only accounts for some spaces. While the bridge sits in an ideal tourist location, not all of the places where cantantes performed are situated where people can conveniently find them.

3. Madsen's study focuses specifically on the residents of Hidalgo County, located on the Texas-Mexico border. Though his interviewees do not come from the region I discuss, their narratives speak to ways that ethnicity, class, citizenship, and gender intersect and play out in their daily lives. William Madsen, *The Mexican-Americans of South Texas*, 2nd ed. (New York: Holt, Rinehart and Winston, 1973), 41–42.

4. *The Sentinel*, Works Progress Administration Map 3280, 1941, Mexican Migratory Workers of South Texas.

5. Tejano scholar Arnoldo De León argues that the Mexican American population in Houston never fit the larger Texas Mexican model; instead, Houstonians rooted themselves in their Mexican identity. Although De León terms these Houston Mexicans "Texas Mexican," he is explicitly drawing on a notion of biculturalism. Houston's Texas Mexican community, he maintains, emerged out of the decisions of organizational leaders to assert explicit ties to Mexico and a nationalist identity, while simultaneously cementing their place on the Texas scene and within the larger Houston economic structure through self-sustaining businesses.

6. Arnoldo De León, *Ethnicity in the Sunbelt: Mexican Americans in Houston* (College Station: Texas A&M Press, 2001), 46.

7. Ibid., 47–48.

8. Tejano scholar Américo Paredes published extensive studies on corridos and their significance in cultural folklore tradition. For a more in-depth reading on style and individual artists, see Américo Paredes, *A Texas-Mexican Cancionero: Folksongs of the Lower Border*, with a new foreword by Manuel Peña (Austin: University of Texas Press, 1995); Manuel Peña, *The Texas-Mexican Conjunto: History of a Working-Class Music* (Austin: University of Texas Press, 1985), *Música Tejana* (College Station: Texas A&M University Press, 1999, *The Mexican American Orquesta* (Austin: University of Texas Press, 1999); Maria Herrera-Sobek, *The Mexican Corrido: A Feminist Analysis* (Bloomington: Indiana University Press, 1990); Guadalupe San Miguel, *Tejano Proud: Tex-Mex Music in the Twentieth Century* (College Station: Texas A&M University Press, 2002); and Ramiro Burr, *The Billboard Guide to Tejano and Regional Mexican Music* (New York: Billboard Books, 1999).

9. Paul S. Taylor, *An American-Mexican Frontier: Nueces County, Texas* (New York: Russell and Russell, 1971), 146. Notes in brackets added by Villarreal.

10. Ramiro Burr, "Play Honors Legendary Singer," *The Houston Chronicle*, Star Edition, November 4, 1991.

11. Interview with Carmen Marroquin by Dr. Clary Shorkey, March 19, 1988. Texas Music Museum.

12. The story of the Carter Family, noted as the first country music family and founders of country music, illustrates the larger significance of travel and the spread of music through recordings. As they returned home from Bristol, Tennessee, where they had recorded with Victor Records, "the rickety car died while fording a stream and had to be pushed out by the trio to dry." Mary A. Bufwak, *Finding Her Voice: Women in Country Music, 1800–2000* (Country Music Foundation, 2003) p. 46. Similar to Texas Mexican musicians, those from the Appalachian region had to be willing to travel significant distances in whatever kind of transportation they could afford as part of their investment in the new recording opportunities.

13. Early scholarship and primary documents refer to Mexican Americans and Mexican nationals as "Latin" or as being of "Latin extraction."

14. Mendoza, Strachwitz, and Nicolopulos, *Lydia Mendoza: A Family Autobiography.* Strachwitz's oral history interviews with Mendoza contain many small nuggets of information that allow us to continue mapping her family's travels and ask questions about how their culture "traveled" with them.

15. Tejana singing superstar Selena Quintanilla Perez was catapulted into a popularity that overshadowed the "early women"—those who recorded in kitchens and other makeshift studios. Contrary to the misconception that early women cantantes played only supporting roles in the music industry, their performances garnered attention for record labels and contributed to their household incomes. The historical emphasis on male musicians has resulted in female singers remaining nameless and on the fringe of the industry. Finding them in music history proved difficult due to their anonymous status in photos and in the larger narrative. As my interviewees reached deep into their memories, I discovered that their stories disrupted the narrative of our Tejano imagination, a myth in which great male musicians shaped the future of the music. It was not until the appearance of a smattering of legends like Lydia Mendoza, and later, Selena, that women received some mention for their contribution.

16. Peirce Lewis, "Taking Down the Velvet Rope: Cultural Geography and the Human Landscape," in *Past Meets Present: Essays about Historic Interpretation and Public Audiences*, ed. Jo Blatti (Washington, D.C.: Smithsonian Institution Press, 1987), 23.

17. Lewis, "Taking Down," 40.

18. De León, *Ethnicity in the Sunbelt.*

19. As evidenced by a flyer, held in the Chairez Family collection, that advertises the 1929 dance.

20. Chairez Family Collection, 1918–78, MS 94, Houston Metropolitan Research Center, Houston Public Library (hereinafter Chairez Coll., Houston Publ. Lib.)

21. Premont, like Alice, is located in Jim Wells County, which is adjacent to Nueces County.

22. Homero S. Vera, "Premont, Texas: The Mexican Heritage," *El Mesteño* 4 (January 2001), 4. The magazine has articles in both Spanish and English.

23. Homero S. Vera, "Teatro Alameda," *El Mesteño* 4 (February 2001).

24. Mendoza, Strachwitz, and Nicolopulos, *Lydia Mendoza: A Family Autobiography*, 121.

25. Homero Vera, "Pachangas," *El Mesteño* 4 (February 2001), 18.

26. Interview with Carmen Marroquin by the author and Deborah Vargas, July 7, 2000.

27. KSAT 12 interview, courtesy of Mario Orellana.

28. Historian Vicki L. Ruiz discusses the family oligarchy and the way in which elders, both men and women, collaborated to restrict the movement of adolescent girls and to protect family honor.

29. Sofia Rodriguez noted in an interview that Chelo Silva often sang for free when she was out for a night with friends. Though Silva had a remarkable relationship with her audiences, her insistence on managing her career as she saw fit, singing in bars and for free, worked in opposition to the demands of the music industry and has left a tainted memory of her contributions.

30. Selden Menefee, *Mexican Migratory Workers of South Texas*, Report of the Works Progress Administration (Washington, D.C.: U.S. Government Printing Office, 1941), 21.

31. Interview with Sofia Rodriguez by the author, March 28, 2001.

32. For a lengthier examination, see Virginia Scharff, "Women at the Wheel in the 1920s," in *Taking the Wheel: Woman and the Coming of the Motor Age* (Albuquerque: University of New Mexico Press, 1992). She examines both the personal and sexual freedom that the automobile created for middle-class Euro-American women. Scharff includes a photo of three Mexican American women in a touring car, which gives the impression that they owned the car. However, the photo appears to be posed at a state or county fair.

33. Pomeroy describes the ease with which people could travel by automobile and stay in a roadside camp overnight: "Corollary to the automobile was the auto camp, which was common enough by the 1920's so that one might undertake a long trip in the West with fair assurance of finding a suitable place to pitch a tent within reach of the main highways." Earl Pomeroy, *In Search of the Golden West: The Tourist in Western America*, 2nd reprint ed. (Lincoln, Neb.: Bison Books, 2010). Because of prevailing racial segregation, Texas Mexican travelers had to rely on open homes or places such as churches to find lodging on their journeys. Small towns such as Fredericksburg or Halletsville, for example, were known for their anti-Mexican attitudes.

34. Pomeroy, *In Search of the Golden West*, 121.

35. Russell Sanjek's multivolume work on the history of popular manufactured music offers a detailed look at the growth of the industry from its early experimental days to the present-day multimillion-dollar conglomerates. Russell Sanjek, *Pennies from Heaven: The American Popular Music Business in the Twentieth Century* (Boston, Mass.: Da Capo Press, 1996). From the beginning, Sanjek points to the difficulty of undertaking a project such as this, because of the geographical dispersion of the recordings of the independent specialty labels. Further, the disappearance of trade papers such as *Talking Machine World* and *Phonograph Review* affects any possibility of historical continuity. Because of the size of the project, Sanjek is unable to elaborate on the connection between the expansion of the record industry and the transformation of radio programming.

36. Sanjek, *Pennies*, 30.

37. Ralph Peer of Victor Records had a rival, Frank Walker, who was in charge of "race" records at Columbia as well as the Blue Bird label.

38. Columbia archival documents.

39. Eleuterio Escobar Papers, Benson Latin American Collection, University of Texas at Austin (hereinafter UT Austin).

40. Jo Blatti, Introduction to *Past Meets Present: Essays about Historic Interpretation and Public Audiences*, ed. Jo Blatti (Washington, D.C.: Smithsonian Institution Press, 1987), 5.

41. Sofia Gonzalez, conversation with author, January 8, 2002.

42. Ibid.

43. Ibid.

44. Gonzalez's youngest son, Cruz, died from leukemia in 1954 at the age of seventeen.

45. Remaining unmarried for the next fifty-three years, San Juanita Flores died in April 1999, three months shy of her ninety-third birthday.

46. Paul Taylor writes in *Mexican Labor in the United States: Valley of the South Platte, Colorado* (Berkeley: University of California Press, 1929), 146, that in a season of working the beet fields, an experienced man could work ten acres and a woman seven acres.

47. Mendoza, Strachwitz, and Nicolopulos, *Lydia Mendoza: A Family Autobiography*, 36.

48. Ibid.

49. Menefee, *Mexican Migratory Workers*, xiv.

50. Arnoldo De León, *Mexican Americans in Texas: A Brief History* (Arlington Heights, Il.: Harlan Davidson, 1993), 82.

51. Earle and Roberts, *Houston Housing, 1939*, 62.

52. De León, *Ethnicity in the Sunbelt*, 33.

53. For more information on the Pecan Shellers Strike, see Richard Croxdale, "Pecan-Shellers' Strike," Handbook of Texas Online, tshaonline.org/handbook/online/articles/oep01.

54. Escobar Papers, UT Austin.

55. María L. de Hernández, vertical file, Benson Latin American Collection, General Libraries, University of Texas at Austin.

56. Taylor, *American-Mexican Frontier*, 90.

57. Ibid., 90.

58. Mendoza, Strachwitz, and Nicolopulos, *Lydia Mendoza: A Family Autobiography*, 271.

59. Texas State Employment Service, *Survey of Farm Placement in Texas, 1936 and 1937* (Austin, Tex.: Texas State Employment Service, 1938), 1.

60. "Ex-Labor Agent Sees Little Labor Importation, *The Sentinel* 1, no. 14 (March 5, 1948). E. E. Mireles and Jovita Gonzalez Mireles Papers, Special Collections and Archives, Bell Library, Texas A&M University–CC.

61. Francisco E. Balderrama and Raymond Rodríguez, *Decade of Betrayal: Mexican Repatriation in the 1930s* (Albuquerque: University of New Mexico Press, 1995), 136.

62. De León, *Mexican Americans*, 95.

63. Mario Barrera, *Race and Class in the Southwest: A Theory of Racial Inequality* (Notre Dame, Ind.: University of Notre Dame, 1979), 106.

64. Texas State Employment Service. *Survey*, 45.

65. Ibid., 40.

66. Ibid., 41.

67. U.S. Bureau of the Census, *Population in 1940.* Population of the major Texas cities was: Houston 384,514; Austin 87,930; Corpus 57,301, and San Antonio 253,854.

68. U.S. Bureau of the Census, *Fifteenth and Sixteenth Censuses of the United States: 1930–1940 Population.* The Mexican population dropped from 266,354 to 159,266.

69. For more on the demands made on the Texas government to take action and the organizational relationships that emerged, see Thomas Guglielmo, "Fighting for Caucasian Rights: Mexicans, Mexican Americans, and the Transnational Struggle for Civil Rights in World War II Texas," *Journal of American History* 92, no. 4 (March 2006), 1212–37.

70. *San Antonio Express News*, June 8, 1958. Special magazine on the Fiesta Noche del Rio.

71. "Stars of the 'Fiesta Noche' to St. Louis," *San Antonio Express*, October 16, 1968. Fernández Papers, UTSA.

72. Ibid.

5. MAPPING COMMUNITIES

Epigraph. Dora Mirabal Collection, Special Collection and Archives, Bell Library, Texas A&M University–CC.

1. Communication scholar Lisa A. Flores examines the rhetoric of need, an argument used to increase the number of Mexican laborers called up and the burden placed on Mexican workers in the public discourse during this period. See "Constructing Rhetorical Borders: Peons, Illegal Aliens, and Competing Narratives of Immigration," *Critical Studies in Media Communication* 20, no. 4 (December 2003), 362–87.

2. Several important studies examine the external influences on Mexican Americans in Los Angeles, including the work of George Sánchez, David Gutierrez, Eric Davila, and Matt Garcia. All of these authors situate Mexican Americans at the center of cultural shifts in identity. Their micro-level case studies map race, ethnicity, and profession in urban spaces.

3. For more on Mexican American women's work during the Depression, see Julia Kirk Blackwelder, *Women of the Depression: Caste and Culture in San Antonio, 1929–1939* (College Station: Texas A&M University Press, 1999).

4. Studies of Mexican American populations in Los Angeles, San Antonio, and Houston draw the most attention, while studies in Chicago are now emerging at a faster rate.

5. David Montejano, *Anglos and Mexicans in the Making of Texas, 1836–1986* (Austin: University of Texas Press, 1987), 167.

6. George O. Coalson, "Kingsville, Texas," *The Handbook of Texas Online*, http://www.tshaonline.org/handbook/online/articles/hdk02. Accessed January 29, 2015. The land set aside is the original town site of Kingsville, named after Richard King.

7. The original Tejano identity has ties to the pre-1848 population of Mexican elites who lived in Tejas. I use the term Tejano as a reconstruction of cultural identity and citizenship with an emphasis on Mexican as culture, not Mexico as a place. De León argues in *Ethnicity in the Sunbelt* that biculturalism did not apply to Texas Mexicans who did not see themselves as part of Texas.

8. Historian David Montejano describes the early twentieth century as a time when an increasing number of *mexicanos* became migrant laborers on Euro-American commercial farms and small farms in the Southwest, Oklahoma, and Arkansas.

9. George J. Sánchez, *Becoming Mexican American: Ethnicity, Culture, and Identity in Chicano Los Angeles, 1900–1945* (New York: Oxford University Press, 1993), 12.

10. Emilio Zamora, "Mutualist and Mexicanist Expressions of a Political Culture in Texas," in *Mexican Americans in Texas History*, ed. Emilio Zamora et al. (Austin: Texas State Historical Association, 2000), 88. See also Emilio Zamora, *The World of the Mexican Worker in Texas* (College Station: Texas A&M University Press, 1993).

11. Barbara Rozek, "The Entry of Mexican Women into Urban Based Industries," in *Women and Texas History*, ed. Fane Downs and Nancy Barker (Austin: Texas State Historical Association, 1993), 27.

12. Rozek asks significant questions: "Did women work full-time or part-time, and what number of hours helps render precisely that designation? When women worked outside the home, were they adding to the family income or serving as the primary wage earner? How do we deal with the lack of consistent terms to identify the general Spanish-speaking population through such sources as the census records? And how can we compare one decade to another when the terminology varies and seems imprecise?" p. 16.

13. Work Projects Administration in the State of Texas [hereinafter WPA], Writers' Program, *Texas: A Guide To The Lone Star State* (New York: Hastings House, 1940), including the revised edition: Harry Hansen, ed., New York: Hastings House, 1969. Helen Simons and Cathryn A. Hoyt, eds., *Hispanic Texas: A Historical Guide* (Austin: University of Texas Press, 1992).

14. WPA, *Texas*, 88.

15. Ibid., 645, 652.

16. Ibid., 653.

17. The *Texas Handbook Online* gives an overview of business transactions in New Gulf, Texas, including the sale of the New Gulf Sulfur company and the financial troubles, but tells little of its residents.

18. Interview with Rosita Fernández by Deborah Vargas, August 18, 1999.

19. Vicki L. Ruiz, *From Out of the Shadows: Mexican Women in Twentieth Century America* (New York: Oxford University Press, 2008), 50.

20. William Madsen, *The Mexican-Americans of South Texas*, 2nd ed. (New York: Holt, Rinehart and Winston, 1974), 33.

21. Sara Evans. *Born for Liberty* (New York: Free Press, 1991), 185.

22. Rosales, F. Arturo, *Chicano: The History of the Mexican American Civil Rights Movement* (Houston, Tex.: Arte Público Press, 1997), 95. Rosales addresses patterns of segregation throughout the twentieth century. He specifically examines de jure segregation through the categorization of Mexicans as "colored" in his chapter, "The Mexican American Generation." See also Sánchez, *Becoming Mexican American.*

23. Montejano, *Anglos and Mexicans*, 160.

24. At the time of Taylor's study, LULAC was in its infant years as an organization. Taylor notes that LULAC is a small group that identifies itself as Mexican American but believes that the use of the term will grow over time. Taylor also notes that Nueces County led all Texas counties in picking cotton, and by 1930 led all counties in the United States. Paul Taylor, *An American Mexican Frontier: Nueces County, Texas* (Chapel Hill: University of North Carolina Press, 1934), xi). It would be interesting to see figures of cotton production in the surrounding counties of Jim Wells, San Patricio (south of Refugio), and Kleburg.

25. Montejano, *Anglos and Mexicans*, 167.

26. Marquez, *LULAC*, 29.

27. Andrés Tijerina, *History of Mexican Americans in Lubbock County, Texas*, Graduate Studies 18 (Lubbock: Texas Tech Press, 1979), 36.

28. Taylor, *American Mexican Frontier*, 120.

29. Tijerina, *History of Mexican Americans*, 37.

30. I originally heard about this system from my grandfather, Raymond H. Villarreal, whose two younger siblings, a brother and a sister, were sent to work for separate families.

31. *The Sentinel*, May 7, 1948. La Verdad, Texas A&M–CC.

32. For a further elaboration on the alliances between the Mexican government and Mexican Americans, see Guglielmo, "Fighting for Caucasian Rights," 1212–37.

33. Fernández's father had served as a captain in the Mexican army before moving his family to San Antonio. There he worked for the Works Progress Administration (WPA, later called Work Projects Administration) created by Franklin D. Roosevelt's New Deal.

34. Interview with Rosita Fernández by author, March 2001.

35. Mendoza, Strachwitz, and Nicolopulos, *Lydia Mendoza: A Family Autobiography*, 332.

36. Kathleen May Gonzalas, "The Mexican Family in San Antonio, Texas," undergraduate thesis, University of Texas, 1928.

37. Menefee, *Mexican Migratory Workers*, ix.

38. Ibid.

39. R. Garcia, *Rise of the Mexican American*, 19.

40. Emilio Zamora, "Mutualist and Mexicanist Expressions of a Political Culture in Texas," in *Mexican Americans in Texas History*, ed. Emilio Zamora, Cynthia Orozco, and Rodolfo Rocha (Austin: Texas State Historical Association, 2000), 84.

41. Emilio Zamora, *The World of the Mexican Worker in Texas* (College Station: Texas A&M University Press, 1993), 95. The layers of ethnic identity have been the subject of extensive studies, with arguably mixed results depending on gender, class, and region studied. See, for example, Gabriela F. Arredondo, "'What! The Mexicans, Americans?' Race and Ethnicity, Mexicans in Chicago, 1916–1939," Ph.D. diss., University of Chicago, 1999.

42. Garcia, *Rise of the Mexican American*, 88.

43. Marquez, *LULAC*, 48.

44. Neil Foley, "Partly Colored or Other White: Mexican Americans and Their Problem with the Color Line," in *Beyond Black and White: Race, Ethnicity, and Gender in the U.S. South*, ed. Stephanie Cole, Alison Marie Parker, and Laura F. Edwards (College Station: Texas A&M University Press, 2004), 2.

45. Foley's work focuses on the fight to change Mexican American racial identity in government records from "colored" to "white" in El Paso and other urban areas in Texas.

46. Cynthia Orozco documents the debate over who could become a member in *No Mexicans, Women, or Dogs Allowed: The Rise of the Mexican American Civil Rights Movement*, Austin: University of Texas Press, 2009.

47. Foley, "Partly Colored," 4.

48. Marquez, *LULAC*, 49.

49. "The Readers Forum," *The Sentinel*, May 7, 1948 (vol. 1, no. 18). Garcia Papers, Texas A&M—CC.

50. The May 1, 1942, newspaper article refers to the applicants in this manner. A look at articles in the following days indicates that "and others" refers to the directors of the celebration event. Under certain circumstances, particularly when celebrating a Mexican holiday, the Mexican consulate general would intervene on behalf of Mexican Americans.

51. "Ban on Beer for Mexican Fete Studied," *San Antonio Light*, May 1, 1942.

52. Ibid.

53. Ibid.

54. Montejano, *Anglos and Mexicans*, 279.

55. For an analysis of the Longoria incident and its impact on Mexican American activism, see Patrick Carroll, *Felix Longoria's Wake: Bereavement, Racism, and the Rise of Mexican American Activism* (Austin: University of Texas Press, 2003).

56. F. Arturo Rosales, "Mexicans in Houston: The Struggle to Survive, 1908–1975," *The Houston Review: History and Culture of the Gulf Coast* 3 (Summer 1981), 237. Film, music, and theatrical activity also increased after the 1928 opening of Teatro Azteca in California.

57. Perhaps too, after years of doing what they loved, the cantantes came to the same conclusion that "art has neither nationalities nor borders." Quoted in Vicki L. Ruiz, *From Out of the Shadows*, from the March 1927 issue of *La Opinion*.

58. Rosa Linda Alonzo Saenz, "Frank and Ventura Alonzo: Houston Big Band Leaders," family history paper written April 1982. Alonzo Coll., Houston Publ. Lib.

CONCLUSION

1. Julie Neal, "La Villita will reopen with Sidewalk Prophets," *Alice Echo* (Alice, Tex.), May 22, 2013.

BIBLIOGRAPHY

ARCHIVAL COLLECTIONS

Houston Metropolitan Research Center, Houston Public Library
    Frank and Ventura Alonzo Collection, MS 0202
    Chairez Family Collection, 1918–78, MS 994
    Gregorio T. Valerio Collection, MSS 0101–002

Special Collections and Archives, Bell Library, Texas A&M University–
Corpus Christi
    Alejandro Chapa Family / Mexican Chamber of Commerce Papers
    Clifford Edge Papers
    Dr. Hector Garcia Papers
    E. E. Mireles and Jovita Gonzalez Mireles Papers
    El Progreso

Benson Latin American Collection, University of Texas at Austin
    Eleuterio Escobar Papers, 1906–71
    María L. de Hernández vertical file

Archives Library, University of Texas at San Antonio
    Rosita Fernández Papers, 1925–97, MS 18

GOVERNMENT DOCUMENTS

Texas State Employment Service. *Survey of Farm Placement in Texas, 1936 and
    1937.* Austin, Tex.: Texas State Employment Service, 1938.
U.S. Bureau of the Census. *Fifteenth and Sixteenth Censuses of the United States:
    1930–1940 Population.*
U.S. Supreme Court. *Cronin v. Adams*, 192 U.S. 108 (1904)
U.S. Supreme Court. *Crowley v. Christensen*, 137 U.S. 86 (1890)
U.S. Supreme Court. *Goesaert v. Cleary*, 335 U.S. 464 (1948)

INTERVIEWS AND ORAL HISTORIES

Ventura Alonzo, interviewed by author and Deborah Vargas, May 2000, San
    Antonio, Tex.
Rosita Fernández, interviewed by author, March 2001, San Antonio, Tex.

167

Rosita Fernández and Raul Almaguer, interviewed by Deborah Vargas, August 19, 1999, San Antonio, Tex.

Sofia Gonzalez, interviewed by author, March 2001, Corpus Christi, Tex.

Carmen Marroquin, interviewed by author and Deborah Vargas, July 7, 2000, Alice, Tex.

Sofía Rodríguez, interviewed by author, March 28, 2001, Corpus Christi, Tex.

Mary F. Villarreal, interviewed by author, March 29, 2001, Tivoli, Tex.

BOOKS AND ARTICLES

Alamillo, José M. *Making Lemonade out of Lemons: Mexican American Labor and Leisure in a California Town, 1880–1960.* Urbana: University of Illinois Press, 2006.

Aparicio, Frances R. "U.S. Expressive Cultures." In *The Columbia History of Latinos in the United States since 1960*, edited by David G. Gutierrez. New York: Columbia University Press, 2004.

Arredondo, Gabriela F. *Mexican Chicago: Race, Identity, and Nation, 1916–1939.* Urbana: University of Illinois Press, 2008.

———. "'What! The Mexicans, Americans?' Race and Ethnicity, Mexicans in Chicago, 1916–1939." PhD diss., University of Chicago, 1999.

Arreola, Daniel D. *Tejano South Texas.* Austin: University of Texas Press, 2002.

Balderrama, Francisco E., and Raymond Rodríguez. *Decade of Betrayal: Mexican Repatriation in the 1930s.* Albuquerque: University of New Mexico Press, 1995.

Barrera, Mario. *Race and Class in the Southwest: A Theory of Racial Inequality.* Notre Dame, Ind.: University of Notre Dame, 1979.

Blackwelder, Julia Kirk. *Women of the Depression: Caste and Culture in San Antonio, 1929–1939.* College Station: Texas A&M University Press, 1999.

Blatti, Jo. Introduction to *Past Meets Present: Essays about Historic Interpretation and Public Audiences*, edited by Jo Blatti. Washington, D.C.: Smithsonian Institution Press, 1987.

Boris, Eileen. "On the Importance of Naming: Gender, Race, and the Writing of Policy History." *Journal of Policy History* 17 (2005): 72–92.

Broyles-González, Yolanda. *Lydia Mendoza's Life in Music / La Historia de Lydia Mendoza: Norteño Tejano Legacies.* New York: Oxford University Press, 2001.

Bufwak, Mary A. *Finding Her Voice: Women in Country Music, 1800–2000.* Country Music Foundation, 2003.

Burr, Ramiro. *The Billboard Guide to Tejano and Regional Mexican Music.* New York: Billboard Books, 1999.

Carranza, Vicente. "Las Hermanas Góngora," *La Voz Latina* 4, no. 40 (April 1999).

Carroll, Patrick. *Felix Longoria's Wake: Bereavement, Racism, and the Rise of Mexican American Activism.* Austin: University of Texas Press, 2003.

Clifford, James. *Routes: Travel and Translation in the Late Twentieth Century.* Cambridge, Mass.: Harvard University Press, 1997.

Coalson, George O. "Kingsville, Texas." *The Handbook of Texas Online.*

Deutsch, Sarah. *Women and the City: Gender, Space, and Power in Boston, 1870–1940.* New York: Oxford University Press, 2000.

Drucker, Susan, and Gary Gumpert. *Voices in the Street: Explorations in Gender, Media, and Public Space.* New York: Hampton Press Communication Series, 1996.

Earle, Huber Dale, and Le Wallace Roberts. *Houston Housing, 1939.* Houston, Tex.: Housing Authority of the City of Houston and Work Projects Administration, 1940.

Fisher, Mary Macmillan. *Rosita's Bridge.* San Antonio, Tex.: Maverick, 2001.

Flores, Lisa A. "Constructing Rhetorical Borders: Peons, Illegal Aliens, and Competing Narratives of Immigration." *Critical Studies in Media Communication* 20, no. 4 (December 2003): 362–87.

Flores, Maria Eva. "The Good Life the Hard Way: The Mexican American Community of Fort Stockton, Texas, 1930–1945." Ph.D. diss., Arizona State University, 2000.

Foley, Neil. "Partly Colored or Other White: Mexican Americans and Their Problem with the Color Line." In *Beyond Black and White: Race, Ethnicity, and Gender in the U.S. South,* edited by Stephanie Cole, Alison Marie Parker, and Laura F. Edwards. College Station: Texas A&M University Press, 2004.

———. *The White Scourge: Mexicans, Blacks, and Poor Whites in Texas Cotton Culture.* Berkeley: University of California Press, 1997.

García, Ignacio M. *Héctor García: In Relentless Pursuit of Justice.* Houston: Arte Público Press, 2002.

Garcia, Mario T. "Mexican Americans and the Politics of Citizenship: The Case of El Paso, 1936." *New Mexico Historical Review* 2 (April 1984).

García, Matt. *A World of Its Own: Race, Labor and Citrus in the Making of Greater Los Angeles, 1900–1970.* Chapel Hill: University of North Carolina, 2001.

Garcia, Richard A. *Rise of the Mexican American Middle Class: San Antonio, 1929–1941.* College Station: Texas A&M University Press, 1991.

Gonzalas, Kathleen May. "The Mexican Family in San Antonio, Texas." Undergraduate thesis, University of Texas, 1928.

Guglielmo, Thomas. "Fighting for Caucasian Rights: Mexicans, Mexican Americans, and the Transnational Struggle for Civil Rights in World War II Texas." *Journal of American History* 92, no. 4 (March 2006).

Herrera-Sobek, Maria. *The Mexican Corrido: A Feminist Analysis.* Bloomington: Indiana University Press, 1990.

Jacobson, Matthew Frye. *Whiteness of a Different Color: European Immigrants and the Alchemy of Race.* Cambridge, Mass.: Harvard University Press, 1998.

Kaplowitz, Craig A. *LULAC, Mexican Americans, and National Policy.* College Station: Texas A&M University Press, 2005.

Kells, Michelle Hall. *Héctor P. García: Everyday Rhetoric and Mexican American Civil Rights.* Carbondale: Southern Illinois University Press, 2006.

Kwolek-Folland, Angel. *Incorporating Women: A History of Women and Business in the United States.* Woodbridge, Conn.: Twayne, 1998.

León, Arnoldo de. *Ethnicity in the Sunbelt: A History of Mexican Americans in Houston.* College Station: Texas A&M Press, 2001.

———. *Mexican Americans in Texas: A Brief History.* Arlington Heights, Ill.: Harlan Davidson, 1993.

Lewis, Peirce. "Taking Down the Velvet Rope: Cultural Geography and the Human Landscape." In *Past Meets Present: Essays about Historic Interpretation and Public Audiences,* edited by Jo Blatti. Washington, D.C.: Smithsonian Institution Press, 1987.

Limón, José L. *Dancing with the Devil: Society and Cultural Poetics in Mexican-American South Texas.* Madison: University of Wisconsin Press, 1994.

Lipsitz, George. "Land of a Thousand Dances: Youth Minorities and the Rise of Rock-n-Roll." In *Recasting America,* edited by Larry May. Chicago: University of Chicago Press, 1989.

Madsen, William. *The Mexican-Americans of South Texas.* 2nd ed. New York: Holt, Rinehart and Winston, 1973.

Marquez, Benjamin. *LULAC: The Evolution of a Mexican American Political Organization.* Austin: University of Texas Press, 1993.

Mendoza, Lydia, Chris Strachwitz, and James Nicolopulos. *Lydia Mendoza: A Family Autobiography.* Houston, Tex.: Arte Público Press, 1993.

Menefee, Selden. *Mexican Migratory Workers of South Texas.* Report of the Works Progress Administration. Washington, D.C.: U.S. Government Printing Office, 1941.

Montejano, David. *Anglos and Mexicans in the Making of Texas, 1836–1986.* Austin: University of Texas Press, 1987.

O'Rear, Mary Jo. *Storm over the Bay:* The People of Corpus Christi and Their Port. Corpus Christi, Tex.: Gulf Coast Books, 2009.

Orozco, Cynthia E. *No Mexicans, Women, or Dogs Allowed: The Rise of the Mexican American Civil Rights Movement.* Austin: University of Texas Press, 2009.

Paredes, Américo. *A Texas-Mexican Cancionero: Folksongs of the Lower Border.* Austin: University of Texas Press, 1995.

Pathak, Archana. "Being Indian in the U.S.: Exploring the Hyphen as an Ethnographic Frame." *International and Intercultural Communication Annual* 31 (2009).

Peña, Manuel. *The Mexican American Orquesta.* Austin: University of Texas Press, 1999.

———. *Música Tejana: The Cultural Economy of Artistic Transformation.* University of Houston Series in Mexican American Studies. College Station: Texas A&M University Press, 1999.

————. *The Texas-Mexican Conjunto: History of a Working-Class Music.* Austin: University of Texas Press, 1985.

Perales, Alonso. *Are We Good Neighbors?* San Antonio, Tex.: Artes Gráficas, 1948.

Pomeroy, Earl. *In Search of the Golden West: The Tourist in Western America.* 2nd reprint ed. Lincoln, Neb.: Bison Books, 2010.

Ramos, Henry A. J. *The American GI Forum: In Pursuit of the Dream, 1948–1983.* Houston, Tex.: Arte Público Press, 1998.

Ramos, Raúl A. *Beyond the Alamo: Forging Mexican Ethnicity in San Antonio, 1821–1961.* Chapel Hill: University of North Carolina Press, 2008.

Rodríguez-Estrada, Alicia. "Dolores Del Rio and Lupe Velez: Images On and Off the Screen, 1925–1944." In *Writing the Range: Race, Class, and Culture in the Women's West,* edited by Elizabeth Jameson and Susan Armitage. Norman: University of Oklahoma Press, 1997.

Rosales, F. Arturo. *Chicano: The History of the Mexican American Civil Rights Movement.* Houston, Tex.: Arte Público Press, 1997.

————. "Mexicans in Houston: The Struggle to Survive, 1908–1975." *The Houston Review: History and Culture of the Gulf Coast* 3 (Summer 1981).

Rozek, Barbara. "The Entry of Mexican Women into Urban Based Industries." In *Women and Texas History,* edited by Fane Downs and Nancy Barker. Austin: Texas State Historical Association, 1993.

Ruiz, Vicki L. *From Out of the Shadows: Mexican Women in Twentieth Century America.* New York: Oxford University Press, 2008.

————. "La Malinche Tortilla Factory." In *Privileging Positions: The Sites of Asian American Studies,* edited by Gary Y. Okihiro, et al. Pullman: Washington State University Press, 1995.

————. "Situating Stories: The Surprising Consequences of Oral History." *Oral History Review* 25 (Summer–Fall 1998): 72–73.

Sacks, Karen. *Caring by the Hour.* Chicago: University of Illinois Press, 1988.

San Miguel, Guadalupe. *Tejano Proud: Tex-Mex Music in the Twentieth Century.* College Station: Texas A&M University Press, 2002.

Sánchez, George J. *Becoming Mexican American: Ethnicity, Culture, and Identity in Chicano Los Angeles, 1900–1945.* New York: Oxford University Press, 1993.

Sanchez, Joanne Rao. "From Familial Shelter to Expanding Horizons." In *Beyond the Latino World War II Hero: The Social and Political Legacy of a Generation,* edited by Maggie Rivas-Rodríguez and Emilio Zamora. Austin: University of Texas Press, 2009.

Sanjek, Russell. *Pennies from Heaven: The American Popular Music Business in the Twentieth Century.* Boston: Da Capo Press, 1996.

Sarris, Greg. *Mabel McKay: Weaving the Dream.* Berkeley: University of California Press, 1994.

Scharff, Virginia. *Taking the Wheel: Women and the Coming of the Motor Age.* Albuquerque: University of New Mexico Press, 1992.

Schein, Richard H. "Race and Landscape in the United States." In *Landscape and Race in the United States*, edited by Richard H. Schein. New York: Routledge, 2006,

Simons, Helen, and Cathryn A. Hoyt, eds. *Hispanic Texas: A Historical Guide.* Austin: University of Texas Press, 1992.

Taylor, Paul. *An American-Mexican Frontier: Nueces County, Texas.* Chapel Hill: University of North Carolina Press, 1934. Reprinted New York: Russell and Russell, 1971.

————. *Mexican Labor in the United States: Valley of the South Platte, Colorado.* University of California Publications in Economics 6, no. 2. Berkeley: University of California Press, 1929.

Tijerina, Andrés. *History of Mexican Americans in Lubbock County, Texas.* Graduate Studies 18. Lubbock: Texas Tech Press, 1979.

Vargas, Deborah R. *Dissonant Divas in Chicana Music: The Limits of La Onda.* Minneapolis: University of Minnesota Press, 2012.

Vargas, Zaragosa. *Labor Rights Are Civil Rights: Mexican American Workers in Twentieth-Century America.* Princeton, N.J.: Princeton University Press, 2005.

Vera, Homero. "Premont, Texas: The Mexican Heritage." *El Mesteño* 4, no. 40 (January 2001).

————."Pachangas." *El Mesteño* 4, no. 41 (February 2001).

————. "Teatro Alameda," *El Mesteño* 4, no. 41 (February 2001).

Villarreal, Mary Ann. "Becoming San Antonio's Own: Reinventing 'Rosita.'" *Journal of Women's History* 20, no. 2 (2008).

————. "Finding Our Place: Reconstructing Community through Oral History." *Oral Historian* 33, no. 2 (2006).

————. "Life on the 'Hill': Entrepreneurial Strategies in 1940s Corpus Christi." In *An American Story: Mexican American Entrepreneurship and Wealth Creation*, edited by John Sibley Butler, Alfonso Morales, and David L. Torres. Lafayette, Ind.: Purdue University Press, 2009.

Williams, Norma. *The Mexican American Family: Tradition and Change.* New York: Rowman and Littlefield, 1990.

Work Projects Administration in the State of Texas. Writers' Program. *Texas: A Guide to the Lone Star State.* New York: Hastings House, 1940. Rev. ed., edited by Harry Hansen. New York: Hastings House, 1969.

Zamora, Emilio. *The World of the Mexican Worker in Texas.* College Station: Texas A&M University Press, 1993.

Zamora, Emilio, Cynthia Orozco, and Rodolfo Rocha, eds. *Mexican Americans in Texas History.* Austin: Texas State Historical Association, 2000.

INDEX

CPSIA information can be obtained
at www.ICGtesting.com
Printed in the USA
LVOW11s0325090318
569207LV00001B/27/P